Community and Authority

Community and Authority

The Rhetoric of Obedience in the Pauline Tradition

Cynthia Briggs Kittredge

Trinity Press International

HARRISBURG, PENNSYLVANIA

Community and Authority
Harvard Theological Studies 45

Produced at the office of the *Harvard Theological Review*
Managing Editor: Marianne Palmer Bonz
Copyeditor: Melanie Johnson-DeBaufre
Book Design and Typesetting: Anne Custer
Cover Design by: Trude Brummer
Cover Art: Fresco from the Catacomb of Priscilla in Rome,
used by permission of the publisher Rizzoli (Sansoni), Milan
Harvard Theological Studies Series Editors: Allen D.
Callahan, John B. Carman, David D. Hall, Helmut Koester,
Jon D. Levenson, Francis Schüssler Fiorenza, Ronald F.
Thiemann

Library of Congress Cataloging-in-Publication data
Kittredge, Cynthia Briggs
    Community and authority: the rhetoric of obedience in the
        Pauline tradition / Cynthia Briggs Kittredge
    p.   cm.—(Harvard theological studies: 45)
    Originally presented as the author's doctoral thesis—
        Harvard University, 1996.
    Includes bibliographical references and index.
    ISBN 1-56338-262-8 (paperback: alk. paper)
    1. Obedience—Biblical teaching. 2. Bible. N.T.
        Ephesians—Socio-rhetorical criticism. 3. Bible. N.T.
        Philippians—Socio-rhetorical criticism. I. Title. II.
        Series: Harvard theological studies; no. 45.
    BS2545.6.O2GK58 1998
    224.506—dc21   98-34293
                                              CIP

The paper used in this publication meets the minimum
requirements of the American National Standard for
Informaiton Sciences—Permanence of Paper for
Printed Library Materials.

Manufactured in the USA

02 01 00 99 98 1 2 3 4 5 6 7 8 9 10

For Frank, Rachel, Emily, and Henry

Acknowledgments

This study of the language of obedience, written as my doctoral dissertation at Harvard Divinity School, has grown out of a fascination with Paul's letters and their history of interpretation. Many teachers contributed to my thinking, most especially my thesis advisor, Elisabeth Schüssler Fiorenza, who first encouraged my interest in hermeneutics, challenged me with critical questions, and shared her keen insights throughout the evolution of this project. Allen Callahan assisted me with timely practical and conceptual advice, and Krister Stendahl read my work thoughtfully in its early and later versions. Former Harvard faculty Bernadette Brooten, Richard Horsley, and Larry Wills have advised me helpfully over the years. To the late Professor George MacRae, S.J., I owe thanks for instilling in me an appreciation for the profound and the curious within the New Testament.

I am enormously grateful to Ellen Aitken, Jennifer Berenson Maclean, and Barbara Rossing, whose combined learning, generosity, and humor during our many meetings were vital to the completion of my dissertation and their own as well. Many conversations with other colleagues, Shelly Matthews, Denise Buell, Georgia Frank, and John Lanci have enriched my work. I thank Kathryn Kunkel, Th.D. administrator, and Gretchen Korb and Andrew Ashcroft, at that time students at Gordon College, who helped prepare the dissertation for submission.

In the process of preparing this dissertation for publication as a book, Melanie Johnson-DeBaufre has been a skillful copy editor, and I thank her for her enthusiasm and warmth and for all the ways in which her suggestions have improved the book. I also thank Anne Custer for her careful and untiring typesetting and layout of the manuscript. I am grateful to the editors of Harvard Theological Studies, Allen Callahan and Francis Schüssler Fiorenza, for their interest in my work and to Marianne

Palmer Bonz, managing editor of *Harvard Theological Review*, for her support and supervision of the project.

My attention to research and writing could not be maintained without the support of my extended family. I thank all those who have helped to care for my children and have played other roles in our busy household: Emily Adams, Jessica Brindle, Gretchen Korb, Elliott Buck Thomson, Stacey Hess, and Diane Neal Emmons. The people and clergy of St. John's, Beverly Farms, Emmanuel Church in Manchester-by-the-sea, and the Companions of the Holy Cross have spiritually sustained me and reminded me of the diverse audiences for scholarly work. My good friend Elisabeth Keller urged me on, and Ann Hopfenbeck commented on one chapter at a critical time. From our first days at Harvard Divinity School, Cathy Hagstrom George has given me her perceptive and loyal friendship, which has been essential throughout this project. I thank my parents, Taylor and Jane Briggs, for their encouragement to quietness and confidence. Most of all, I give my deepest thanks and love to my husband Frank, and our children, Rachel, Emily, and Henry.

Contents

Short Titles

Balch, *Let Wives Be Submissive*
  Balch, David L. *Let Wives Be Submissive: The Domestic Code in
  1 Peter.* SBLMS 26. Atlanta: Scholars Press, 1981.

Bassler, *Pauline Theology*
  Bassler, Jouette M., ed. *Pauline Theology*, vol. 1: *Thessalonians,
  Philippians, Galatians, Philemon.* Minneapolis: Augsburg Fortress,
  1991.

Beare, *Philippians*
  Beare, Francis Wright. *A Commentary on the Epistle to the
  Philippians.* London: Black, 1959.

Bloomquist, *Function of Suffering*
  Bloomquist, L. Gregory. *The Function of Suffering in Philippians.*
  JSNTSup 78. Sheffield: JSOT Press, 1993.

Botha, *Subject to Whose Authority?*
  Botha, Jan. *Subject to Whose Authority? Multiple Readings of
  Romans 13.* Emory Studies in Early Christianity. Atlanta: Scholars
  Press, 1994.

Bultmann, *Theology of the New Testament*
  Bultmann, Rudolf. *Theology of the New Testament.* 2 vols. Trans.
  Kendrick Grobel. New York: Scribner's, 1951.

Crouch, *Origin*
  Crouch, James E. *The Origin and Intention of the Colossian
  Haustafel.* Göttingen: Vandenhoeck & Ruprecht, 1972.

D'Angelo, "Colossians"
D'Angelo, Mary Rose. "Colossians." In Schüssler Fiorenza, *Searching the Scriptures*, 313–24.

Fee, *Philippians*
Fee, Gordon D. *Paul's Letter to the Philippians*. Grand Rapids, MI: Eerdmans, 1995.

Fowl, *Story of Christ*
Fowl, Stephen E. *The Story of Christ in the Ethics of Paul: An Analysis of the Function of the Hymnic Material in the Pauline Corpus*. JSNTSup 36. Sheffield: JSOT Press, 1990.

Furnish, *Love Command*
Furnish, Victor Paul. *The Love Command in the New Testament*. Nashville: Abingdon, 1972.

Furnish, *Moral Teaching*
Furnish, Victor Paul. *The Moral Teaching of Paul: Selected Issues*. 2d rev. ed. Nashville: Abingdon, 1985.

Furnish, *Theology and Ethics*
Furnish, Victor Paul. *Theology and Ethics in Paul*. Nashville: Abingdon, 1968.

Garland, "Composition and Unity"
Garland, David E. "The Composition and Unity of Philippians." *NovT* 26 (1985) 141–73.

Käsemann, "Critical Analysis"
Käsemann, Ernst. "A Critical Analysis of Philippians 2:5–11." *JTC* 5 (1968) 45–88.

Käsemann, "Romans 13"
Käsemann, Ernst. "Principles of the Interpretation of Romans 13." In idem, *New Testament Questions of Today*. Trans. W. J. Montague. Philadelphia: Fortress, 1969. 196–216.

Käsemann, *Jesus Means Freedom*
 Käsemann, Ernst. *Jesus Means Freedom*. Trans. Frank Clarke. Philadelphia: Fortress, 1970.

Kittel, "ἀκούω"
 Kittel, Gerhard. "ἀκούω." *TDNT* 1 (1968) 216–25.

Lincoln, *Ephesians*
 Lincoln, Andrew T. *Ephesians*. Word Biblical Commentary 42. Dallas: Word, 1990.

Lincoln, "Stand Therefore"
 Lincoln, Andrew T. "'Stand Therefore . . . ' Ephesians 6:10–20 as *Peroratio*." *Biblical Interpretation* 3 (1995) 99–114.

Lohse, *Colossians*
 Lohse, Edward. *Colossians and Philemon*. Trans. William R. Poehlmann and Robert J. Karris. Hermeneia. Philadelphia: Fortress, 1971.

Louw and Nida, *Greek-English Lexicon*
 Louw, Johannes P. and Eugene A. Nida, eds. *Greek-English Lexicon of the New Testament. Based on Semantic Domains*. New York: United Bible Society, 1989.

Maclean, "Ephesians"
 Maclean, Jennifer Berenson. "Ephesians and the Problem of Colossians. Texts and Traditions in Eph 1:1–2:10." Ph.D. diss., Harvard University, 1995.

Martin, *Slavery as Salvation*
 Martin, Dale B. *Slavery as Salvation: The Metaphor of Slavery in Pauline Christianity*. New Haven: Yale University Press, 1990.

Martin, *Carmen Christi*
 Martin, Ralph P. *Carmen Christi: Philippians 2:5–11 in Recent Interpretation and the Setting of Early Christian Worship*. Cambridge: Cambridge University Press, 1967.

Meeks, "Androgyne"
Meeks, Wayne A. "The Image of the Androgyne: Some Uses of a Symbol in Earliest Christianity." *HR* 13 (1974) 165–208.

Meeks, "In One Body"
Meeks, Wayne A. "In One Body: The Unity of Humankind in Colossians and Ephesians." In Jacob Jervell and Wayne A. Meeks, eds. *God's Christ and His People: Studies in Honour of Nils Alstrup Dahl*. Oslo: University Press, 1977. 209–21.

Meeks, "Man From Heaven"
Meeks, Wayne A. "The Man From Heaven in Paul's Letter to the Philippians." In Birger A. Pearson, ed. *The Future of Early Christianity: Essays in Honor of Helmut Koester.* Minneapolis: Fortress, 1991. 329–36.

Meeks, *Origins of Christian Morality*
Meeks, Wayne A. *The Origins of Christian Morality: The First Two Centuries*. New Haven: Yale University Press, 1993.

Miletic, *One Flesh*
Miletic, Stephen Francis. *"One Flesh"* : *Eph. 5.22–24, 5.31: Marriage and the New Creation*. Rome: Editrice Pontificio Instituto Biblico, 1988.

Mitchell, *Rhetoric of Reconciliation*
Mitchell, Margaret M. *Paul and the Rhetoric of Reconciliation: An Exegetical Investigation of the Language and Composition of 1 Corinthians*. Louisville, KY: Westminster/John Knox, 1991.

Morgan and Barton, *Biblical Interpretation*
Morgan, Robert and John Barton. *Biblical Interpretation*. Oxford Bible Series. Oxford: Oxford University Press, 1988.

Mouton, "Reading Ephesians Ethically"
Mouton, Elna J. "Reading Ephesians Ethically: Criteria Towards a Renewed Identity Awareness?" *Neotestimentica* 28 (1994) 359–77.

Petersen, *Rediscovering Paul*
  Petersen, Norman R. *Rediscovering Paul: Philemon and the Sociology of Paul's Narrative World.* Philadelphia: Fortress, 1985.

Sampley, *One Flesh*
  Sampley, J. Paul. *"And the Two Shall Become One Flesh." A Study of Traditions in Ephesians 5:21–33.* SNTSMS 16. Cambridge: Cambridge University Press, 1971.

Schnackenburg, *Ephesians*
  Schnackenburg, Rudolf. *Ephesians: A Commentary.* Trans. Helen Heron. Edinburgh: T. & T. Clark, 1991.

Schüssler Fiorenza, *Bread Not Stone*
  Schüssler Fiorenza, Elisabeth. *Bread Not Stone: The Challenge of Feminist Biblical Interpretation.* Boston: Beacon, 1984.

Schüssler Fiorenza, *But She Said*
  Schüssler Fiorenza, Elisabeth. *But She Said: Feminist Practices of Biblical Interpretation.* Boston: Beacon, 1992.

Schüssler Fiorenza, *In Memory of Her*
  Schüssler Fiorenza, Elisabeth. *In Memory of Her: A Feminist Theological Reconstruction of Christian Origins.* New York: Crossroad, 1983.

Schüssler Fiorenza, *Revelation*
  Schüssler Fiorenza, Elisabeth. *The Book of Revelation: Justice and Judgement.* Philadelphia: Fortress, 1985.

Schüssler Fiorenza, "Rhetorical Situation"
  Schüssler Fiorenza, Elisabeth. "Rhetorical Situation and Historical Reconstruction in 1 Corinthians." *NTS* 33 (1987) 386–403.

Schüssler Fiorenza, "Rhetoricity of Historical Knowledge"
Schüssler Fiorenza, Elisabeth. "The Rhetoricity of Historical Knowledge: Pauline Discourse and its Contextualizations." In Lukas Bormann, Kelly Del Tredici, and Angela Standhartinger, eds. *Religious Propaganda and Missionary Competition in the New Testament World: Essays Honoring Dieter Georgi*. Leiden: Brill, 1994. 443–69.

Schüssler Fiorenza, *Searching the Scriptures*
Schüssler Fiorenza, Elisabeth, ed. *Searching the Scriptures*, vol. 2: *A Feminist Commentary*. New York: Crossroad, 1994.

Soelle, *Beyond Mere Obedience*
Soelle, Dorothee. *Beyond Mere Obedience*. Trans. Lawrence W. Denef. New York: Pilgrim, 1982.

Stowers, "Friends and Enemies"
Stowers, Stanley K. "Friends and Enemies in the Politics of Heaven: Reading Theology in Philippians." In Bassler, *Pauline Theology*, 105–21.

Watson, "Rhetorical Analysis"
Watson, Duane. "A Rhetorical Analysis of Philippians and Its Implications for the Unity Problem." *NovT* 30 (1988) 57–88.

White, "Morality"
White, L. Michael. "Morality Between Two Worlds. A Paradigm of Friendship in Philippians." In David L. Balch, Everett Ferguson, and Wayne A. Meeks, eds. *Greeks, Romans and Christians: Essays in Honor of Abraham J. Malherbe*. Minneapolis: Fortress, 1990. 201–15.

Wire, *Corinthian Women*
Wire, Antoinette Clark. *The Corinthian Women Prophets: A Reconstruction through Paul's Rhetoric*. Minneapolis: Fortress, 1990.

The Rhetoric of Obedience
in the Pauline Tradition

Influential New Testament exegetes and theologians such as Rudolf Bultmann, Ernst Käsemann, and Victor Furnish have claimed that obedience is a key concept for interpreting Pauline theology and ethics.[1] Exegesis of the Pauline letters, especially the letters to the Romans and to the Philippians, supports this assertion that for Paul obedience is equivalent to faith. The emphasis of these scholars on the importance of obedience and the particular way in which they understand obedience continues to have an impact on treatments of Christian ethics and spirituality, especially in Christian traditions that value Paul highly. Their views of obedience is adapted and reiterated by scholars such as Wayne Meeks and Dale Martin, who approach the discussion of New Testament ethics from a different perspective.[2]

The traditional treatments stress the centrality of obedience as a mode of Christian life and sharply distinguish between Christian and Jewish obedience to the commandments. For example, Rudolf Bultmann contrasts faith with the obedience of Jewish legalism.[3] Understood as an act of faith, obedience is not obedience to the commandments but a total way of submitting to the will of God. For Bultmann and others, obedience has no specific content. It is merely an attitude or stance toward God. For example, in the section on ὑπακούω in the *Theological Dictionary of the New Testament*, Gerhard Kittel explains that:

---

[1] Bultmann, *Theology of the New Testament*; Käsemann, *Jesus Means Freedom*; Furnish, *Theology and Ethics*. See also Käsemann, "Romans 13," 206.

[2] Meeks, *Origins of Christian Morality*; Martin, *Slavery as Salvation*.

[3] Bultmann, *Theology of the New Testament*, 1. 315.

Similarly at Phil. 2:12, in connection with the obedience of Jesus in v. 8 (*infra*), recollection of the ὑπακούειν [obedience] of the community can describe its positive religious state: καθὼς πάντοτε ὑπακούσατε [as you have always obeyed], just as believers in Ac. 5:32 can be called: οἱ πειθαρχοῦντες (θεῷ) [those who obey (God)].[4]

Phil 2:8, which refers to Jesus' obedience, illustrates the obedience urged for the Christian. In *Theology and Ethics in Paul*, Victor Furnish begins by discussing Christ's obedience in Phil 2:8 and in Rom 5:19. Christ's obedience is primarily "obedience to death." In Christian obedience, those who belong to Christ participate in Christ's obedience. Using other texts about love from the Pauline letters, Furnish concludes that faith's obedience is surrender to love: "In the vocabulary of Pauline theology faith is obedience, and obedience is love."[5] Furnish's interpretive move, which makes obedience equivalent to love, spiritualizes obedience and leaves unanswered questions about the content and object of obedience and about the difference between obedience and love.

In discussions of Pauline theology, not only is obedience in Paul's writings differentiated from obedience in Judaism but the obedience in the undisputed letters of Paul is assumed to be different from the injunctions to obey in later letters in the Pauline tradition. Although Greek words for "obey" occur in the household codes, which preach obedience of children to parents and slaves to masters in Ephesians and Colossians, scholars of Pauline theology do not treat these occurrences as meaningfully related to Christian obedience in Philippians and Romans. Even though the writers of Ephesians and Colossians saw themselves in continuity with Paul, commentators do not give enough attention to that continuity. They overlook the aspects of obedience in the later writings that clearly draw on Pauline language and explicitly involve submission of a weaker to a stronger authority.

The restriction of the discussion of obedience to the genuine letters of Paul and the accompanying minimization of the importance of obedience language in the letters of the Pauline tradition is both a theoretical

---

[4]Kittel, "ακούω," 224.
[5]Furnish, *Theology and Ethics*, 182–206.

and a practical-theological problem. The theoretical problem is caused by the distancing of the "religious" and "social" in the analysis of religious language. The theological problem is whether celebrating the "free obedience" in Paul's letters while overlooking the strong links between that language and the maintenance of a specific social system as illustrated in Ephesians is a useful theological strategy in contemporary discussion of Paul's ethics.

This study investigates the influential Pauline theologians' major claims about obedience and their reconstruction of the development of the language of obedience in the Pauline tradition. These claims are reexamined in light of recent methodological contributions, particularly rhetorical criticism and historical work on the diversity of early Christian languages and viewpoints. I proceed in two related steps. First, I examine the work of several influential interpreters of Paul in order to identify the operative hermeneutical frameworks. This exploration high lights both the broad features of these interpretive frameworks and certain specific Pauline texts critical to their arguments. Next, I present an alternative framework for interpretation and analyze two of these Pauline texts, the letter to the Philippians and the letter to the Ephesians.

Context of this Study

The design of this book is conceived within the context of the broad discussion of hermeneutical and theological issues within New Testament studies. Students of New Testament hermeneutics have demonstrated the critical role played by the choice of interpretive framework in reading biblical texts.[6] In interpretation, both the historical context of the text and of the interpreter must be brought into relation with one another. For exegetes, reading New Testament texts is not simply a matter of determining what the text *meant* and then leaving interpre-

---

[6]See Anthony C. Thiselton, *The Two Horizons: New Testament Hermeneutics and Philosophical Description with Special Reference to Heidegger, Bultmann, Gadamer, and Wittgenstein* (Grand Rapids, MI: Eerdmans, 1980); Paul Ricoeur, *Essays on Biblical Interpretation* (ed. and intro. Lewis S. Mudge; Philadelphia: Fortress, 1980); Fernando F. Segovia and Mary Ann Tolbert, eds., *Reading From This Place*, vol. 1: *Social Location and Biblical Interpretation in the United States* (Minneapolis: Fortress, 1995).

tation for preaching and teaching what it *means* to the preacher and theologian. The stance of the interpreter affects the reading of what the text meant historically. In most Christian traditions the historical meaning of a text is normative for its contemporary meaning, thus it is not possible to separate so strictly what a text meant from what it means.[7] It is logical that the interpretive framework of Pauline theologians, including their evaluation of the Pauline letters, their presuppositions about earlier and later traditions, and their understanding of the relationship between Judaism and Christianity, would be relevant in determining what they interpret as central to Pauline theology. This study views biblical interpretation as expressing the values and priorities of the interpreter and not as a value-neutral presentation of the "facts."[8]

Feminist and liberation theologians have highlighted the way in which theological interpretation is a committed enterprise. It cannot be neutral because interpretation involves the power to select some readings and exclude others. They have called on theologians and exegetes to be explicit about their own social position and rhetorical situation.[9] In the debates about the complexity of the horizon of the contemporary interpreter, the question of the role of obedience is particularly significant. Obedience in the context of the exhortations to submission in the Pauline letters explicitly refers to a structured relationship of power between a superior and an inferior. Thus, it is important to consider the social position and perspective of Pauline theologians when examining their analysis of obedience as "free."[10]

Methodological Perspective

The "language of obedience" refers to the discourses of obeying and submitting that appear in the arguments of the letters of Paul and of

---

[7]See Krister Stendahl, "Method in the Study of Biblical Theology," in J. Philip Hyatt, ed., *The Bible in Modern Scholarship* (Nashville, TN: Abingdon, 1965) 196–209. See also the critique of this position in Schüssler Fiorenza, *Bread Not Stone,* 23–42.

[8]Schüssler Fiorenza, "Rhetoricity of Historical Knowledge," 443–69.

[9]Elisabeth Schüssler Fiorenza, "Commitment and Critical Inquiry," *HTR* 82 (1989) 1–11.

[10]In her study of *mimesis* in Paul, Elizabeth Castelli (*Imitating Paul: A Discourse of Power* [Louisville, KY: John Knox, 1991]) asks how readings of New Testament texts perpetuate or challenge the power relationships expressed in the text.

those who wrote letters in Paul's name to early Christian churches. This language of obedience depends upon relationship—it is a feature of social relationships. These may be between people or between people and God or Christ, but both kinds of relationships depend for their meaningfulness on a social context in which humans obey one another. The language of obedience both occurs within social relations and constructs social relations. Obedience is a feature of a relationship of super- and subordination in which one of inferior status obeys one of superior status.

Thus, I begin with the basic insight from the sociology of knowledge that social arrangements and symbolic arrangements are related. The language of obedience is part of the language of social relations. Theological language about Christ obeying God or about obedience as a spiritual attitude of a Christian derives from the world of social relationships. In this sense, the language of obedience is part of the symbolic universe of early Christian communities. The term "symbolic universe" refers to the world as it is known by members of a community or culture. In his work on Paul, Norman Petersen makes the distinction between theology and symbolic universe. The symbolic universe is the world "as it is viewed," while theology is "systematic reflection on that symbolic universe." Peterson explains that "a symbolic universe is the world as it is viewed, not as something which exists apart from the way we view it."[11] That symbolic universe is ordered in a particular way. Its social roles draw upon the language of roles within society.

The language of obedience naturally occurs within the context of the marriage, slavery, and parent-child relationships that make up the kyriarchal family. In the ancient world the family was a hierarchical structure in which inferior members were linked to higher members by relationships that required obedience. This conception of the Greco-Roman patriarchal family has been elaborated by historians.[12] Elisabeth Schüssler Fiorenza argues that patriarchy should be understood not simply as the sex/gender system in which all men dominate all women but in the classical sense of a "complex pyramidal political structure of domination and subordination" or "kyriarchy" in which the father/master rules

---

[11]Petersen, *Rediscovering Paul*, 29–30.
[12]Page DuBois, *Centaurs and Amazons: Women and the Pre-History of the Great Chain of Being* (Ann Arbor: University of Michigan Press, 1982).

and the subordinates (wives, slaves, children) obey.[13] Language about obedience to God as part of slavery to God, marriage with God, and being a child of God is metaphorical language that draws on the relationships within the classical kyriarchal family. The early Christians attempted to describe their new self-understanding and its consequences for their status, their relationships, and their understanding of their communities by using the language, images, and metaphors from the surrounding cultural context, which included the kyriarchal family. They described their experience with a variety of metaphors and employed traditional metaphorical language in new ways. They used the language of obedience and the metaphors of slavery, marriage, and parent-child relations as well as the language of Spirit, wisdom, and freedom. Using and developing a Christian language, they were both living within and constructing a new symbolic universe.

Early Christian History

This study takes as its starting point a conception of early Christian history as a struggle between an emerging Christian movement with a vision of equality and the forces of the dominant patriarchal ethos of the Greco-Roman world.[14] It does not view the development of early Christianity as a unilinear development towards patriarchalization necessitated either by the development of "orthodoxy" or, in sociological terms, by the need for institutional survival. Rather, the New Testament canon in general and the letters of Paul in particular give evidence of both the impulse toward equality and the movement towards patriarchalism. If one reads the evidence in Paul's letters in light of this struggle, one can see that the competing visions of community are articulated with different cultural languages and social metaphors. The language of obedience and the metaphors drawn from the patriarchal family play a role in that struggle.

Therefore, I understand Paul's letters to the early Christian churches as part of an ongoing debate and discussion that took place in the con-

---

[13]Schüssler Fiorenza, *But She Said*, 115.

[14]Schüssler Fiorenza, *In Memory of Her*, 92. Schüssler Fiorenza (*But She Said*) has developed this alternative framework in her more recent works, which situate her feminist biblical criticism in the context of biblical interpretation and feminist theory.

text of various interpretations of the meaning of Christ. Rather than using a model that sees Paul's letters as a timeless source of orthodox
teaching or reconstructs the historical situation behind the letters as Paul
arguing with his "opponents," this investigation seeks to recover the
theology and symbolic universe of the audience of Paul's letters and the
early Christian communities of which they are a part. Paul's letters are
read as rhetorical arguments, designed to persuade, that take place within
the public discourse of the *ekklesia* and seek to deal with competing
claims.[15]

As rhetorical texts, Paul's letters depend upon a shared symbolic
universe while also constructing one that the reader may accept and live
within. Paul's letters can be read as a source for his symbolic universe,
that is, the "world" in which Christ and God are related and act on a
symbolic plane.[16] Paul builds the symbolic universe of his letters around
his understanding of the gospel and speaks of it in scriptural, conventional, and social language and metaphors that were known and used by
early Christians. For his rhetoric to be effective, Paul counts on sharing
at least some elements of the symbolic universe of his audience. While
they probably shared some elements, they may have construed others
differently. Paul writes to create and construct that shared knowledge of
the symbolic universe. Within the rhetoric of Paul's letters, there is evidence of points of conflict. Those points of conflict constitute the
exigencies of the rhetorical situation.[17]

While some rhetorical approaches restrict themselves to exploring
and elucidating the way the author's text works to persuade, my
approach seeks to understand the early Christian communicative situation as a whole. Therefore, I shall focus not on the author alone but on
the Christian community to whom and with whom the author speaks.
The audience of a Pauline letter has contributed to that communication,
not only in terms of its expectations of genre or formal categories of
rhetorical arrangement but by its own ways of constructing symbolic
universes, of using language and metaphor. The only way a letter can be

---

[15]Schüssler Fiorenza, "Rhetoricity of Historical Knowledge," 443–69.

[16]Petersen, *Rediscovering Paul*, 204.

[17]Petersen (ibid., 273 n. 11) acknowledges the competition between different
symbolic universes, but he does not investigate Paul's letters for evidence of the
contours of that competition.

persuasive is by connecting with the knowledge and understanding possessed by its audience. This study seeks to use the author's rhetoric to gain access to the counter arguments and theological understandings of the community. This approach understands that there may be tension between the audience and the author, that the audience does not passively accept the author's writing.

Rhetorical Criticism

While some who practice rhetorical criticism[18] focus on analysis of the New Testament texts according to the categories of classical rhetoric and use classical rhetoric as a prescriptive method, others use rhetoric in the broader sense, a method corresponding to the terms "modern rhetoric" or "New Rhetoric."[19] The ancient discipline of rhetoric was established in antiquity and discussed in the rhetorical theory of Plato, Isocrates, Aristotle, and Quintilian. Ancient rhetoric dealt with the means of persuasion and the science of speaking adequately. The science of ancient rhetoric was oriented toward the creation of speeches and the instruction of those wishing to communicate.[20] New Rhetoric understands that the guidelines of classical rhetoric are not prescriptive structures but tools for analyzing the text's means of persuasion.[21] Rhetoric is understood as persuasive political discourse and as argument. In modern rhetorical analysis the focus has shifted from the author of a text to the reader or the audience.[22] The author's message is interpreted through the situation in which it is given. Modern rhetoric understands rhetoric as it was used by Paul to be a flexible, extremely fluid discipline.[23] This

---

[18]The many varieties of methods included under the heading of "rhetorical criticism" have been discussed and distinguished in recent work. See Botha, *Subject to Whose Authority?* 121–37; Burton Mack, *Rhetoric and the New Testament* (Minneapolis: Fortress, 1990); Wire, *Corinthian Women,* 197–99. Antoinette Wire's use of rhetorical criticism in analyzing 1 Corinthians has influenced its use in this project. See Schüssler Fiorenza, "Rhetorical Situation," 386–403.

[19]See discussion in Botha, *Subject to Whose Authority?* 121–27, 134–37.

[20]Ibid., 125.

[21]Schüssler Fiorenza, *Revelation,* 22.

[22]Botha, *Subject to Whose Authority?* 125.

[23]Stephen Kraftchick, "Why Do the Rhetoricians Rage?" in Theodore W. Jennings, ed., *Text and Logos: The Humanistic Tradition of the New Testament* (Atlanta: Scholars Press, 1990) 78.

perspective uses classical categories as tools to understand Paul's letters as argument and stresses the importance of the context of the speech.[24]

Here, rhetorical analysis interrogates Paul's rhetoric to gain access to the early communities in which he wrote. The analysis begins with the author's arguments but will take the further step of historical reconstruction. Reconstruction of the historical situation using a different framework of analysis is necessary in order to get beyond the inscribed rhetorical situation of the text. Analyses that limit themselves to elucidating the androcentric perspectives of a text function to reinscribe those perspectives and discourses.

This analysis attempts to understand and to describe the place of obedience language within Paul's rhetoric and to put that rhetoric into the broader context of historical debate. It will do so by taking seriously the character of Pauline texts as rhetorical texts that construct a picture of history. Elisabeth Schüssler Fiorenza elaborates this perspective extensively in her work: "Historical writings such as the Pauline letters do not reflect historical reality; rather as prescriptive-persuasive texts they construct it. Paul's texts do not merely respond to the rhetorical situation, but also create it."[25] In order to recover the voices submerged in the text one must move from rhetorical analysis to reconstruction of the historical situation. The distinction between the inscribed rhetorical situation and the possible historical situation is critical: the inscribed rhetorical situation is inscribed in the text itself; the historical situation must be reconstructed from other sources as well.[26]

This study builds critically upon recent work on Paul's symbolic universe that has treated obedience within its metaphorical and symbolic contexts. Norman Petersen explores the letter to Philemon and the other undisputed Pauline letters using the categories of symbolic universe and social relations.[27] He points out how the world and the church are two realms and two separate domains within Paul's narrative world.[28] In Petersen's reconstruction, the two main features of Paul's symbolic universe are the social master-slave system and the anthropo-

[24]Schüssler Fiorenza, *Revelation*, 21.
[25]Schüssler Fiorenza, "Rhetoricity of Historical Knowledge," 456.
[26]Ibid., 447.
[27]Petersen, *Rediscovering Paul*.
[28]Ibid., 25.

logical kinship system. God as "our Father" and Christ as "our Lord" are the organizing metaphors of Paul's symbolic universe. After exploring the relevant texts from Paul's letters, Petersen concludes that "the master-slave system is related to the kinship system as one symbolic representation of a stage within which God adopts his children."[29] The master-slave system is mediated by its temporary character.[30] Peterson's analysis does not recognize how the master-slave and kinship system are related as two aspects of the same kyriarchal system in which father and master rule over child and slave. The perspective of this study is that obedience is a feature of both the master-slave system and the kinship or patriarchal system and must be analyzed as kyriarchal language. Petersen's analysis treats all Pauline texts as roughly equivalent pieces of data for reconstructing Paul's symbolic universe. Petersen does not take into account the rhetorical function of Pauline language within the individual letters in their historical situation.[31]

In his treatment of the metaphor of slavery in *Slavery as Salvation*, Dale Martin discusses Paul's use of the metaphor in 1 Corinthians in the context of the topos of the enslaved leader in Greco-Roman sources. He investigates why an early Christian would have wanted to be a "slave of Christ." He argues that the slavery metaphor in Paul's first letter to the Corinthians expresses both status elevation for those who are of low status and lowering of status for those who are of high status. In addition, he explains how slavery can have a positive soteriological use in the early Christian context. Martin does not treat the metaphor of marriage in his discussion of slavery. He sees Paul's use of the metaphor of slavery as a response to the language of his "opponents." In his reconstruction of the opponents, however, he does not credit them with an alternate symbolic universe to Paul's. Rather he sees them as representing a position of "love patriarchalism." Martin's treatment of the metaphor of slavery and the attendant language of obedience explicitly does not address the concrete social implications of soteriological language but restricts itself to slavery as a soteriological metaphor.[32]

---

[29]Ibid., 212.

[30]Ibid., 214.

[31]For example, in his discussion of Paul's notion of "the form of a slave" (ibid., 251), Petersen discusses and conflates Phil 2:7, Gal 4:5, and Rom 8:2 without considering the rhetorical context of the different texts from which he quotes.

[32]Martin, (*Slavery as Salvation*, xiv) restricts his focus in this way: "Nor do I intend to

The investigation of obedience in this study takes place amid vigor-ous discussion about how to construct Pauline theology. Bultmann, Furnish, and Käsemann represent an earlier confidence in the straight-forward task of describing such a theology. After a period of the denial of any coherence in Paul's theology, new insights have begun to emerge about how to describe Paul's theology, such as the effort to determine the theology of single letters and the community for which they were written, only then beginning to synthesize.[33] Another such effort is the shift from trying to identify the "center" of Pauline theology to describ-ing the "balance between fundamental matters in his thought world."[34] With all of these reconstructions of the theology of Paul, whether in one letter or in many, interpreters seek to rearticulate or to amplify the voice of Paul the author. I use a rhetorical method to distinguish Paul's voice, or the author's voice in the case of Ephesians, and to place it in relation-ship with other voices that can be reconstructed from the text.

Format of this Study

This exploration begins by investigating several representative treat-ments of obedience in Pauline scholarship and describing their hermeneutical frameworks. Usually unacknowledged or denied in the traditional historical critical method, a hermeneutical framework shapes how one reads texts. The "commentary" of the biblical interpreters forms part of the rhetoric of the tradition. This chapter highlights some of the features of the theological frameworks of these treatments and constructs an alternative framework for interpretation.

---

shed any great light on the narrower subject of the relation of early Christianity to slavery—to describe, for example, early Christian attitudes toward slavery, Paul's stance on the institution of slavery, or the position of slaves in the social structure of Christian house churches." Martin's limitation of the subject has consequences for the conclusions he draws.

[33]The Pauline Theology Group of the Society of Bibilical Literature has undertaken this effort. Their results are compiled in Bassler, *Pauline Theology*; David M. Hay, ed., *Pauline Theology*, vol. 2: *1 & 2 Corinthians* (Minneapolis: Augsberg Fortress, 1993); David M. Hay and E. Elizabeth Johnson, eds., *Pauline Theology*, vol. 3: *Romans* (Min-neapolis: Augsberg Fortress, 1995).

[34]See J. Paul Sampley, "From Text to Thought World: The Route to Paul's Ways," in Bassler, *Pauline Theology*, 6.

Most treatments of obedience in Paul have sharply distinguished between different vocabulary for obedience. The second chapter sketches the semantic field of obedience language in the ancient world, using several Greek authors, in order to show what words and concepts comprise the field. The investigation attends to the terms ὑπακούειν ("to obey") and ὑποτάσσεσθαι ("to subject oneself"), verbs that are traditionally separated in treatments of obedience. The word ὑπακούειν is judged to be typical of the undisputed letters of Paul and the word ὑποτάσσεσθαι to be characteristic of "early catholicism" as represented by the author of Ephesians. The second chapter explores the semantic field of obedience in the letters of the Pauline tradition and how that field indicates the contours of a symbolic universe.

Chapters three and four investigate one incidence of obedience language in one of Paul's letters that has been extremely influential in the discussions of obedience in Pauline thought. The narrative of Christ in Phil 2:6–11 and its use by Paul in the context of the letter to the Philippians has been esteemed as one of the premier texts on which the theory of "free obedience" is based. Employing a method of rhetorical analysis, the third chapter sketches the rhetorical situation inscribed in the letter. The fourth chapter reconstructs the possible historical situation in order to explore how Paul utilizes the rhetoric of Christ as "obedient to the point of death" and the congregation as "obeying" within the dynamics of the argument of the letter.

The fifth and sixth chapters explore a letter from a later point in the Pauline tradition, the letter to the Ephesians. It is the example that many Protestant exegetes contrast most sharply with obedience in Paul's genuine letters. They cite the difference in vocabulary for obedience and the context of this language in a household code as key reasons to contrast them. Chapter five analyzes its argument rhetorically, and chapter six reconstructs its historical situation. I will show how the language of obedience functions in the struggle of competing visions of community.

The final chapter compares the conclusions about the roles of obedience language in the analyses of Philippians and Ephesians in both their rhetorical and historical situations and proposes an alternate way of describing the function of the language of obedience in the Pauline tradition.

CHAPTER 1

The Hermeneutical Framework
of the Interpretation of Obedience in Paul

Recent work in epistemology in general and in biblical studies in particular has focused on the importance of frameworks of interpretation. What one emphasizes, what one subordinates, and how one reconstructs the narrative of a text shape the reading of texts. Even "scientific" methods operate with frameworks, models, and metaphors in order to analyze, categorize, and interpret data. Initially conceived as an Enlightenment challenge to ecclesiastical dogmatism and presented as a reasonable and scientific method, historical criticism is itself a product of certain values, ways of seeing, and theological and ethical aims.[1] Many scholars have challenged the positivism of historical criticism in biblical studies. Elisabeth Schüssler Fiorenza has outlined three different paradigms for biblical studies: the doctrinal, historical, and pastoral-theological.[2] She has challenged all biblical scholars to make explicit their frameworks of interpretation and to bring them to the table of debate and discussion. One of the tasks of rhetorical criticism as she describes it is to delineate the frameworks of interpretation that shape the rhetoric of biblical studies.

[1]For history of the rise of historical criticism, see James Barr, *The Bible in the Modern World* (New York: Harper & Row, 1973); Raymond E. Brown, *The Critical Meaning of the Bible* (New York: Paulist, 1981); Stephen Neill and Tom Wright, *The Interpretation of the New Testament 1861–1961* (2d ed.; New York: Oxford University Press, 1988).

[2]Elisabeth Schüssler Fiorenza, "'For the Sake of Our Salvation . . .' Biblical Interpretation and the Community of Faith," in idem, *Bread Not Stone*, 23–42. See also idem, "Text and Reality-Reality as Text: The Problem of a Feminist Social and Historical Reconstruction on the Basis of Texts," *StTh* 43 (1989) 19–34; idem, *But She Said*, 80–88.

Theological explications of obedience over the past century operate with certain premises, assumptions, and ways of viewing the world. The resulting treatments of obedience support and strengthen those assumptions. Despite the fact that theologians and exegetes have disputed some details, all participants in the debate have shared a similar hermeneutical framework. Therefore, the discussion of obedience operates within specific boundaries in which some readings are possible and others unthinkable.

The discourses of the Pauline letters and the hermeneutical frameworks of Pauline theologians are closely related. Interpreters of Paul, the majority of whom accept Paul's authority as a premise of their work, take their clues from the author's rhetoric in the letters in order to reconstruct the historical situation behind the letter, the theological issue in dispute, and the position Paul takes. Thus, these interpreters reflect and amplify certain features of Paul's rhetoric. The subject of obedience provokes a subtle and interesting interplay between Paul's rhetoric and the rhetoric of the Pauline theologians. When interpreting Paul's role in the community, his relationship with his audience, and his relationship to other views, scholarly commentary authoritatively interprets Pauline language and strengthens certain features in the text.

The following analysis focuses on several influential scholars who have written about obedience in Paul's letters. It identifies some of the common features of the discussion of obedience that reveal the framework within which these critics are working in order to show how far the discussion has advanced and to indicate in what direction it may proceed.

Radical Obedience

In his New Testament theology, Rudolf Bultmann (1887–1976) attempted to translate the language of the New Testament into the language of contemporary experience so that he could convey the message of this collection of ancient religious texts.[3] Bultmann's exposition of the role of obedience in his *Theology of the New Testament* has

---

[3]For Bultmann's contribution to the discipline of New Testament theology, see Hendrikus Boers, *What is New Testament Theology?* (Philadelphia: Fortress, 1979). Also John R. Donohue, S.J., "The Changing Shape of New Testament Theology," *TS* 50 (1989) 314–35; James F. Kay, "Theological Table-talk Myth or Narrative?: Bultmann's New Testament and Mythology Turns Fifty," *TToday* 48 (1991) 326–32.

influenced later interpreters of Pauline theology. Although writing in a German context, the translation and publication of his works into English in the 1950s made his influence strongly felt in American biblical studies.[4] His interpretation of the major Pauline texts, Rom 5:18–19 and Phil 2:6–11, set the groundwork for future discussions of the centrality of obedience in Pauline theology and ethics. His understanding of the development of obedience from Judaism through "genuine" Paul and into the deutero-Pauline tradition remains a feature of many contemporary treatments of obedience in Paul.[5] For example, Don B. Garlington's book on Romans begins with Bultmann's formulation that faith is obedience as a premise for the study of the phrase "the obedience of faith" in the Septuagint.[6]

The prominent role of obedience in Bultmann's theology is bound up with his Lutheran tradition's assertion of salvation by faith alone and his existentialist focus on the individual's relation to God. His understanding of Paul is explicitly a "theological" interpretation.[7] The particular theological interests and the hermeneutical framework with which Bultmann operates shape his exegesis of Paul.

Bultmann values "radical" obedience above both Jewish "boasting" and obedience as a "work." For Bultmann, radical obedience is the attitude of "man under faith." It is the individual's response to God's gift. In defining radical obedience, Bultmann distinguishes it from "formal" obedience, that is, obedience to the commandments. With this distinction, Bultmann opposes Christian obedience to Jewish "legalism" :

> "Faith's obedience" is the genuine obedience which God's Law had indeed demanded, but which had been refused by the Jews by their misuse of it to establish "their own righteousness," using it as a means for "boasting."[8]

---

[4]For essays from several perspectives on the influence of Bultmann, see Edward C. Hobbs, ed., *Bultmann: Retrospect and Prospect: The Centenary Symposium at Wellesley* (Philadelphia: Fortress, 1985).

[5]For example, Neil Elliot employs Bultmann's insights about the structure of Romans in his recent study of obedience in that letter (*The Rhetoric of Romans: Argumentative Constraint and Strategy and Paul's Dialogue with Judaism* [JSNTSup 45: Sheffield: JSOT Press, 1990] 70).

[6]Don B. Garlington, *"The Obedience of Faith"* (WUNT 2d ser., 38; Tübingen: Mohr, 1991) 10.

[7]See the discussion of theological interpretation in Morgan and Barton, *Biblical Interpretation*, 109.

[8]Bultmann, *Theology of the New Testament*, 1. 315.

Boasting, or relying on achievement for justification before God, is a result of formal obedience. Bultmann's construction of Judaism sets up Jewish obedience as a foil for Jesus' obedience or Christian obedience.[9] Bultmann's schema stresses the discontinuity between obedience in Christian life and Jewish obedience more than it highlights the symbolic continuities between obedience as understood by a Jewish audience and the way that Paul describes it in Romans.

Because obedience as adherence to prescriptions would make of obedience a meritorious work and not a radical relationship, Bultmann stresses that obedience, like faith, is an *attitude* toward God.[10] God's grace, and not faith, is the decisive moral act.[11] Thus, obedience for Bultmann does not have specific content, rather the moral conduct of the believer has the *character* of obedience:

> As true obedience, "faith" is freed from the suspicion of being an accomplishment, a "work." As an accomplishment it would not be obedience, since in an accomplishment the will does not surrender but asserts itself; in it, a merely formal renunciation takes place in that the will lets the content of its accomplishment *be dictated by an authority lying outside of itself*, but precisely in so doing thinks it has a right to be proud of its accomplishment. "Faith"—the radical renunciation of accomplishment, the obedient submission to the God-determined way of salvation, the taking over of the cross of Christ—is the free deed of obedience in which the new self constitutes itself in place of the old. As this sort of decision, it is a deed in the true sense: In a true deed the doer himself is inseparable from it, while in a "work" he stands side by side with what he does.[12]

Radical obedience is radical for Bultmann because it is a relationship between God and human that is *unmediated*. No intermediary authority such as law or institution stand between the man of faith and God's

[9]Samuel Sandmel, "Bultmann on Judaism," in Charles W. Kegley, ed., *The Theology of Rudolf Bultmann* (New York: Harper & Row, 1966) 211–20.

[10]Bultmann, *Theology of the New Testament*, 1. 315.

[11]Rudolf Bultmann, "Das Problem der Ethik bei Paulus," *ZNW* 13 (1924) 128–29.

[12]Bultmann, *Theology of the New Testament*, 1. 315–16 (my emphasis). See also idem, *Jesus and the Word* (trans. Louise Pettibone Smith and Erminie Huntress Lantero; New York: Scribner's, 1934) 65; originally published as *Jesus* (Berlin: Deutsche Bibliothek, 1926).

grace. It is submission to God and not to any human superior. In this way, Bultmann intends "radical obedience" to relativize and criticize obedience to social superiors. Because it is submission to an external authority, the obedience recommended in Eph 5:21–22 would be understood by Paul to be a "work" and not "free obedience" as in the undisputed Pauline letters. Obedience to Paul is the only exception to this principle of unmediated obedience. Bultmann accepts Paul's demand for obedience as proof of Christian obedience to Christ (2 Cor 10:5–6).[13] According to Bultmann, Paul holds a position as an appropriate intermediary between a Christian and God.

Obedience is also radical because it occurs in the moment of encounter with God and in the event of decision. It is not obedience to a doctrine but acceptance of "*kerygma*, personal address, demand, and promise."[14] It is not based on knowing what the past requirements have been in order to predict what obedience will mean in the future. Rather, obedient response to God comes about in direct encounter with one's neighbor. Bultmann's conception of faith as direct encounter with God relies on Barth's emphasis on the Word of God confronting "man" and on Heidegger's stress on the human existence in time being characterized by decision in the moment.

Bultmann distinguishes between obedience in Paul and in the early church. In the development of the early church, he says, the basis for radical obedience was lost. Obedience was viewed as a meritorious work. Radical obedience, therefore, is sharply different from both the Judaism that preceded it and the later Pauline tradition that followed it. Thus, Bultmann's reconstruction of early Christianity reflects his vision of obedience as an existential decision in the moment. It is cut off from past experience and future promises. He does not question why radical obedience degenerated so rapidly, nor how the later Pauline tradition was able to incorporate obedience so smoothly into its injunctions to maintain social hierarchy in the family and in society.

Obedience summarizes Bultmann's view of ethics. It holds together the eschatological and the ethical.[15] It is free from moral authority out-

---

[13]Bultmann (*Theology of the New Testament*, 1. 308) states: "Nevertheless, in the function of an apostle he must demand that the congregation's 'obedience to Christ' prove itself in obedience to him (2 Cor 10:5f)."

[14]Ibid., 319.

[15]See the discussion by Thomas C. Oden, *Radical Obedience: The Ethics of Rudolf*

side the human and is an inward assent to the demand of God.[16] Love is enacted, not in specific works but in an attitude of obedience. Obedience of love is identical with obedience of faith, which is grounded in the saving act of God.[17] Human freedom from oneself makes one free to love the neighbor.

Although not directed primarily at his exegesis, Dorothee Soelle's critique of Bultmann's theology highlights Bultmann's hermeneutical framework, which she describes as one that is individualistic and that does not question power relations and ideology. Her observations about his theology raise questions for the investigation of the Pauline texts on obedience.

Soelle criticizes Bultmann's understanding of obedience on theological and ethical grounds. She argues that when obedience is drained of objective content, it becomes a technique or goal in itself.[18] Only when it is related concretely to the requirements for justice in a political and social situation can it be meaningful. When it becomes a value in itself, it leads to passivity in the face of injustice and maintains the arrangements of human authorities. She points out how the conventional picture of Jesus places his obedience and self-denial in the foreground.[19]

Soelle takes Bultmann's own concept of demythologization and charges that the idea of obedience itself should be seen as a myth that protects certain interests above others:

> In mythical thought where God appeared directly in summons and command, in natural phenomena and changes of fortune, a concept like obedience had a different meaning than it does in the modern view of self-determination. That which had its rightful place in mythology becomes an ideological relic in our post-mythological age. Such a relic tends to cloak the interests of those who care for and pass on dead myths. The assertion that "the essence of faith is obedience" is as formal as it is empty, and requires ideological critique rather than interpretation.[20]

Bultmann (Philadelphia: Westminster, 1964) 88–93.

[16] Walter Schmithals, *An Introduction to the Theology of Rudolf Bultmann* (Minneapolis: Augsburg, 1968) 282.

[17] Ibid., 290.

[18] Soelle, *Beyond Mere Obedience*.

[19] Ibid., 56–57.

[20] Ibid., 69–70.

The various features of Bultmann's understanding of obedience in his theology of Paul are closely related. The sharp distinction he draws between Paul and the Judaism of his time is consistent with his picture of the "man of faith" radically obedient to God, but with little connection to his network of social relationships and cultural and religious identities.[21] His effort to see Paul as discontinuous with Judaism affects his assertion that obedience lacks content because in Judaism it so obviously has content. When he minimizes the importance of the later Pauline tradition as turning obedience into a "work," Bultmann does not adequately take into account how a relational concept like obedience is embedded in its social and cultural context.

Bultmann's interpretation of obedience in the Pauline texts exemplifies a reconstruction of the development of the use of obedience language that will arise again in other discussions, that is, a separation of obedience language in Paul's undisputed letters from later tradition and an evaluation of Paul's understanding as superior.

Freedom and Obedience

Like Bultmann, Ernst Käsemann (1906–1998) emphasized obedience as a central theme in Pauline theology. Käsemann's particular understanding, however, reflects his interpretation of the Pauline texts and is closely connected with his theological differences from his teacher, Bultmann.[22] Obedience plays a key role in Käsemann's theological effort

---

[21]Bultmann's lack of interest in the social and political context of theology in general has been identified by others in addition to Soelle. See also Dieter Georgi, "Rudolf Bultmann's *Theology of the New Testament* Revisited," in Edward C. Hobbs, ed., *Bultmann: Retrospect and Prospect: The Centenary Symposium at Wellesley* (Philadelphia: Fortress,1985) 75–87. His claim that the cataclysmic events of his time had little effect on his thinking is formally reflected in his theology. See also Stephen R. Haynes, "'Between the Times': German Theology and the Weimar Zeitgeist," *Soundings* 74 (1991) 9–44; Elisabeth Schüssler Fiorenza, "The Ethics of Interpretation: Decentering Biblical Scholarship," *JBL* 107 (1988) 3–17.

[22]For the relationship between the thought of Bultmann and Käsemann, see J. Christiaan Beker, *Paul the Apostle: The Triumph of God in Life and Thought* (Philadelphia: Fortress, 1980) 276–77. See also Morgan and Barton, *Biblical Interpretation,* 118. For Käsemann's own reflection on his debate with Bultmann, see Ernst Käsemann, "What I Have Unlearned in 50 Years as a German Theologian," *Cur-*

to correct what he sees as Bultmann's focus on anthropology by asserting the primacy of christology.[23] More explicitly than Bultmann, Käsemann chooses the Pauline strand of the tradition as authoritative and uses this "canon within the canon" to critique other expressions. He uses obedience to Christ as Lord to assert the primacy of christology over ecclesiology and against what he sees as the early catholic interpretation of Paul in Ephesians and Colossians and in the Pastoral Epistles.

Obedience in Paul helps to stake out the position Käsemann wants to define as the heart of Paul's gospel, between "enthusiasm" on the one hand, which characterizes the opponents of Paul, and "early catholicism" on the other, characterized by Luke and Ephesians. According to Käsemann, bodily life is of no importance for the Christian enthusiasts. For the early catholics, the church must accommodate to the surrounding culture. Rather than having Christ as its Lord, the church takes over the position of Christ.

Käsemann upholds what he understands to be the heart of Paul's gospel against the threat of enthusiasts and early catholics by describing the dialectical relationship between freedom and obedience. Obedience to Jesus as Lord means freedom from all earthly lords, including church institutions. Yet that freedom, made possible by Jesus' obedience, is not isolation from social responsibility but solidarity with creation.[24] Indeed obedience is freedom. Freedom is the ultimate expression of the Protestant spirit. In *Jesus Means Freedom,* Käsemann traces the theme of freedom throughout the New Testament, identifying all elements that would try to limit it. At the same time, however, obedience and "the new obedience" recur frequently in Ernst Käsemann's work, often explicitly explained as Paul's response to the excesses of enthusiasm. Obedience to God assures that freedom will not be pursued at the expense of others.[25]

Käsemann's understanding of obedience as Paul's response to enthusiasm grows out of his interpretation of 1 Corinthians. From Paul's

---

rents in Theology and Mission 15 (1988) 325–35.

[23]Morgan and Barton, *Biblical Interpretation,* 118.

[24]Ernst Käsemann, *Commentary on Romans* (trans. Geoffrey W. Bromiley; Grand Rapids, MI: Eerdmans, 1980) 179.

[25]Ernst Käsemann, "On the Subject of Primitive Christian Apocalyptic," in idem, *New Testament Questions of Today* (trans. W. J. Montague; Philadelphia: Fortress, 1969) 124–37.

preaching, the enthusiasts understood that the resurrection meant freedom, but they saw that freedom as implying that bodily life did not matter. Christ was Lord for them but not the one they serve.[26] Unlike the opponents, Paul does not preach from anthropology and soteriology but from Christ. To oppose the enthusiasts, Paul "will therefore have to describe the essence of Christian faith as obedience, as hope, as love; and thus he will set bounds to the arbitrariness of the enthusiasts."[27] Paul preaches the theology of the cross to put freedom where it should be, "between blind obedience and enthusiasts' excesses."[28] The exalted one is thus the crucified one. Käsemann concludes that "this state in God's love becomes essentially a state of obedience."[29]

Against Bultmann, Käsemann argues that the earthly Jesus cannot be dispensed with for faith. In fact he repeatedly states that the saving facts of the gospel point to Jesus himself and not vice versa.[30] Therefore, he traces the New Testament's proclamation of freedom to Jesus himself. Jesus, the "liberal," rejects the scribes' belief that obedience to God takes precedence over all earthly things.[31] Responsibility to one's neighbor is more important than obedience to the law if, for example, it would prohibit helping a person in need on the Sabbath. Jesus tolerated no other gods and fulfilled the first commandment, first as promise, then as obedience.

When Käsemann discusses obedience, he refers primarily to the New Testament passages that use the word ὑπακούειν ("to obey"). In his analysis of Rom 13:1–7, he stresses that ὑποτάσσεσθαι ("to subject oneself, to submit") refers to the order of earthly relationships:

> ὑπεταγή is the obedience we owe because it is inherent in some specific τάγμα, i.e., it arises out of given earthly relationships, while ὑπακοή simply designates obedience as an achievement.[32]

This distinction allows Käsemann to avoid addressing Col 3:18–4:1 and Eph 5:21–6:9 directly when discussing obedience.

---

[26]Käsemann, *Jesus Means Freedom,* 65. See also idem, "Romans 13," 206.
[27]Käsemann, *Jesus Means Freedom,* 66.
[28]Ibid., 73.
[29]Ibid., 76.
[30]Ibid., 38.
[31]Ibid., 25.
[32]Käsemann, "Romans 13," 207.

Like Bultmann, Käsemann understands obedience in Paul as obedience to God *instead of* obedience to human superiors. For Käsemann, obedience to God is obedience to Christ as Lord, the Christ of the christological hymns who is exalted above the heavens and enthroned as universal sovereign. The Christ hymns for Käsemann are the most basic expression of early Christian theology.[33] God's power is proclaimed through Christ's lordship over the world and believers. In their proclamation of Christ as Lord, they deny power to all other lords. Obedience to Christ as Lord, therefore, does not allow obedience to other lords.

Besides the so-called enthusiasts, Käsemann's other theological opponents are those New Testament authors who represent what he calls early catholicism. Among these authors Käsemann includes Luke and the authors of Ephesians, Colossians, and the Pastoral Epistles. In these texts, the radical freedom of the Christian gospel disappears under the pressure to accommodate to the surrounding culture. Here the church becomes ascendant. Although these authors take their cue from themes in Paul, they develop them in the direction of salvation history and toward organizing ministry into offices, which are opposite to Paul's message in his genuine letters.[34]

Käsemann is highly critical of this development in the New Testament canon. Eph 1:20–23, which he describes as consistent with Eph 5:23–24, is an important text for him on the subject of the increasing importance of the church. He describes it as a place where "the gospel is domesticated."[35] Rather than being its judge, Christ is the mark toward which the church is growing. Although the passage stresses that Christ is "head over all things for the church," Käsemann understands the statement that the head cannot exist without the body as a move that diminishes the lordship of Christ. Likewise, he sees the ideal of mutual submission proclaimed in Ephesians as a threat to Christ as sovereign Lord. Although he mentions that the church is seen as a prototype of

---

[33]See the discussion of Col 1:15–20 in Ernst Käsemann, "A Primitive Christian Baptismal Liturgy," in idem, *Essays on New Testament Themes* (trans. W. J. Montague; Studies in Biblical Theology; Napierville, IL: Allenson, 1964) 149–68. See also idem, *Jesus Means Freedom*, 48; idem, "A Critical Analysis of Philippians 2:5–11," *JTC* 5 (1968) 45–88.

[34]Ernst Käsemann, "Paul and Early Catholicism," in idem, *New Testament Questions of Today* (trans. W. J. Montague; Philadelphia: Fortress, 1969) 245–46.

[35]Käsemann, *Jesus Means Freedom*, 89.

Christian marriage and he refers to the coming of a patriarchal system,[36] he does not pursue the connections between this christological development in which marriage is seen as the model for the Christ-church relationship and the social system of patriarchy. The author of Ephesians says wives submit to your husbands, as Christ is head of the church. As Käsemann interprets it, however, it is the presence of the church (wife) in relationship with Christ (husband) that is the domestication of the gospel. He does not reflect on the use of obedience to commend social roles and sexual hierarchy.

Käsemann analyzes Hebrews as a document of early catholicism in which the Christian message is adapted "for the long road." The author of Hebrews understands Jesus' obedience, not as the antithesis of Adam's disobedience but as a sign of humility linking Jesus with human beings.[37] The message of Jesus' obedience is the universal truism: "learn by suffering." Käsemann criticizes this reinterpretation of obedience as having a pedagogical purpose of making Jesus a model for faith. This move demotes Jesus from Lord of believers and denies the true place of the cross. Speaking of God's pedagogy works to the detriment of christology and must be corrected by the Spirit.[38]

However, in contrasting Paul with the author of Hebrews, Käsemann admits that:

> According to Paul, too, the Son creates sons, the Obedient One creates obedient people. And so the disciples are urged to become like their Lord in suffering. But the Apostle speaks of the manifestation of the new obedience which bears the stamp of the new world. Since Christ there has once more been an earth that listens to its Creator.[39]

Käsemann asserts, but does not explain, how the obedience in Paul wherein Christ creates obedient sons is different than obedience in which humans are obedient like Christ. Although the former stresses creation and the latter imitation, they seem to be more closely related than Käsemann admits.

---

[36]Ibid., 96.
[37]Ibid., 25.
[38]Ibid., 114.
[39]Ibid., 105.

Käsemann envisions the controversy in the New Testament canon very much in terms of the contemporary theological debates of his time.[40] In asserting the primacy of the Protestant doctrine of justification by faith as the center of Pauline theology in Romans, he is preaching his theological viewpoint against others, such as Krister Stendahl, who would read Romans with a salvation history perspective.[41] Many times in his writing, "existentialists" who argue from anthropology and soteriology could be substituted for "enthusiasts." Influenced by Barth, Käsemann criticizes the collapsing of christology into soteriology. Like Barth, his commentary on Romans is explicitly theological and rhetorical rather than confined to exegetical questions.[42]

In Käsemann's work, obedience functions to give an ethical, social dimension to the freedom preached by Paul and to provide a check against what Paul perceives to be enthusiastic excesses. True obedience for Käsemann means obedience to Christ as Lord and not to human authorities. Obedience to church authority or societal convention is excluded from this obedience. He does not consider how obedience is used in later Pauline tradition to justify structures of authority.

Käsemann's discussion of the role of obedience in Paul's theology depends upon his identifying the enthusiasts in the church in Corinth as the Other to whom Paul is opposed. Not only does Käsemann read Paul's rhetoric in 1 Corinthians as accurately describing a historical situation, but, for rhetorical reasons of his own, he intensifies the opposition between "enthusiasm" and obedience. The voices of those in Corinth whom Paul opposes are criticized with the notion of obedience. Käsemann summarizes the relationship of obedience language and enthusiasm:

---

[40]Käsemann relates his study of the New Testament to the social needs of his times in "What I Have Unlearned in 50 Years as a German Theologian," *Currents in Theology and Mission* 15 (1988) 325–35.

[41]Morgan and Barton, *Biblical Interpretation,* 118; Krister Stendahl, "The Apostle Paul and the Introspective Conscience of the West," in Samuel H. Miller and G. Ernest Wright, ed., *Ecumenical Dialogue at Harvard: the Roman Catholic-Protestant Colloquium* (Cambridge, MA: Belknap, 1964).

[42]Robert Jewett, "Major Impulses in the Theological Interpretation of Romans Since Barth," *Int* 34 (1980) 17–31. See also Joseph A. Fitzmyer, S.J., review of *An die Römer,* by Ernst Käsemann, *TS* 35 (1974) 744–47.

In this area Paul always acts as the representative of the
conservative attitudes of a view of existence we must call patriarchal—a view which, historically borrowed from the synagogue
of the diaspora, bases social ordinances on theological principles.
Where the apostle is not simply and naively reproducing these
attitudes, he is having to sharpen them because in his concrete
situation he is confronted with an eschatological enthusiasm.[43]

The issue of the struggles around Paul's authority in Corinth is not addressed.

Käsemann's analysis of the anti-enthusiastic function of obedience re-
veals an important dynamic of Pauline interpretation—the construction
of an Other against whom Paul directs his language of obedience. According to Käsemann, the alternative theological position in the
debate with Paul believes the body to be of no moral account or that social roles are meaningless. The rhetoric of obedience is construed as a
necessary corrective to such interpretations of the meaning of the gospel.

Neil Elliott employs this interpretive strategy in the conclusion of
his book on Romans. He concludes that Paul's letter to the Romans is
not directed at Jewish boasting but at Gentile boasting:

> From beginning to end, the argumentation of Romans is Paul's
> sustained critique of the Hellenistic *kerygma*, subordinating the
> doctrines of expiation of sins in Christ and freedom from the
> Law to the call for "the obedience of faith." Paul has, so to
> speak, perceived already the problem of generating a positive
> obligating ethic from the theologoumena of "freedom," and his
> solution is to abandon that language, at least in Romans, and
> speak instead ("because of your weakness," 6.19) of "slavery to
> righteousness" and the transfer to a new dominion.[44]

In his conclusion about the theological position that Paul is criticizing
in Romans, Elliott takes the opposite position of Bultmann. In his
construction of an opposing theological position, however, Elliott
employs the same strategy as Bultmann, who constructs the Jews as
the Other, and Käsemann, who understands the so-called enthusiasts

---

[43]Käsemann, "Romans 13," 209.

[44]Neil Elliott, *The Rhetoric of Romans: Argumentative Constraint and Strategy
and Paul's Dialogue with Judaism* (JSNTSup 45; Sheffield: JSOT Press, 1990) 298.

as Other. The prominence of the construction of the Other in previous studies of obedience points to an important line of investigation for the analysis of Philippians and Ephesians: how does the language of obedience, as Paul uses it, contribute to the construction of identity and of otherness within the letters?

Obedience as Love

Victor Paul Furnish explores the relationship between the New Testament and ethics in order to stimulate dialogue between scripture and contemporary ethical questions.[45] Because of his moderate position, his use of historical criticism in interpreting ethical issues in the New Testament, and his concern to relate them to contemporary ethical questions, he is widely read as an influential voice in New Testament ethics. For the purpose of this study, Furnish's work is notable both for its emphasis on the pervasiveness of obedience as a theme in the New Testament and for its acceptance of the metaphor of marriage and the social system on which it is based.

Obedience is a recurring theme in Furnish's work. First, he names it as one of the major themes in Paul's preaching and claims that it is equivalent to love.[46] In later work, where he focuses on Jesus' command to love, Furnish emphasizes the human response to that command, which he calls obedience. To obey the command is "to give oneself utterly in the obedience of love."[47] With this claim, Furnish spiritualizes obedience. By harmonizing obedience and love, he does not distinguish between Paul's use of the language of love and the language of obedience in particular rhetorical situations.

Furnish's method leads to such equations. Although he avoids the classic word study method, which may, for example, focus on the word *agape* in the New Testament, and he is attentive to the context of Jesus' statements in the various gospels, Furnish does not deal with the communities in which this literature developed, with their social structure, or with the community function of affirming love of one's enemies.

---

[45]See Furnish, *Theology and Ethics*; idem, *Moral Teaching*; idem, *Love Command*.
[46]Furnish, *Theology and Ethics*, 202.
[47]Furnish, *Love Command*, 92.

Rather, he pays most attention to verbal patterns and the logical relationships between these patterns.[48]

Furnish illustrates his method through his treatment of obedience as a major theme of Paul's preaching in *Theology and Ethics in Paul*. For Furnish, faith, love, and obedience are in a vital relationship.[49] He discusses the two references to obedience of Christ in Rom 5:19 and Phil 2:8 and argues that since Adam's transgression was disobeying God's commandment, then Christ's obedience is following God's commandment. Since Gal 1:4 suggests that God's will for Christ was that he give himself up, then Christ's obedience is his obedience to death, made explicit in the Christ hymn.[50] Here Furnish defines terms in Pauline theology by using one text to explain another rather than by examining the language of obedience within its own context. He concludes his discussion of Pauline themes with the statement: "in the vocabulary of Pauline theology faith is obedience and obedience is love."[51] With this equation, the distinctiveness of the structure of obedience and of the images associated with it is lost.

Furnish concentrates on the undisputed letters of Paul when he is defining Pauline theology. He does not deal with the development between the undisputed letters of Paul and 2 Thessalonians, Ephesians, and Colossians, or the question of whether the deutero-Pauline letters should be considered authoritative sources for theology.[52] He concludes that a study of the love ethic in these epistles neither upholds nor overthrows the judgment that they are not Paul's own work.[53] In other words, he admits the possibility of a continuity of thought between Paul and the Pauline school.

Furnish does not ask about the connection between obedience of the Christian to God or to Christ as Lord and obedience of wife to husband in Ephesians because he accepts that there is harmony between the earlier and later traditions. He takes for granted the metaphor of marriage

---

[48]Wayne A. Meeks, review of *The Love Command in the New Testament*, by Victor Paul Furnish, *Int* 27 (1973) 95–100.

[49]Furnish, *Theology and Ethics*, 182.

[50]Ibid., 186.

[51]Ibid., 202.

[52]Bruce C. Birch and Larry L. Rasmussen, review of *The Moral Teaching of Paul*, by Victor Paul Furnish, *Int* 34 (1980) 417–20.

[53]Furnish, *Love Command*, 130.

and the hierarchical relationship it entails. Furnish's treatment of marriage epitomizes his harmonization of the Pauline and deutero-Pauline letters. To illustrate how obedience is a result and not a condition for salvation, Furnish uses Paul's metaphor of the believer as Christ's bride (Rom 7:1–6; 2 Cor 11:2–3). He interprets the subordination of the Christian to God and the wife to the husband as "mutuality":

> The Christian "belongs to his Lord" in a way analogous to that in which a wife in Paul's day belonged to her husband. The husband's care for her and the wife's obedience to him constitute the essence of their new life together. Their life as husband and wife consists precisely in the continuing mutuality of this relationship, to which love constantly brings its unrelenting gift and claim. The marriage does not "progress" to some distant day when the gift need no longer be given or the claim no longer heeded. The marriage endures in the ever repeated giving and receiving, claiming and obeying. Just so for the believer who belongs to Christ. The reality of his new life is not separable from the powerful claim which Christ's lordship now exercises over him.[54]

Because of his strong theological commitment to the theme of the sovereign God who commands and to whom believers submit in obedience to those commands, Furnish does not question the positive character of marriage as a model for the God-human relationship. The sovereignty of this God is a positive force that could never be misused or corrupted. Obedience to God relativizes obedience to all other lords. Furnish is indebted to Käsemann for this understanding of the dialectical relationship of "indicative" statements about salvation and "imperative" ethical injunctions.[55]

In his later work for a wider audience, where he explicitly grapples with questions of sex and marriage and the role of women in the church, Furnish does not elaborate the unequal model of marriage that he suggests in his discussion of the bride of Christ.[56] Rather, he stresses Paul's

---

[54]Furnish, *Theology and Ethics*, 226.

[55]Furnish (ibid., 225 n. 44) expresses his debt to Käsemann for this emphasis.

[56]It is noteworthy that in his article "Belonging to Christ: A Paradigm for Ethics in First Corinthians" (*Int* 44 [1990] 145–57), Furnish does not speak of the metaphor as

principle of mutuality, distinct from both Greek and Jewish conceptions of marriage. Paul expresses this mutuality in 1 Corinthians 7 as does the author of Ephesians 5.[57] Mutuality characterizes Paul's vision of marriage. Furnish asserts that the injunctions for women's submission in the Pastorals and in 1 Corinthians 14 are by an author living in a time after Paul. He summarizes Paul's treatment of the governing authorities in Rom 13:1–7 by concluding that for the Christian "subjection to governing authorities is secondary to her or his obedience to the will of God."[58] Throughout his work, Furnish relies on obedience as an overarching way to describe human relationship with God. By equating obedience and love, however, Furnish does not recognize the distinctive way that obedience language constructs relationships. His reading of the rhetoric of Eph 5:21–6:9 may influence his formulation of obedience as equivalent to love. Furnish's discussion of Paul's use of the metaphor of marriage illustrates how an interpreter can accept and reinscribe kyriarchal language in his commentary.

Bultmann, Käsemann, and Furnish represent an approach to New Testament theology and ethics that focuses on building a rational system out of the variety of language and expression within Paul's letters. Therefore they isolate the language of obedience from its social and symbolic contexts. Their investigations of obedience are shaped by their commitment to a certain view of the development of early Christian history from the unstructured community of Paul to the more hierarchically structured early catholicism, which they either reject, as in the case of Bultmann and Käsemann, or simply acknowledge, as in the case of Furnish.

Slavery as Metaphor

More recent work in the area of early Christian ethics has sought a different approach to the study of early Christianity. Rather than using the rational language of ethics and the method of Furnish, these schol-

---

related to gender. Rather, he says "belonging to Christ means conforming one's life to the new identity which is given when he is accepted as one's Lord." In his commentary on 2 Corinthians he lists the passages that refer to the bride of Christ as 2 Cor 11:2; 1 Cor 7:2; Eph 5:22; and Rom 7:4 (*II Corinthians* [AB 32; New York: Doubleday, 1984] 486).

[57]Furnish, *Moral Teaching,* 47.

[58]Ibid., 138.

ars have understood Christian morality as developing within community and as using language and symbol in the socialization process to shape moral behavior. Wayne Meeks utilizes cultural-anthropological categories to discuss the development of Christian morality in his *The Origins of Christian Morality: The First Two Centuries*. Meeks's approach is more suited to an explanation of the language of obedience because it understands obedience as operative within the metaphors of marriage and slavery, which are also social institutions.[59] For example, Meeks does not discuss obedience as a topic but treats slavery as a metaphor for salvation and the image of God as owner. He emphasizes baptism as the ritual of conversion in which loyalty was transferred from one set of social relations to another.[60] Thus, the early Christian sect opposed itself to the morality of the world by adopting a different kind of behavior. However, Meeks uses the category of "ambivalence" to describe early Christian views about adapting to the morality of the surrounding culture:

> All the ambivalence and tensions that we have noticed between this movement of self-described converts and the moral world of the Greek city were focused and concentrated in the very houses where they held their "own meetings of God." The formulas of their baptismal ritual proclaimed that they had taken off their "old human" and put on "the new," that the old connections had been replaced by a new family of the children of God, brothers and sisters, a family in which there was no longer "Jew or Greek, slave or free, male and female" (Gal 3:28). But life in the house continued. Christian brothers and sisters still had siblings of flesh and blood who might or might not also be Christians. Christian slaves had masters and Christian wives had husbands, and a householder incurred obligations to his or her patrons and clients and equals in the social network of the city. True, a prophet of the lowest social class might receive in a trance a "revelation of the Lord" and with it the right to speak and give direction to the household assembly—but everyone still knew to whom the house belonged. True, women sometimes took on exceptional roles of leadership in the new movement—but there were soon strong reactions against that. True, in an exceptional case the apostle

[59]Meeks, *Origins of Christian Morality*, 166–72.
[60]Ibid., 31.

could write to a householder that he should welcome back his
delinquent slave "no longer as a slave, but more than a slave, a
beloved brother . . . both in the flesh and in the Lord" (Philem
16), but elsewhere he treats slavery as a matter of indifference:
"You were a slave when called? Never mind" (1 Cor 7:21). Soon
Paul's disciples and other leaders as well would be repeating the
old rules of Greek household management, "Slaves, be submissive in all fear to your masters . . . . ; Likewise wives, be submission to your own husbands . . ." and so on (1 Peter 2:18–3:7).[61]

Meeks treats the points at which the early Christian vision challenged
the social structures of society as exceptions to the general trend toward
accommodation. He contrasts interpreters of Paul who interpret him in
an ascetic direction, such as those in the Thomas tradition, with those
interpreters, such as the authors of Ephesians and Colossians, who lean
"more and more in the direction of adopting the commonsense universe
of popular morality."[62]

Meeks discusses the metaphor of slavery under the heading "God as
Owner."[63] Noting that the metaphor of slavery is used positively by Paul
in 1 Corinthians 9 and Romans 6, he points out that slavery in the Greco-
Roman world was flexible and multifaceted and could be a means of
status mobility.[64] He does not emphasize the fact that there were other
metaphors and language to describe salvation in early Christianity but
assumes that being promoted as the slave of a different master was the
only "advance" possible within the early Christian symbolic universe.
Although Meeks begins with baptism and conversion as basic to early
Christianity and recognizes the sharp tension between the early Christian community and its culture, he does not stress that some Christians
understood baptism as abolishing the categories of slave and free, male
and female. By immediately elaborating on the category of ambivalence,
Meeks's reconstruction undercuts the concreteness of the early Christian claim of equality and of freedom. Thus, his analysis tends to
reinscribe the conservative strands of the New Testament sources.

[61]Ibid., 49–50.
[62]Ibid., 64.
[63]Ibid., 169.
[64]Here Meeks cites the work of Dale B. Martin, which will be discussed below.

Meeks's view of the centrality of Paul contributes to his stress on ambivalence. Although Meeks emphasizes the importance of the community for shaping morality, when discussing Paul's communities, he gives more weight to Paul's language than Paul's audience. For example, he argues that the Christian house communities, especially at Corinth, have leadership crises unrelated to Paul himself to which Paul responds with the flexible metaphor of the cross:

> When Paul writes to the various communities he founded, it is invariably to suggest, cajole, argue, threaten, shame, and encourage those communities into behaving, in their specific situation, in ways somehow homologous to that fundamental story. In the process, Paul uses older stories and older rules, maxims, customs, and moral commonplaces to interpret the Christ-story—but simultaneously uses the Christ-story to transform those older stories, rules, maxims, customs, and commonplaces. That led to a certain polyphony in Paul's discourse.[65]

Meeks's framework, in which Paul is at the center, cannot take into account the way the community might contribute to such polyphonic discourse.

The method Meeks uses to discuss early Christian morality is more useful for the study of obedience language than the construction of a system in which obedience is one element. However, features of the framework of earlier Pauline theologians continue in his analysis despite his different methodology. First, he focuses on Paul's voice as the source of all creative use of language in the tradition and discounts the contribution of early Christian communities. In this respect, Meeks's work shares Bultmann and Käsemann's identification of Paul as the genuine and authoritative moment in the tradition.

Although Meeks discusses the author of Ephesians's interpretation of Paul, he does not focus on the role of the language of obedience and the metaphors of slavery and marriage in the development towards accommodation to the universe of popular morality. To the extent that Meeks's framework takes the kyriarchal language in which God is parent, owner, and king for granted and construes Paul as the chief interpreter of that language, Meeks's framework of interpretation is the same as that of Furnish, despite the difference in their method.

---

[65]Meeks, *Origins of Christian Morality*, 196.

In his study of the metaphor of slavery in its context in Greco-Roman rhetoric, Dale Martin investigates how the metaphor of slavery can have a positive soteriological role for early Christians.[66] At the outset, in his definition of his subject, Martin separates slavery as a metaphor from early Christian stances towards slavery.[67] First, he establishes that as part of a patronal system, Greco-Roman slavery was multifaceted and ambiguous, a system in which one could advance in status by becoming slave to a higher master. Within that system it was less important that you were a slave and more important whose slave you were.[68] On this basis Martin argues that in 1 Corinthians 9 Paul confirms his authority with the self-identification "slave of Christ" and then lowers himself with the expression "slave of all." In his analysis Martin does not give attention to the other soteriological metaphors in early Christianity except to argue that in 1 Corinthians Paul was arguing against those who saw themselves as strong and as "reigning." He argues that although there were more egalitarian voices and metaphors in early Christianity, the Christian movement saw itself along the lines of a patronal structure from the very beginning.[69] In his discussion of Paul's use of the enslaved leader in 1 Corinthians 9, he concludes that Paul "uses patriarchal language to make a non-patriarchal point."

> Modern persons imbued with ideas similar to the democratic ideology of Paul's world may not find Paul's implication radical, but to those Greeks and Romans whose symbolic universe was more informed by benevolent patriarchalism, Paul's advice was disturbing and unacceptable.[70]

In Martin's reconstruction, Paul is using the topos of the enslaved leader to oppose those who support love patriarchalism.

By exploring the social context of Paul's language, Martin arrives at an interpretation that differs from other readings of how Paul uses sla-

---

[66]Martin, *Slavery as Salvation*, xiv.

[67]Ibid.

[68]Ibid., 132. Martin's analysis of Greco-Roman slavery does not refer to the work of Orlando Patterson whose sociological study of slavery across cultures presents features of slavery that challenge Martin's reconstruction of Greco-Roman slavery. See Orlando Patterson, *Slavery and Social Death: A Comparative Study* (Cambridge, MA: Harvard University Press, 1982).

[69]Martin, *Slavery as Salvation*, 58–59.

[70]Ibid., 128.

very language as a rhetorical strategy in a specific situation in Corinth. But like earlier interpreters, Martin's reconstruction constructs an Other to which Paul's rhetoric is directed. Martin takes into account the social-political context in his treatment of slavery as a metaphor, but he does not discuss the image of marriage that Paul also employs in 1 Corinthians nor does he refer to the debates about sexuality at issue in Corinth. When he defines his topic as discussion of the "metaphor" of slavery, his focus is too narrow to include issues of concrete behavior of women or slaves within the community.

In recent discussions of Pauline theology, theologians have noted the difficulty of systematizing Paul's use of the slavery metaphor. They identify obedience and the related slavery metaphor as one of the "contradictions" in Pauline theology. Richard Hays speaks of "Slavery and Freedom" as one of the "loose ends" or "synthetic challenges" that must be addressed by those who wish to make a synthesis in Pauline theology.[71] He points out the paradox that while Paul's exhortation to Philemon to receive Onesimus back "no longer as a slave but more than a slave, as a beloved brother . . . both in the flesh and in the Lord" (Phlm 16) implies that "the symbolic world of the gospel impinges on and reshapes social relations," in other parts of his letters Paul uses the slavery metaphor positively: urging Christians to "become slaves of one another" (Gal 5:13) and referring to himself and Timothy as "slaves of Christ Jesus" (Phil 1:1).[72] J. Christiaan Beker speaks of Paul's conflict between two convictions:

> a) the conviction of the presence of the Spirit within the communal body of Christ, which establishes a pneumatic democracy in the body of Christ and in turn explains the lack of normative "offices" in the Pauline church; and b) the conviction of his unique apostolic call and authority, which establishes Paul as the normative interpreter of the gospel who requires the church to be obedient to his own construal of coherence-contingency relations.[73]

---

[71]Richard Hays, "Crucified with Christ: A Synthesis of the Theology of 1 and 2 Thessalonians, Philemon, Philippians, and Galatians," in Bassler, *Pauline Theology*, 244.

[72]Richard Hays (ibid., 245) states: "Obviously Paul uses the slavery metaphor in different ways, but the uses would seem to work against one another, particularly at the level of discerning the practical social implications of the gospel story."

[73]J. Christiaan Beker, "Recasting Pauline Theology," in Bassler, *Pauline Theology*, 23.

In the framework of Hays and Beker, Paul is the source for Pauline theology, therefore contradictions within Paul's use of language can be described as a "paradox" or attributed to an inner "conflict of convictions." The fact that the system of Hays and Beker cannot account for the different uses of the language of obedience in Paul's letters indicates the limitations of their frameworks and points to the need for an alternative framework of interpretation.

Conclusions and Alternate Framework

This review of influential interpreters of obedience language in the Pauline tradition has shown that these treatments of obedience share five major features. First, they draw a sharp distinction between obedience in Paul's letters and subordination and obedience in the letters of the Pauline tradition, particularly Ephesians and Colossians. This is related to the second common feature: a focus on the "spiritual" dimension of obedience rather than on the way it implies and constructs social relationships. Third, their analysis takes for granted the social system in which the language of obedience operates, that is, the sex/gender system and the kyriarchal family. In some instances this language is amplified. Fourth, Paul's call for obedience is constructed as a necessary response to a social or theological "problem" : enthusiasm, gnosticism, or kerygmatic Hellenistic libertinism. Finally, they emphasize the role of human will when they conclude that Pauline obedience is "free obedience," "voluntary obedience," or obedience as "love." By this formulation, they deal with the contradiction or tension in the letters between the language of freedom and the language of mutuality.

These common features allow us to describe the framework with which these interpreters are working as one that takes the kyriarchal metaphor of slavery and marriage as a given aspect of early Christian language represented by Paul. If Paul's conservative position with respect to the patriarchal system is a difficulty, as it appears to be for Käsemann, it is explained by a reconstruction of a historical situation in which Paul's so-called opponents present a problem such as "enthusiasm," to which Paul responds with the language of obedience. If the interpreter takes a sociological approach, such as Wayne Meeks, the language of obedience used to reinforce patriarchal relationships is an inevitable accommodation to the surrounding culture. In various ways, commentators rationalize Paul's use of this language as necessary. Thus, these studies have supported the assumptions with which they have begun: that obedience language and the symbolic world it evokes—of ruler and ruled, master and slave, and husband and wife—is early Christian language that had no viable alternatives. However, the way they interpret Paul's rhetoric and reconstruct his historical situation renders evidence of viable alternatives invisible. Because all of these exegetes accept Paul as the authoritative center of the early Christian tradition, they have not investigated critically Paul's use of the language of obedience to construct relationships between himself and the members of his audience.

Coming from a feminist perspective, this study questions both the inevitability of the symbolic universe of kyriarchy within early Christian language and the enormous emphasis and privilege given to Paul's voice at the expense of others in the reconstruction of the history of early Christianity from his letters. Within the diverse context of the early Christian movement, a vision of equality struggled for expression within the dominant patriarchal culture. This study explores how the language of obedience operates in specific situations, at particular moments within this struggle. I do this by a method of rhetorical criticism and historical reconstruction that can understand, rephrase, and amplify not only Paul's voice but the voices of other Christians in the community.

CHAPTER 2

The Semantic Field of Obedience:
the Verbs ὑπακούειν and ὑποτάσσεσθαι

E xegetes who have discussed the concept of obedience in Paul have distinguished Paul's use of the language of obedience (for example, in Rom 5:18–19 and 6:12–19 and Phil 2:6–12) from the obedience language in later Pauline writers by limiting the discussion to passages that use the word ὑπακούειν ("to obey"). They do not consider texts in either the undisputed Pauline letters or in the later letters in which the word ὑποτάσσεσθαι ("to subject oneself, to submit") appears because these passages are thought to be about subjection or subordination rather than obedience. Exegetes base their arguments heavily on the difference in vocabulary between ὑπακούειν, which they consider to be characteristic of genuine Pauline letters, and ὑποτάσσεσθαι, which appears frequently in the pseudonymous letters. For example, in commenting on Romans 13, Ernst Käsemann quotes Gerhard Delling: "Whereas ὑπακούειν usually designates free obedience, ὑποτάσσεσθαι emphasizes more strongly the fact that divine order rules in the divinely established world and that this entails super- and sub-ordination."[1] Among the exegetes discussed in chapter one, Käsemann explicitly claims that the distinction between obedience and submission is based on the distinction in vocabulary. Bultmann also makes the implicit distinction when he distinguishes between radical obedience and the obedience that is commanded by an authority outside the self. The word ὑπακούειν connotes the qualities of freedom and deci-

---

[1]Gerhard Delling, *Romer 13, 1–7 innerhalb der Briefe des NT* (Berlin: Evangelische verlagsanstalt, 1962) 39. Quoted by Ernst Käsemann, *Commentary on Romans* (trans. Geoffrey W. Bromiley; Grand Rapids, MI: Eerdmans, 1980) 351.

sion that Bultmann says characterize radical obedience, while ὑποτάσσεσθαι refers to that obedience mediated by a hierarchy of human authorities. The restriction of discussions of obedience in the Pauline tradition to passages with ὑπακούειν and an elimination or marginalization of passages that use ὑποτάσσεσθαι is very common, particularly among Protestant exegetes. The adoption of this distinction pervades Pauline studies and therefore must be addressed directly before proceeding to explore the language of obedience in Philippians and Ephesians. I argue that the sharp distinction drawn between the two words is a false one, based upon the exegetes' convictions about Paul and not upon the evidence of the language of the time.

The distinction between vocabulary for obedience and for subordination rests upon the fact that ὑπακούειν and its cognates ὑπακοή and ὑπήκοος ("obedience" and "obedient") occur more frequently in the undisputed Pauline letters,[2] while ὑποτάσσεσθαι predominates in the deutero-Pauline and Pastoral Epistles.[3] Of the occurrences of ὑποτάσσεσθαι in these latter letters, eleven of them occur in passages that are known as the household codes. The difference in the roots of the two words: ἀκούω ("hear") for ὑπακούειν and ταττ-, ταγ- ("order") for ὑποτάσσεσθαι has been used to argue for a fundamental difference of meaning.[4] The increase in the occurrences of the word ὑποτάσσεσθαι in the apostolic fathers,[5] where it is used in the context of submission to bishops and presbyters, has also contributed to the opinion that ὑποτάσσεσθαι has a fundamentally different meaning than ὑπακούειν.

The actual distribution of these two different expressions in the Pauline letters, however, shows exceptions to these general rules, which call into question this distinction. The word ὑποτάσσεσθαι does occur in Paul's undisputed letters (Rom 8:7, 20, 10:3, 13:1, 5; 1 Cor 14:32, 34, 15:27, 28, 16:16; and Phil 3:21). Of these instances both 1 Cor 14:32 and 34 and Rom 13:1 and 5 refer to social relationships.[6] 1 Cor 15:27–

---

[2] Verb: Rom 6:12, 16, 17, 10:16; Phil 2:12. Noun: Rom 1:5, 5:19, 6:16 (twice), 15:18, 16:19, 26; 2 Cor 7:15, 10:5, 6; Phlm 21. Adjective: 2 Cor 2:9; Phil 2:8.

[3] Eph 1:22, 5:21, 24; Col 3:18; 1 Pet 2:13, 18, 3:1, 5, 22, 5:5; Tit 2:5, 9, 3:1.

[4] Kittel, "ἀκούω," 224.

[5] Ignatius Poly. 2.1; Eph. 2.2, 5.3; Magn. 2; Trall. 2.1–2, 13.2; 1 Clem. 57.

[6] The Pauline authorship of both of these texts is disputed. Besides the textual evidence, one of the main arguments for 1 Cor 14:35 as a later interpolation is that the language of the injunction, particularly the verb ὑποτάσσεσθαι, is typical of later Pauline

28 argues for the hierarchical relation between God and Christ. In addition, the deutero-Pauline letters contain the word ὑπακούειν (Eph 6:1, 5 and Col 3:20, 22). In these instances both verbs occur in the same context, within several verses of one another.[7] In order to challenge the view that these occurrences are exceptions to the general distinction, I shall investigate the language of obedience in the Greek of Paul's time to see how the two words are related to one another. I argue that an exploration of the language of obedience must include consideration of the whole semantic field of obedience, which contains both words.

The Semantic Field of Obedience

The concept of a semantic field derives from the study of linguistics and the philosophy of language and has been developed in New Testament studies.[8] Within a semantic network, various member words express different aspects of central concepts. Semantic networks may change over time and various networks may exist simultaneously. In this understanding of language, words do not have an essential meaning in themselves but gain their meaning through their relationship with the other words in context. Therefore it is not sufficient when one investigates obedience to study the word ὑπακοή as a single word with a single meaning. Rather, one must study the various words used to describe obedience, their relationship to each other, and the way in which context determines difference in meaning.

Investigating the semantic field of obedience differs from a word study approach, which focuses on one word, such as ὑπακοή, and groups it with others of similar etymology.[9] The semantic field approach is especially promising in the case of obedience, which is expressed by a range

---

writings. Thus, the validity of the distinction is maintained by appealing to the distinction. In the case of Rom 13:1–7, a text that has caused interpreters enormous problems, the resemblance between Paul's advice here with that in 1 Pet 2:13–17 is used to argue that this text is also a later interpolation.

[7]In addition, the word ὑπακούειν occurs in 1 Pet 3:6 and Heb 5:9, 11:8.

[8]See James Barr, *The Semantics of Biblical Language* (London: Oxford University Press, 1961); Eugene A. Nida and Johannes P. Louw, *Lexical Semantics of the Greek New Testament: A Supplement to the Greek-English Lexicon of the New Testament Based on Semantic Domains* (Atlanta: Scholars Press, 1992).

[9]See, for example, the article by Kittel, "ἀκούω," 216–25.

of words with various connotative and associative meanings and tensions between figurative and literal meanings.[10] Semantic field analysis allows one to explore three aspects of the previous discussions of obedience. First, it calls into question the sharp distinction between obedience to God and obedience to social superiors. Second, it helps to redraw the map of obedience language. Third, it shows how the different words in their contexts are related to one another.[11]

Taking up James Barr's challenge that theological thinking is done in larger linguistic structures and sentences,[12] scholars have sought to go beyond a word study approach to biblical language, such as that represented by the *Theological Dictionary of the New Testament*, and have developed lexicons to reflect an alternate understanding of language. A major work that employs the concept of semantic field is the lexicon of the New Testament based on semantic domains by Johannes P. Louw and Eugene A. Nida. The authors place ὑπακούειν and ὑποτάσσεθαι (middle and passive) and their synonyms in one domain and ὑποτάσσειν ("to subject") in the active voice in another. They point out that, although in some languages it is difficult to determine the difference between "leading" and "ruling or governing," the two sets of interpersonal relationships must be distinguished.[13] Louw and Nida make this distinction by placing ὑπακούειν and ὑποτάσσεθαι under the domain that they call "Guide, Discipline, Follow."[14] They place ὑποτάσσειν (active) and words for ruling and serving (βασιλεύειν and δουλεύειν) under the subdomain of "Control, Rule." The former category suggests voluntary action in response to a benign authority, while the latter connotes the necessity of the use of force under a coercive authority.

---

[10]See the principles of semantic analysis described in the introduction to Louw and Nida, *Greek-English Lexicon*, v–xx.

[11]As it begins to understand religion as a language or a complex web of cultural meanings, New Testament studies has moved away from an emphasis on vocabulary to an appreciation of language as a field. The work of Wayne Meeks demonstrates this sensitivity. See Wayne Meeks, *The First Urban Christians: The Social World of the Apostle Paul* (New Haven: Yale University Press, 1983).

[12]James Barr, *The Semantics of Biblical Language* (London: Oxford University Press, 1961) 231–34.

[13]Louw and Nida, *Greek-English Lexicon*, 466. See also Botha (*Subject to Whose Authority?* 12–61) who discusses Rom 13:1–7 from a linguistic perspective.

[14]Louw and Nida, *Greek-English Lexicon*, 465.

Investigating the use of the words in several representative Greek authors provides comparative evidence to analyze Louw and Nida's distinction. By establishing the semantic field in the Greek language at the time of Paul, we may broaden the understanding of obedience beyond the very restricted definition of Delling, taken over by Bultmann and Käsemann. Even more importantly, broadening the field, focusing on the context, and looking at the other words that appear with the major words for obey and obedience can provide a glimpse into the symbolic universe in which obedience makes sense. Once one moves away from viewing ὑπακούειν as an exclusively theological word with a theological meaning, one can begin to see the various social contexts in which obedience language is at home.

The following exploration is not an exhaustive study of the place of obedience in the work of each specific author but an assessment of the range of Greek words and their contexts both in the Greek of Plato and Aristotle and in Greek-speaking contemporaries of Paul. I begin by looking at Plato and Aristotle's use of words for obey because authors who write at the time of Paul appropriate their categories of thought in a revival of Platonic and Aristotelian thought.[15] I then examine the contexts of these words in several representative Greek authors: the Stoic philosopher Epictetus, the rhetorician Dionysius of Halicarnassus, and the Jewish apologists Philo and Josephus.

Plato and Aristotle

Authors of the time of Paul revive the rhetoric of Plato and Aristotle, including the contexts in which they use the language of obedience.[16] Before the Hellenistic period, the verb ὑποτάσσεσθαι does not occur. The verb ὑπακούειν appears in contexts that denote "to answer" and "to obey." In Plato, ὑπακούειν may mean "to answer the

---

[15]On the rediscovery of Aristotle in the first century, see Elizabeth A. Clark, *Clement's Use of Aristotle: The Aristotelian Contribution to Clement of Alexandria's Refutation of Gnosticism* (New York: Mellen, 1977). See also John M. Dillon, *The Middle Platonists: A Study of Platonism 80 BC to AD 220* (London: Duckworth, 1977).

[16]The influence of Aristotle's view of household management upon the household code tradition of the New Testament has been shown convincingly by Balch, *Let Wives Be Submissive.*

door,"[17] "to agree,"[18] or "to comply" to a request.[19] In *Leges* it is used with "new laws" as its object.[20] It can be used figuratively to mean "answer the call" of a country when it calls people to duties.[21] Elsewhere, Plato uses ὑπακούειν in a discussion of teaching people virtue. Here the verb occurs in the negative to refer to "the one who does not obey" (ὃς δ' ἂν μὴ ὑπακούῃ) such punishment and instruction.[22]

In Aristotle, ὑπακούειν means "to answer" or "to obey."[23] In one passage in *Politica*, the discussion of rulers and ruled is the context for the verb. In a discussion of two parts of the soul, the verb ὑπακούειν refers to the part of the soul that can "obey reason." "For the soul is divided into two parts, of which one is in itself possessed of reason (λόγος) while the other one is not rational in itself, but is capable of obeying reason."[24] Although the specific word is ὑπακούειν and not ὑποτάσσεσθαι, the implication is that obedience is a feature of the relationship of ruled to ruler. The one who is ruled obeys the one who rules.[25]

From the first century BCE to the first century CE, Greek authors use both ὑπακούειν and ὑποτάσσεσθαι.[26] Relationships of ruling and being ruled are the context for both verbs.

Epictetus and Dionysius of Halicarnassus

The Stoic philosopher Epictetus (ca. 50–130 CE) uses the word ὑπακούειν

---

[17]Plato *Phaed.* 59e.4. For the following references, see *Plato* (LCL; 12 vols.; Cambridge, MA: Harvard University Press, 1914–27).

[18]Plato *Crito.* 43a.6.

[19]Plato *La.* 200d.7.

[20]Plato *Leg.* 708d.4.

[21]Plato *Ep.* 358a.7.

[22]Plato *Prot.* 325a.8.

[23]Aristotle *Ath.* 32.3.6. See Aristotle *Athenaion politeia* (ed. F. G. Kenyon; 3d ed.; London: Longmans, 1892).

[24]Aristotle *Pol.* 7.1333b. See *Aristotle* (LCL; vol. 23; Cambridge, MA: Harvard University Press, 1967).

[25]Elsewhere in *Politica*, Aristotle explains that the body is to be governed by the soul (*Pol.* 1.1254b).

[26]Results of a *Thesaurus Linguae Graecae* search show that in the first century BCE, both verbs occur in Philo, Diodorus Siculus, Dionysius of Halicarnassus, Strabo, and Appolonius Citiensis. In the first century CE, Plutarch, Josephus, Epictetus, Dio Chrysostom, Clement of Rome, Ignatius, and Aesop all use both verbs. Both are used in the New Testament and within the Pauline letters.

as "to answer a call" and as a response to commands of a king.[27] The word occurs in reference to the behavior of a slave and of a son. In *Diss.* 1.13.2, a slave is said to obey or not to obey a request: "And when you have asked for warm water, and the slave does not obey you; or if he does obey you but brings in tepid water" (ὅταν δὲ θερμὸν αἰτήσαντός σου μὴ ὑπακούσῃ ὁ παῖς ἢ ὑπακούσας χλιαρώτερον ἐνέγκῃ). This discussion is in the context of ruling: "Do you, not remember what you are and over whom you rule?" (οὐ μεμνήσῃ τί εἰ καὶ τίνων ἄρχεις). The relationship between the slave and the master determines whether one should be angry or not when the slave does not obey. Epictetus also uses the word ὑπακούειν in the context of a son in relationship to his father. "To obey in all things" (πάντα ὑπακούειν) is a feature of being a son.[28] Clearly, in Epictetus's use, the obedience is not "radical," but conventional, as it occurs in the social relationships of master and slave and of father and son. In *Diss.* 4.1.154, ὑπακούειν and πείθεσθαι ("to obey") are synonyms in the context of the obedience that one should yield to a country: "nor would he have suffered another to yield them more obedience and submission" (οὐδὲ παρεχώρησεν ἄλλῳ μᾶλλον πείθεσθαι αὐτοῖς καὶ ὑπακούειν).

Epictetus uses the verb ὑποτάσσεσθαι less frequently than ὑπακούειν. It appears twice in the active voice to mean "to classify" or "to lay down a premise" in an argument.[29] In the passive, it means "to be subservient" or "to be subject": "Remember that it is not merely desire for office and wealth which makes men abject and subservient to others (ταπεινοὺς ποιεῖ καὶ ἄλλοις ὑποτεταγμένους)."[30] The meaning of the passive sense of the verb appears to overlap with the meaning of ὑπακούειν in that one who subjects oneself to another is also one who would obey that one.

In the work of the rhetorician Dionysius of Halicarnassus (d. 8 BCE), ὑπακούειν can mean "agree," "hear," or "heed."[31] The negative denotes "not to obey" or "to decline." The verb ὑποτάσσεσθαι is used in political contexts to mean "to be subject." For example, in discussing the

---

[27]Epictetus *Diss.* 1.11.20, 2.6.16 and Diss. 1.25.8, 14 (trans. W. A. Oldfather; LCL; 2 vols.; London: Heinemann, 1926–29).

[28]Ibid., 2.10.7.

[29]Ibid., 2.17.11 and 4.1.61.

[30]Ibid., 4.4.1.

[31]For example, Dionysus of Halicarnassus *Ant. Roma.* 2.37.4.5, 2.50.3.6, 3.4.3.7, 4.27.1.4 (trans. Earnest Cary; LCL; 7 vols.; Cambridge, MA: Harvard University Press, 1940–51).

relationship of colonies to the mother-cities, Dionysius says: "Indeed, there are many races of mankind among which the mother-cities do not rule over their colonies but are subject to them" (πολλά γέ τοι φῦλά ἐστιν ἀνθρώπων, παρ' οἷς αἱ μητροπόλεις οὐκ ἄρχουσιν ἀλλ' ὑποτάττονται ταῖς ἀποικίαις).[32] The verb also is used to refer to the soul subjected to the body in *Ant. Roma.* 5.67.4, a passage similar to the one in which Aristotle speaks of the two parts of the soul in which one obeys the other.

The verb ὑποτάσσεσθαι and a cognate of ὑπακούειν occur in the same context in a discussion of a military leader, Mettius, who does not want to be under another leader: "[This man] disdaining now to hold any longer a command that was subject to another's command or to be subordinated rather than himself to lead" (οὐκ ἀχιῶν ἔτι ἀρζὴν ἔχειν ἑτέρας ἀρχῆς ὑπήκοον οὐδὲ ὑποτάττεσθαι μᾶλλον ἢ οὐκ αὐτὸς ἡγεῖσθαι). The overlapping meanings of the two words is evident in this passage. The adjectival phrase "being obedient (ὑπήκοον) to the command of another" and the infinitive "being subordinated" (ὑποτάττεσθαι) share the common feature that they represent the opposite of "leading."[33]

Philo and Josephus

Paul's near contemporaries, the Jewish philosopher Philo of Alexandria (20 BCE– 40 CE) and the Jewish historian Flavius Josephus (37– ca. 100 CE), use both verbs to express the concepts that in English would be called "obedience," "subjection," and "subordination." The semantic field of obedience in Philo ranges across the contexts of political life, the subjection of citizens or captives to rulers, agricultural life in which animals are subject to their masters, and relationships within the family. A survey of Philo's usage of ὑπακούειν and ὑποτάσσεσθαι shows that these words describe relationships among people of unequal power or authority. These relationships include subject and ruler, slave and master, animals and humans, and wife and husband. In these relationships, the one who is in an inferior position, the subject or the ruled, obeys the one who rules.

[32]Ibid., 3.11.2.2.
[33]Ibid., 3.23.3.3.

In Philo, the primary Greek words expressing obedience are ὑποτάσσεσθαι, ὑπακούειν and πειθάρχειν. The meanings of these three words overlap considerably including "to obey," "to be subject," or "to follow a command." In general, ὑπακούειν describes the action characteristic of one who is subjected to another. Both ὑποτάσσεσθαι and ὑπακούειν have cognates that mean "a subject." In two texts in Philo, cognates of both verbs appear together in the same context. The first, τοῦ ὑπηκόου in *Hypothetica* 7.5, means the "subject" of a ruler, parallel with wife of a husband and son of a father. Being a ὑπήκοος, an "obedient one," is here equivalent to being a subject of a ruler:

The same holds of any other persons over whom he has authority (ὧν κυριεύει). If a man has devoted his wife's sustenance to a sacred purpose he must refrain from giving her that sustenance; so with a father's gifts to his son or a ruler's to his subjects (ἐὰν ἄρχων τοῦ ὑπηκόου).[34]

In *De Agricultura* 47, ὑπήκοος connotes "subject" of a ruler:

We gain nothing from the rule and governance (ἀρχαί τε καὶ προστασίαι) of men who are too good and gentle. For kindness is a quality open to contempt, and injurious to both sides, both rulers and subjects (ἄρχουσί τε καὶ ὑπηκόοις). The former, owing to the slight esteem in which they are held by those placed under their authority (ἐκ τῆς τῶν ὑποτεταγμένων) are powerless to set right anything that is wrong either with individual citizens or with the commonwealth.[35]

In the second sentence, τῶν ὑποτεταγμένων refers to the same subjects using a synonym of ὑπήκοος. These two instances in Philo illustrate the overlapping meaning of ὑποτάσσεσθαι and ὑπακούειν in the context of ruler and obedient subjects. When one is a subject, one obeys.

Philo's *De Abrahamo* provides another example of obedience as characteristic of subject peoples. Captive nations obey the orders of the king.

---

[34]*Hypothetica* 7.5. See *Philo* (LCL; 10 vols.; Cambridge, MA: Harvard University Press, 1929–62).

[35]On Philo's discussion of democracy in terms of the mind ruling the body, see Samuel Sandmel, *Philo's Place in Judaism: A Study of Conceptions of Abraham in Jewish Literature* (New York: Ktav, 1971) 148 n. 222.

The four great kings are described as those "whom the nations of the east obeyed" (οἷς ὑπήκουεν ἔθνη τὰ ἐῷα). Proof of the nations' subjection lies in their obedience to the orders of the king (πειθαρχοῦντα τοῖς τῶν βασιλέων ἐπιτάγμασι).[36]

The examples discussed in which ὑπήκοος stands for "a subject" show the overlapping meanings of ὑπακούειν and ὑποτάσσεσθαι in Philo. There are other texts where one or the other words stands alone. Philo utilizes ὑπακούειν without ὑποτάσσεσθαι to mean to obey commands and oracles.[37] He uses ὑποτάσσεσθαι to mean "subjects" and "under which category."[38] The contexts of these words do not differ significantly.

The widespread use of slavery as an example and as a metaphor for the relationship of obedience is apparent in Philo. Paul makes use of slavery as the context of obedience, notably in Rom 6:16–23 and Phil 2:6–8. Philo also chooses the master-servant relationship as a metaphor for the relationship between God and human.[39] Philo comments on Gen 26:5 (LXX) where "to obey" is translated as ὑπακούειν. Abraham, the slave (δοῦλος) of God, will speak boldly to his master only when he knows that his words will benefit his master. Philo describes the paradox of a servant of God feeling more joy than if he were king over the whole human race. Later Philo attributes Moses' frankness of speech (παρρησία) to friendship.[40] Philo goes on to qualify this relationship, however, by saying that this confidence is tempered with piety. Moses addresses God as δεσπότης, or master, rather than κύριος, as an example of that piety. Philo explains that δεσπότης is derived from the word "to fear" and therefore means "fearful lord" (φοβερὸν κύριον). Philo describes the combination of fear and confidence with which Moses addresses his master. His explanation assumes that fear of subordinate to superordinate is natural in relationships of subjection.

Philo interprets certain relationships of superiority and inferiority as natural. He uses Genesis 1–3 to justify and establish the correct hierarchy of power. In his interpretive retelling of the creation story he utilizes the complex of elements typical of the semantic field of obedience: rul-

---

[36]Philo *Abr.* 226.
[37]Philo *Congr.* 68 and *Fug.* 21.
[38]Philo *Leg. Gaj.* 51, 314 and *Decal.* 168, 171.
[39]Philo *Rer. Div. Her.* 6.
[40]Ibid., 21.

ing, being king, serving, obeying, authority, and power. In *Op. Mund.* 142, he describes Adam as "worthy of the rule (ἡγεμονίας) of the creatures of the earth." All mortal things "had been taught or compelled to obey him as their master" (καὶ ὑπακούειν ὡς δεσπότῃ δεδιδαγμένων ἢ βιασθέντων). Later in *Op. Mund.* 148, Philo explains that Adam names the animals because Adam was a king (βασιλεύς), and it is appropriate for a ruler to give titles to his subordinates (τῶν ὑπηκόων). Human beings, Adam's descendants, are still masters of animals (δεσπόζουσι τῶν ἀλόγων).[41] In Philo's symbolic world, ruling over subjects and mastering obedient creatures is the proper role of man, Adam's descendant.

When the hierarchical relationships of slavery, marriage, or parenthood intersect, it is necessary to determine what hierarchies take precedence over others. For example, in *Hypothetica* 7.8 Philo says that the relationship between husband and wife must be maintained even in slavery, and between parents and children even in captivity. His exhortation describes two hierarchical relationships nesting within one another. The hierarchy of the slave couple is preserved within the hierarchy of the master and slave relationship. The relationship of parents over children remains intact in the overarching state of captivity.

Whether free will or coercion plays a role in the semantic field of obedience is an important question because of the emphasis on radical obedience in Pauline theology. In Philo's use of language, ὑπακούειν appears to describe a response demanded in the context of a particular relationship rather than a choice. However, "obeying the commands of virtue" is something the wise man strives to do.[42] There is an element of choice involved. "To be subjected" (ὑποτάσσεσθαι) is not used in contexts where there is choice. Rather, it describes where one fits in the order of creation or where one is subjected to a political or military ruler. Although the element of choice or voluntary response may be slightly greater with ὑπακούειν, the majority of texts in Philo indicate

---

[41]Philo's understanding of ὑποτάσσεσθαι depends upon the LXX, which uses the verb in the active voice to describe God putting certain people under others. Ps 8:7, in which God is said to have subordinated all things to ἄνθρωπος, is an example in the LXX that becomes significant to New Testament writers. The interpretation of this text in Paul's letters will be addressed below, pp. 123–24. For one reading of the trajectory of interpretation of the verb, see Terence Y. Mullins, "The Use of ὑποτάσσειν in Ignatius," *SecCent* 2 (1982) 35–39.

[42]Philo *Congr.* 63.69.

that both words express obligations of particular relationships in nature.

Philo's interpretation of Adam's role in Genesis describes the origin of this natural order. The relationship of obedience exists for a lesser power who is subject to and who obeys the ruler or master. The hierarchical power arrangement is modified in particular cases by a servant of God who, because of an exemplary relationship with that master, is able to speak frankly with him, or by a master who treats a captive woman with gentleness. The meaning of ὑπακούειν and ὑποτάσσεσθαι overlap because obedience of inferior to superior is expected in a divinely ordered hierarchy.

The language that clusters around words for obedience are words that express the various aspects of ruling and serving: βασιλεύειν, κυριεύειν, κρατεύειν, and δουλεύειν. Words for king and master (βασιλεύς and δεσπότης), rule (ἡγεμονία), and power (δύναμις) often appear. Fear is associated with the inferior in relationships of unequal power. Words for commands or orders (ἐπιτάγμασι) occur in the context of obedience and are sometimes contained or implied in the verb ὑπακούειν.

An exploration of the semantic field of obedience in Josephus shows that, although he does not discuss obedience and subjection philosophically as Philo does, the contexts in which obedience words are found and the variety of vocabulary used to express obedience are very similar.

As in Philo, the meanings of ὑποτάσσεσθαι and ὑπακούειν overlap significantly in Josephus. For example, in an extended speech in the *Jewish War*, Josephus uses ὑποτάσσεσθαι and ὑπακούειν nearly synonymously to mean obey. He asks, "Will you to whom obedience (ὑπακούεῖν) is hereditary, you whose resources fall so far short of those who first tendered their submission (τῶν πρῶτον ὑπακουσάντων), will you, I say, defy (ἀνθίστοσθε) the whole Roman empire?"[43] The word that the Loeb translator renders as submission here could be as correctly translated as "obedience." Later in the speech, Josephus asks his audience if they would refuse to serve "those to whom the universe is subject?" (οἷς ὑποτέτακται τὰ πάντα).[44] Serving (δουλεύειν) and obeying (ὑπακούειν)

[43]Josephus *Bell.* 2.357. See *Josephus* (trans. H. St. J. Thackeray; LCL; 9 vols.; Cambridge, MA: Harvard University Press, 1927–65).

[44]Ibid., 361. Another example of those who are subjected having to obey orders is in ibid. 367–68.

are requirements of subjects. Obeying orders as in a military setting or obeying the will of one to whom one is subject politically happens within a relationship of unequal power. The word "master" is used to describe the powerful party.[45] Obedience is the signal of the relationship of subjection.

Several texts in Josephus speak of the proper order signified by obedience when that order is for some reason altered or reversed. Josephus describes individuals who have irregularly elected high priests who then must obey (ὑπακούειν) those who have given them honor.[46] In a speech about the Romans, Josephus asks ironically whether his people have "fallen in love with slavery and with our masters" (φιλόδουλοι δὲ καὶ φιλοδέσποτοι γεγόναμεν). He asks whether submission (τὸ ὑποτάσσεσθαι) was inherited from ancestors.[47] Submission, slavery, and having masters are equivalent relationships.

The association of submission to inequality of power or rank is shown in *Bell.* 1.31, where Josephus discusses dissension among Jewish nobles: "as one of equal rank could tolerate subjection to his equals." Similarly in *Bell.* 4.393, cohorts of John are said to "have scorned being subjected to a former equal" (δεινὸν ἡγουμένων ὑποτετάχθαι τὸ πρὶν ἰσοτίμῳ). In *Bell.* 5.5, Eleazer could not "bear submission to a tyrant junior to himself." Subjection is among unequals.

In the contexts of subjection, where Josephus uses the language of obedience, "voluntary" or "free" obedience is not a category that makes sense. Superior power operates in the response of obedience within the condition of subjection. Disobedience is used metaphorically to refer to a wall that does not succumb to battering force.[48] To obey means to collapse or to cave in to force.

In Josephus's discussion of the Essenes,[49] ὑποτάσσεσθαι and ὑπακούειν are used in different places. First Josephus says that the Essenes will keep faith with the powers (τοὺς κρατοῦσιν) since no one rules (τινὶ τὸ ἄρχειν) except by the will of God. If one is to rule, he does not abuse his authority (ἐχουσία) nor outshine his subjects (ὑποτεταγμένους

[45]Ibid., 4.175.
[46]Ibid., 149.
[47]Ibid., 175.
[48]Ibid., 6.26.
[49]Ibid., 2.140, 146.

ὑπερλαμπρυνεῖσθαι). The context of ruling and of hierarchy of power is evident. The Essene properly takes his place below the powers instituted by God and above his subjects, but not ostentatiously so. The Essenes honor God, their lawgiver Moses, and obey (ὑπακούειν) their elders.[50] The superiority of God and Moses extends by implication to the elders to whom obedience is due.[51]

Josephus's discussions of the relationship the between husband and wife demonstrates that proper order and obedience is expected in the family context as well as in the political and military contexts. The injunction to women in *Ap.* 2.201 to "let her obey" (ὑπακουέτω), because God has given the rule (τὸ κράτος) to man, is absolutely consistent with the pattern of the organization of power and authority in other occurrences of obedience. The chain or hierarchy pervading this semantic field is that of God over humans, and elders, fathers, and rulers over children, subjects, and wives.

Conclusions

The exploration of the context of the words ὑπακούειν and ὑποτάσσεσθαι in several representative Greek authors has shown that obedience occurs in the context of military, political, and domestic subjection. The symbolic universe that is both assumed and constructed by the language of obedience is a kyriarchal one in which father/Lord/husband rules and wife/children/slaves/captives are ruled or obey. As is well known, Philo and Josephus—the two authors who are closest to Paul in time and background—use the language of obedience in a way that supports the hierarchical structure of society. Research on the household codes in both Josephus and Philo support the finding that they urge a benevolent patriarchalism and use submission in apologetic contexts.[52]

---

[50]Ibid., 146.

[51]Josephus *Ap.* 2.206.

[52]See Balch, *Let Wives Be Submissive.* See also the work of Daniel Boyarin who understands Philo to be the writer closest to Paul in his understanding of gender on the spiritual and carnal levels. See Daniel Boyarin, *The Radical Jew: Paul and the Politics of Identity* (Berkeley and Los Angeles: University of California Press, 1994). Also, Daniel Boyarin, *Galatians and Gender Trouble: Primal Androgyny and the First Century Origins of a Feminist Dilemma* (Protocol of the Colloquy of the Center for Hermeneutical Studies 1; Berkeley: Center for Hermeneutical Studies, 1995).

An investigation of ὑπακούειν and ὑποτάσσεσθαι in the Greek of Epictetus, Dionysius of Halicarnassus, and of Philo and Josephus shows that they do not have substantively different meanings, nor is one context characteristic of one more than the other. Those who maintain that Paul is using the verb ὑπακούειν to mean "free obedience" or obedience outside the social hierarchy that organized his world must refute the quantity of evidence from these contemporary authors that suggests that Paul, in line with the use of the language of his time, uses both words to designate "obedience" as a feature of relationships of subordination. The claim that the two verbs have different meanings is not supported by contemporary Greek literature. Therefore, when Bultmann, Käsemann, Delling, and Kittel claim that Paul uses the word ὑπακούειν in a way distinct from ὑποτάσσεσθαι, they are making a theological distinction that asserts that Paul uses ὑπακούειν without the conventional connotations of subordination, or that he deliberately challenges the validity of those connotations and the symbolic universe they construct. I shall question this claim by reexamining key texts from the letters of the Pauline tradition. I consider both ὑπακούειν and ὑποτάσσεσθαι within the language of obedience. Rather than generalizing about all the occurrences of the language of obedience in Paul, however, the next part of this study examines two particular instances of the use of this language in their rhetorical and social contexts. I have chosen to examine the use of obedience language in the undisputed letter of Paul to the Philippians and in the pseudonymous letter to the Ephesians. I treat both these texts as rhetorical works that assume and construct symbolic universes, and I examine how the language of obedience operates to support or to challenge the conventional connotations and contexts of such language.

CHAPTER 3

Paul's Letter to the Philippians:
Rhetorical Analysis and Rhetorical Situation

In Phil 2:5–12, the language of obedience refers both to Jesus, who is described as "having become obedient to the point of death" (γενόμενος ὑπήκοος μέχρι θανάτου), and to the congregation who has "always obeyed" (πάντοτε ὑπηκούσατε). This has been one of the key passages in discussions of obedience in Paul's theology among the exegetes discussed in chapter one. For Ernst Käsemann, the obedience of Christ in Phil 2:8 is the paradigm for "free obedience."[1] Victor Furnish cites Phil 2:6–11 as one of the two places in which Paul refers to Christ's obedience. Furnish elaborates on this passage to develop one of the themes of Paul's preaching: "faith as obedience."[2] He recognizes that in its context Paul connects Christ's obedience with the obedience of those Paul addresses. Elsewhere, Furnish uses Phil 2:1–12 to argue that Christ's obedience is the paradigm for Christian obedience:

> Moreover, the apostle intends Christ's obedience to be paradigmatic
> for the believer. What he has done becomes an "incentive of love"
> (vs. 1 RSV), a "paraclesis" (vs. 1 RSV: "encouragement") in the
> double sense of gift and demand. The believers' obedience—to which
> Paul summons them in vss. 12–13—is made both possible and
> imperative by God's working within and among them (vs. 13), and
> its character is to be that of Christ's own obedience.[3]

[1]Käsemann, "Critical Analysis," 72.
[2]Furnish, *Theology and Ethics*, 182–87.
[3]Ibid., 218.

Wayne Meeks also connects Christ's obedience described in Philippians with Christian obedience. He states:

> Christ's becoming obedient to the point of death (ὑπήκοος μέχρι θανάτου [v.8]) sets the parameters of the obedience Paul expects of the readers (ὑπηκούσατε [v.12], with the implied imperative in the following phrase).[4]

Both Furnish and Meeks point out that Paul draws conclusions about Christian obedience from the description of Christ in Phil 2:6–11. Paul urges obedience from those he addresses and by extension obedience for Christians in general. The relationship between the believer and Christ is one of imitation in general terms. Thus, Furnish calls Christ's obedience paradigmatic. Along with other commentators, Furnish and Meeks assume that in the ambiguity of Phil 2:12 it is natural for Paul to merge obedience to God with obedience to himself.[5]

Claims about Paul's use of the metaphor of slavery in Philippians play a significant role in Dale Martin's discussion of slavery as a metaphor of salvation and its particular use in 1 Corinthians 9. Martin describes the slavery metaphor in Paul's theology of humiliation and exaltation. He recognizes Paul's key role as the intermediary example of obedience in the symbolic universe of Philippians. Christ's movement of humiliation and exaltation is imitated by Paul and then by the Philippians.[6] Martin does not present detailed support for his reading of the slavery theme in Philippians, but his emphasis upon Philippians indicates the importance of that letter in discussions of obedience as part of the metaphor of slavery. Likewise, Norman Petersen depends upon the text of Philippians for his conclusions about the symbolic universe of Paul in which the believer is liberated from one form of enslavement only to be temporarily enrolled in another—that is, to Christ as Lord.[7]

---

[4]Meeks, "Man From Heaven," 335.

[5]The following example illustrates how one commentator reads the ambiguity in Phil 2:12: "Just as you have always obeyed—as in v. 8 above, the verb is used without an object. Here the sense is probably of obedience to the gospel (2 Thess i. 8), the obedience of faith which the apostolic commission promotes (Rom i. 5), or more concretely of obedience to the Apostle's counsels and directions, accepted as carrying all the authority of the God who gave him the grace of the apostolate" (Beare, *Philippians,* 89).

[6]Martin, *Slavery as Salvation,* 131.

[7]Petersen, *Rediscovering Paul,* 246.

The letter to the Philippians, particularly Phil 2:5–12, is one of the very significant New Testatment texts in discussions of obedience in the Pauline tradition. This chapter explores Paul's use of obedience language within the rhetorical argument of the letter as a whole. Unlike many scholarly discussions of the narrative of Christ and its epistolary context in Phil 2:5–12, however, I interpret Paul's letter within an environment of diverse understandings and competing claims. Tensions within the language and imagery of the letter serve as clues to the audience of the letter. Observing Paul's rhetorical strategies and their effects sheds light on how Paul uses and adapts the language of obedience to a specific audience. This leads to a reexamination and reevaluation of the claim that Paul uses the language of obedience in a radical manner.

Procedure in this Chapter

After a discussion of two introductory matters, that is, the problem of the unity of the letter and the relationship between rhetoric and epistolography, I begin with the rhetorical analysis of the argument of the letter. This entails looking at the overall argument of Philippians in order to see how the narrative in which Christ is described as "obedient to the point of death" functions as a model for the behavior of the community. The rhetorical analysis examines the arrangement of topics and traces how the author develops the argument throughout each successive part of the letter. I identify and explore the dynamics of how the letter portrays author, audience, and opponents, and the role of Phil 2:5–12 in that strategy. This exploration may provide additional insights into a common feature of many of the historical reconstructions of exegetes discussed in chapter one, that is, the construction of a theological Other to which the language of obedience is a response. After having placed the narrative of Christ in Phil 2:6–11 into the context of Paul's argument as a whole, I look at the hymn as a pre-Pauline tradition quoted by Paul in order to investigate how Paul adapts the understanding of obedience within the hymn. I interpret Paul's deployment of the Christ hymn in his letter to the Philippians in concert with other rhetorical strategies brought to light in the rhetorical analysis in order to describe the inscribed rhetorical situation.

An exploration of Paul's rhetorical strategies within the letter to the Philippians must consider two key problems in recent Philippians scholarship. Both have to do with the historical situation of the letter, and both are based on a certain way of reading Paul's rhetoric. The first is the relationship between so-called internal opposition to Paul within the community and conflict with enemies from outside the community. The source of this problem is the tension in the language of the letter between warm expressions of friendship and affection toward the audience and strong statements of threat and opposition. Many recent treatments of Philippians emphasize the friendship motifs and read the expressions of friendship inscribed in the letter as accurately describing the historical situation. But these reconstructions cannot account for the extremity of language applied to "opponents" and "enemies." The second problem that has not been directly or successfully addressed is the tension between the language of obedience and the language of friendship. Commentators explain this tension as a paradox. Thus, the obedience to earthly lords is transformed into obedience to a heavenly Lord, and Paul asks the Philippians to obey within the context of friendship. When commentators describe the coincidence of friendship and obedience language as a paradox, they assume Paul himself to be the single source for both kinds of language and do not consider that some expressions may derive from the Christian communities with whom Paul is communicating. This investigation explores these problems first by maintaining the distinction between the rhetorical and historical situation, and second by attempting to construct a possible historical situation based not only upon how Paul constructs the situation but upon other evidence about the early Christian communities within which Paul worked. After analyzing the inscribed rhetorical situation, I begin to reconstruct the historical situation in chapter four.

Reading the Letter as a Unity

The scholarly debate over whether canonical Philippians is one letter written by Paul to Philippi or fragments of three letters to the same city that were modified slightly and compiled by a later redactor continues without resolution. Recent monographs and articles summarize the debate and reassert the validity of the partition theory of Philippians.[8]

---

[8]See, for example, Philip Sellew, "*Laodiceans* and the Philippians Fragments Hypothesis," *HTR* 87 (1994) 17–28. See also Lukas Bormann (*Philippi: Stadt und*

Some present new arguments to support the partition theory of the letter. At the same time, other work on Philippians proceeds to analyze the letter in its present form without employing a theory of partitions.[9] Both sides claim that inconsistency is a sign of the weakness of the alternate position. Those who see the letter as a unity point out that those who divide it can come to no agreement on where the fragments begin and end. Those who claim the opposite refer to the lack of consensus on the rhetorical divisions of the final letter.[10] Settling the question of the integrity of Philippians is not the purpose of this study; but clarifying the assumptions and the aims of the debate is necessary before proceeding with a rhetorical analysis of the letter.

The contrasting approaches of those who read the letter as a unity and those who see it as a compilation of fragments represent different ways of reading texts. One uses source and redaction criticism to explain "problems" within the text. It sees tension in the text as representing different layers of composition rather than as rhetorical strategy or as evidence of the rhetorical situation. For example, the abrupt shift in tone between Phil 3:1 ("Finally, my brothers and sisters, rejoice in the Lord. To write the same things to you is not troublesome to me and for you it is a safeguard"[11]) and Phil 3:2 ("Beware of the dogs, beware of the evil workers, beware of those who mutilate the flesh!"[12]) is explained by an event in the history of the composition of the text.

Christengemeinde zur Zeit des Paulus [NovTSup 78; Leiden: Brill, 1995]), who argues that the letter is made up of fragments. An influential formulation of the fragments hypothesis is Helmut Koester, "The Purpose of the Polemic of a Pauline Fragment (Phil III)," *NTS* 8 (1961–62) 317–32. Recently, however, Jeffrey T. Reed ("Philippians 3:1 ⟶ and the Epistolary Hesitation Formulas: The Literary Integrity of Philippians, Again," *JBL* 115 [1996] 63–90) argues that a comparative study of the "hesitation formula" offers more evidence that Philippians is originally a single composition and not multiple letters.

[9]For example, Fee (*Philippians*) argues against partition theories and analyzes the letter as a whole. While admitting the problems presented by the possibility that the letter is composed of fragments, other scholars proceed to investigate themes and continuities in the letter as a whole. See, for example, Pheme Perkins, "Philippians: Theology for a Heavenly Politeuma," in Bassler, *Pauline Theology*, 89–104.

[10]Fee, *Philippians*, 21–23.

[11]Phil 3:1: τὸ λοιπόν, ἀδελφοί μου, χαίρετε ἐν κυρίῳ. τὰ αὐτὰ γράφειν ὑμῖν ἐμοὶ μὲν οὐκ ὀκνηρόν, ὑμῖν δὲ ἀσφαλές.

[12]Phil 3:2: βλέπετε τοὺς κύνας, βλέπετε τοὺς κακοὺς ἐργάτας, βλέπετε τὴν κατατομήν.

According to this perspective, Phil 3:1 and 3:2 are lines from what were originally two different letters that have been spliced together to form one. Scholars with this view point out that in 3:1 Paul says "finally" (τὸ λοιπόν) as though he were about to conclude the letter. The expression τὸ λοιπόν is repeated in 4:8. "Rejoice" (χαίρετε) occurs in 3:1 and again in 4:4. A further problem is the appearance of Paul's expression of thanks for the Philippians' gift at the end of the letter (4:10–13). The source-critical approach attempts to explain seemingly anomalous features of the present text of Philippians by dividing the text into its original constituent pieces. Although all pieces are from Paul to the community in Philippi, each was written at a different time and, therefore, each has a slightly different historical setting and purpose.[13] Phil 4:10–20, therefore, is a letter of thanks for a gift; 3:2–4:1 is an attack upon opponents; 1:1–3:1 is an apologetic letter from prison. After reconstructing a historical situation for each fragment, this perspective determines a plausible order in which the fragments were written and proposes a hypothetical situation and rationale for the compilation of the fragments.[14]

This method accounts for common language and themes among the fragments by positing the same author and the same audience. It argues that at some time after the writing of the original letters by Paul, the redactor collected the fragments together without tampering with the content and placed them in an order that would appear to be a longer letter to Philippi. This redaction is often explained by the growing respect for Paul's letters as authoritative texts during the time of the redactor.[15]

One consequence of this approach for the interpretation of Philippians is that by reading the letter as three fragments, the polemical fragment (3:2–4:1) receives a less prominent position within the letter. A historical situation is reconstructed behind Phil 3:2–4:1 in which a threat from outside enemies *necessitates* polemical language describing outsiders. Therefore, one can maintain that the relationship between Paul and the

---

[13]I know of no theory of partitions that claims that the fragments are addressed by Paul to different communities.

[14]See, for example, Jean-François Collange, *L'Epître de Saint Paul aux Philippiens* (CNT 10a; Neuchatel: Delachaux and Nestlé, 1973) 24.

[15]For different rationales for the assembling of the fragments of Philippians, see Garland, "Composition and Unity," 156–57. Philip Sellew ("*Laodiceans* and the Philippians Fragments Hypothesis," *HTR* 87 [1994] 26) argues for a second-century redaction.

Philippians is characterized primarily by friendship as the language of partnership and affection would indicate.

In contrast, those who argue for the unity of the letter claim that the problems within the text are not indications of redaction but are stylistic rhetorical features that reveal something about way the argument develops. Those who argue for the unity of the letter point out that τὸ λοιπόν need not mean "finally" but may be used as a transitional particle. "Rejoice in the Lord" (3:1) need not be an expression of farewell. The expression of thanks for the gift is not the main purpose of the letter, and there is no convention that dictates that thanks for a gift must appear first in a letter. Further, unity proponents argue that there is no other example of the kind of literary and editorial activity proposed by the partition theory.[16]

The strongest arguments of those who support the integrity of the letter are based on the reappearance and repetition of key words and themes throughout the letter. The thanksgiving (1:3–11) mentions "partnership in the gospel"[17] and anticipates its verbal occurrence in 4:14 and 15. "In any case it was kind of you to share my distress. . . . No church entered into partnership with me in giving and receiving except you alone."[18] The emphasis on humility and self-abasement, acceptance of suffering, and struggle for progress in the Christian life are paralleled in both Philippians 2 and 3, which are two different fragments according to the partition theory.[19] The paradigmatic narratives of Christ in 2:6–11 and of Paul in 3:4–11 both are used as positive examples for the Philippians' conduct and attitude. For those who hold this position, the evidence of the thematic unity of canonical Philippians justifies reading it as a single rhetorical unit.[20]

Reading the canonical letter of Paul to the Philippians as a rhetorical discourse means reading it as a rhetorical unity. A rhetorical approach

---

[16]Fee, *Philippians*, 22.

[17]Phil 1:5a: ἐπὶ τῇ κοινωνίᾳ ὑμῶν εἰς τὸ εὐαγγέλιον. The NRSV translates κοινωνια as "sharing."

[18]Phil 4:14–15: πλὴν καλῶς ἐποιήσατε συγκοινωνήσαντές μου τῇ θλίψει. . . . οὐδεμία μοι ἐκκλησία ἐκοινώνησεν εἰς λόγον δόσεως καὶ λήμψεως εἰ μὴ ὑμεῖς μόνοι. The NRSV translates ἐκοινώνησεν as "shared."

[19]William S. Kurtz, "Kenotic Imitation of Paul and of Christ," in Fernando F. Segovia, ed., *Discipleship in the New Testament* (Philadelphia: Fortress, 1985) 103–26.

[20]Bloomquist, *Function of Suffering*, 101–18.

to reading Philippians attends to the final form of the text and analyzes how that text works to persuade the audience. The text—as it stands—is designed to be argumentative and persuasive: a reader must follow the cues of the text itself to see how the text functions. It is not necessary, however, to hold a theory of the unity of Philippians in order to analyze it rhetorically. One could assert that the letter is composed of three fragments and look at the rhetorical structure of each. A possible scenario could be reconstructed in which a redactor took a fragment of what appeared to be an *exordium*, for example, and placed it at the beginning of the composition, a *peroratio* at the end, and so on. In this case, the task of rhetorical analysis would be to read the redactor's rhetorical strategy in her/his compilation of the fragments. The analysis would have to propose four different rhetorical situations, each of which would be the basis of a reconstructed historical situation. In my opinion, however, the common themes and argumentative strategies that run throughout the letter point to the activity of one author rather than a redactor who saw the rhetorical possibilities of assembling positive and negative examples and the language of obedience and imitation into a persuasive whole for a new historical situation. If one were to maintain that a redactor pieced together fragments, then one would still have to explain why apparently awkward transitions such as that between Phil 3:1 and 2 were retained.[21]

One could object that the rhetorical arrangement that I will analyze properly belongs to the redactor sometime in the second century rather than to Paul. If such is the case, then the content of the letters could be used as examples of Paul's rhetoric but not the order in which they appear. Words and themes could be said to be characteristic of a Philippian correspondence, and the development of the rhetorical situation at different points in time could be traced. The language of obedience, a feature of one of the fragments, could be attributed to Paul and could be analyzed within its own immediate context. Although this is a possible way to proceed, it has the disadvantage of creating another stage in the development of the Pauline tradition, related to but distinct

---

[21]Of the rhetorical analyses of Philippians, all treat the letter as a rhetorical unit. Watson ("Rhetorical Analysis," 97–103) uses rhetorical analysis to demonstrate that it is a unity. Bloomquist (*Function of Suffering,* 97–103) argues for the unity of the letter on the basis of extensive lexical and thematic parallels.

from Paul. The final effect of such an approach may be to distance the findings of this study about the rhetoric of obedience as evidenced in Philippians from a study of Paul's "genuine" letters. In doing so, one may possibly reemphasize the model of difference between the understanding of "free obedience" in Paul and later hierarchical understandings of obedience. In other words, it may cooperate with the drive toward coherence and unity in Pauline studies that has been described by Elisabeth Schüssler Fiorenza:

> This impetus comes to the fore, for instance, in the attempts of Pauline scholarship to declare texts such as 1 Cor 11:2 16 and 14:34–36 as later interpolations because they do not cohere with the reigning scholarly appreciation of Paul's theology. Or, scholars rearrange the extant text and reconstruct the rhetorical situation of the diverse fragments of Paul's Corinthians correspondence in such a way that the symbolic coherence of Paul's theological argument is safeguarded.[22]

This study explores rather than presumes this reconstructive model.

Rhetoric and Epistolography

Although it is not a speech, Paul's letter to the Philippians uses the persuasive techniques and conventions of Greco Roman rhetoric. Scholars continue to debate whether to consider epistolary conventions or rhetorical conventions as primary in the analysis of Philippians.[23] One possible approach is to read Paul's letters as having an epistolary frame—

---

[22]Schüssler Fiorenza, "Rhetoricity of Historical Knowledge," 465–66. See also the discussion of the interpretive effects of different partition theories of 2 Corinthians by Shelly Matthews, "2 Corinthians," in Schüssler Fiorenza, Searching the Scriptures, 196–217.

[23]See the response to Duane Watson's rhetorical analysis of Philippians by Jeffrey T. Reed, "Using Ancient Rhetorical Categories to Interpret Paul's Letters: A Question of Genre," in Stanley E. Porter and Thomas H. Olbricht, eds., Rhetoric and the New Testament: Essays from the 1992 Heidelberg Conference (JSNTSup 90; Sheffield: JSOT, 1993) 292–324. Reed gives priority to epistolary conventions and argues that Paul worked within the bounds of epistolary traditions and made limited use of technical rhetorical categories. See also the critique of rhetorical criticism by Fee, Philippians, 14–17. Many of the objections raised by these scholars are addressed when one defines the rhetorical categories of analysis functionally and not formally.

opening with prescript and closing with postscript—that encloses a rhetorical arrangement. However, my approach understands rhetoric in a broader sense:

> When both epistolography and rhetoric are redefined in terms of human social behavior, letter writing can be seen properly as a species of the genus rhetoric, and rhetoric therefore encompasses epistolography.[24]

Paul employs epistolary conventions in his overall rhetorical purpose. He also uses forms other than epistolary conventions in his rhetorical argument as seen in the quotation of traditions such as hymns.

It is not necessary to prove that Paul received formal training in rhetoric or employed its forms with conscious intent to show that its patterns influenced his arguments and would have affected the expectations of an audience hearing Paul's letter read. Analysis of Paul's use and adaptation of the conventions of rhetorical speech can work to identify the main proposition of the argument, the proofs that support the proposition, and the arrangement and development of those proofs in order to trace the inscribed rhetorical situation.

The Inscribed Rhetorical Situation

Elisabeth Schüssler Fiorenza argues that rhetorical analysis must distinguish between the rhetorical situation inscribed in the text (the "inscribed rhetorical situation") and the historical situation of the letter.[25] Historical critical studies traditionally reconstruct the historical situation of a Pauline letter as Paul describes it. However, when Paul's letters are read as rhetorical discourses within a public discourse of competing claims, then it is understood that constructing the situation—who Paul is, who the other players are, and what is at stake—is one of the major purposes of Paul's rhetoric itself. Therefore, the historical situation cannot simply be equated with the situation inscribed in the text.

---

[24]Botha, *Subject to Whose Authority?* 138.

[25]Schüssler Fiorenza, "Rhetorical Situation," 386–403. See also idem, "Rhetoricity of Historical Knowledge," 443–69.

The first task of rhetorical analysis is to delineate the inscribed rhetorical situation: the exigency that must be overcome by the speech and the constraints upon the situation. The constraints include the argumentative possibilities of the speaker and the expectations of the audience. Both kinds of constraints affect the rhetoric of the speaker.[26] The author writes to persuade an audience on the basis of arguments and appeals to shared values. These values provide the basis of agreement from which to argue and operate as a constraint upon the author's discourse. Rhetorical analysis seeks to explore those arguments and the values that underlie them and to identify points of tension between the author's symbolic universe and that of the Christian community to whom he is writing. These points of tension indicate the contours of the debate within the early Christian community.

The second task of rhetorical analysis is the reconstruction of the possible historical situation. This reconstruction is done by reading Paul's rhetoric in the letter in light of the understandings of the audience and with information about the historical and social setting from other sources outside the text itself.

Paul's letter to the Philippians is written to a particular situation to persuade a particular audience. Paul's rhetoric portrays himself and the audience and constructs the issues being addressed. This analysis begins by examining Paul's self-portrayal and his portrayal of the audience in the unfolding argument of the letter in order to identify what Paul sees as the central issue—his purpose for writing—and to trace the way that he builds his argument.

The Inscribed Author

At the beginning of the letter, Paul does not apply the title "apostle" to himself as he does in Romans, 1 Corinthians, 2 Corinthians, and Galatians, thereby explicitly claiming apostolic authority. Rather, he identifies himself and Timothy as "slaves [NRSV: servants] of Jesus Christ" (δοῦλοι Χριστοῦ Ἰησοῦ). This phrase will gain significance as the letter progresses, and Christ, who is described in 2:8 as "taking the form of a slave" (μορφὴν δούλου λαβών), becomes a model for congre-

[26]Schüssler Fiorenza, "Rhetorical Situation," 387.

gational behavior. With the phrase "slaves of Jesus Christ," Paul both identifies himself with the authoritative figure of Christ and begins the process of presenting himself as a model to be imitated.

As the author, Paul and his "story" are very evident in the letter itself. Throughout the argument Paul refers to himself, his history, his present situation, and his future. His own narrative biography in 3:4–17 provides an example of renouncing status in contrast to "the dogs" in 3:2. Paul reflects on his own situation in 4:10–20.

In the opening of the letter, as in the early part of a speech, Paul portrays his absence from the community as a problem that his letter is intended to overcome. Three times in the opening of the letter Paul mentions his imprisonment.[27] He first raises the subject of his imprisonment explicitly in 1:12, where he asserts "that what has happened to me has really helped to spread the gospel" (ὅτι τὰ κατ᾽ ἐμὲ μᾶλλον εἰς προκοπὴν τοῦ εὐαγγελίου ἐλήλυθεν). He suggests that his imprisonment ultimately has been positive for the community. He raises his situation in prison again in 1:19–26, when he conveys uncertainty about whether or not he will return to the Philippians. He further alludes to the possibility of his death in 2:17. From his situation in prison, Paul deliberates about sending Timothy (2:19–24) and Epaphroditus (2:25–30) to Philippi. Thus, his imprisonment and resulting absence from the community is a critical feature of his self-portrayal. His situation in prison contributes to the construction of the rhetorical situation.

The Inscribed Audience

Everything Paul says about the audience in 1:3–10 conveys that he has a close and positive emotional relationship with them. Paul uses the emotional expressions "I hold you in my heart" (1:7; NRSV: "You hold me in your heart") and "I long for you all with the compassion of Christ Jesus" (1:8) to convey their close relationship. He thanks them for their "sharing in the gospel" (1:5). He speaks of them as sharing the same struggle (τὸν αὐτὸν ἀγῶνα ἔχοντες, 1:30). They, as "those who share in grace" (συγκοινωνούς μου τῆς χάριτος, 1:7), share common dedication to the gospel of Christ. This gospel is the standard by which conduct is measured throughout the letter. In Phil 4:15, Paul distin-

---

[27]Phil 1:7, 13, 17.

guishes the Philippians from all others when he refers to their "sharing
. . . in the matter of giving and receiving," which refers to a financial
relationship. Paul uses the language of rejoicing (4:4, 10) to describe
his feelings toward them. Paul's references to his past history with the
Philippians operates in his argument to strengthen their relationship in
the present. In the opening verses of the letter, through his use of
emotional language, prayer, and reference to their past association,
Paul describes and establishes a relationship with the audience that
will be the basis of his appeals in the letter.

The distinctive vocabulary of Philippians indicates the common
values of Paul and the community. In the opening verses, Paul invokes
the language of partnership (1:5, 7) and later uses words with the prefix
συν to describe his relationship with the Philippians (4:3, 14). That this
language of partnership appears in Philippians to a degree unknown in
the other letters suggests that it is language characteristic of the community at Philippi and expresses their self-understanding. The financial
relationship described in 4:15, which the Philippians initiated, is further
evidence of the high esteem in which the community holds κοινωνία.
Loyalty to the "gospel" is another common value to which Paul refers at
the outset of the letter.[28]

Paul makes his argument persuasive mainly by the creation of a *relationship* between author and audience and by his portrayal of himself as
it is inscribed in the text. Paul's frequent positive references to his relationship with the Philippians convey that they are in harmony with him
and with one another. At several points in the letter, however, Paul seems
to refer ambiguously to disharmony within the Christian community. At
other points, he implies that there is a threat to the community. The
following analysis of Paul's argument will show how Paul introduces
these anomalous elements and how they function within his argument.

Rhetorical Arrangement

Where form and source criticism see disparate subjects awkwardly
linked, rhetorical criticism sees the main proposition elaborated

---

[28]The significance of the term "gospel" in the letter to the Philippians is observed
by Peter T. O'Brien, "The Importance of the Gospel in Philippians," in idem and David
G. Peterson, eds., *God Who is Rich in Mercy: Essays Presented to Dr. D. B. Knox*
(Australia: Anzea, 1986) 213–33.

successively in different ways in order to build one argument upon another. Various rhetorical analyses of Philippians have identified the elements of the argument as beginning or ending in different places, but for none of these readings have the "shifts" of tone or topic presented a problem.[29] In the overall rhetorical structure of Philippians, the *exordium*, which introduces the main subjects, runs until 1:26. The *narratio*, which gives the history of the matter at hand, continues in 1:27–30. The main body of proofs, or the *probatio*, runs from 2:1 to 3:21, and the *peroratio,* or the summary of the main points and emotional appeal, is contained in 4:1–20. The sections of Philippians correspond with the conventional forms of a rhetorical speech. Knowing what is customary in each one of these sections can help one to appreciate the movement of Paul's argument.

The *Exordium*: Phil 1:1–26

The letter begins with the self-identification of Paul and Timothy, the senders of the letter, as "slaves of Christ Jesus." Paul addresses the letter to "all the saints in Christ Jesus who are in Philippi with the bishops and deacons." This specification of a subgroup—σύν ἐπισκόποις καὶ διακόνοις—within the main group of addressees does not occur in any other undisputed Pauline letter. The word ἐπίσκοποι, used to describe those being addressed, occurs in the Pastoral Epistles.[30] The word διάκονοι occurs throughout the letters of Paul.[31] The designations suggest that Paul is singling out leaders within the Philippian community to address with his letter. He does not name them. By including this form of address in the greeting, Paul notes that he recognizes distinctions between these two titled roles and "all the saints in Christ Jesus."

The *exordium* introduces the main topics of the speech and functions to obtain audience attention, receptivity, and good will.[32] Paul's state-

---

[29]For example, Watson ("Rhetorical Analysis," 67–76) includes 3:2–21 as part of the *probatio* while Bloomquist (*Function of Suffering*, 129–35) includes it in the *argumentio* (*reprehensio*: 3:1–16 and *exhortatio*: 3:17–4:7).

[30]1 Tim 3:2 and Tit 1:7.

[31]Rom 13:4, 15:8, 16:1; 1 Cor 3:5; 2 Cor 3:6, 6:4, 11:15, 23; 1 Thess 3:2.

[32]Watson, "Rhetorical Analysis," 62.

ment in 1:12 that his imprisonment has benefited the advance of the gospel and that many of the community have been strengthened by it (1:13–14) demonstrates that the present topic is of concern to the Philippians themselves and to the whole community. By emphasizing his concern for the Philippians (1:8–11), his past history with them (1:5–7), and their partnership in a common enterprise (1:15), Paul elicits the good will of the audience.

The *exordium* also elicits pathos. Paul's expression of love and yearning for the Philippians in 1:7–9, emphasized by an oath with God as witness in 1:8, generates feeling in the audience toward Paul. Pathos is evoked in 1:19–26, where Paul considers whether he will live or die. Paul portrays himself as preferring to be with Christ (1:23) but choosing instead to remain with the Philippians for their progress and joy in the faith. Paul's description of his predicament and his resolution of that predicament mirrors the description of one who gives up his own interests for the sake of others. Paul exhorts the congregation to do the same in 2:1–4 and interprets Christ's action as similar in taking the form of a slave and being born in human likeness in Phil 2:6–11. Here in the *exordium*, Paul begins the process of showing himself as a positive model. This process culminates in the call to imitate him in 3:17 and 4:9.

The opening of the argument portrays Paul's absence as a problem to be overcome in the letter. In these verses, Paul's argument closely identifies his own presence with unity. For example, in 1:12–13 Paul asserts that his imprisonment has advanced the gospel:[33]

> I want you to know, beloved, that what has happened to me
> has actually helped to spread the gospel, so that it has become
> known throughout the whole imperial guard and to everyone else
> that my imprisonment is for Christ.

---

[33]The following quotations are from Phil 1:12–17: Γινώσκειν δὲ ὑμᾶς βούλομαι, ἀδελφοί, ὅτι τὰ κατ᾽ ἐμὲ μᾶλλον εἰς προκοπὴν τοῦ εὐαγγελίου ἐλήλυθεν, ὥστε τοὺς δεσμούς μου φανεροὺς ἐν Χριστῷ γενέσθαι ἐν ὅλῳ τῷ πραιτωρίῳ καὶ τοῖς λοιποῖς πᾶσιν, καὶ τοὺς πλείονας τῶν ἀδελφῶν ἐν κυρίῳ πεποιθότας τοῖς δεσμοῖς μου περισσοτέρως τολμᾶν ἀφόβως τὸν λόγον λαλεῖν. τινὲς μὲν καὶ διὰ φθόνον καὶ ἔριν, τινὲς δὲ καὶ δι᾽ εὐδοκίαν τὸν Χριστὸν κηρύσσουσιν· οἱ μὲν ἐξ ἀγάπης, εἰδότες ὅτι εἰς ἀπολογίαν τοῦ εὐαγγελίου κεῖμαι, οἱ δὲ ἐξ ἐριθείας τὸν Χριστὸν καταγγέλλουσιν, οὐχ ἀγνῶς, οἰόμενοι θλῖψιν ἐγείρειν τοῖς δεσμοῖς μου.

In verse 14, Paul says that *most* of the brothers and sisters have been emboldened by it:

> And most of the brothers and sisters having been made confident in the Lord by my imprisonment, dare to speak the word of God with greater boldness and without fear.

Immediately following this assertion is the contrast of "some" and "others" in 1:15–17:

> v. 15: *Some* proclaim Christ out of envy and rivalry but *others* from good will.

> v. 16: *Some* [NRSV: these] from love, knowing that I have been put here for the defense of the gospel

> v. 17: *Others* preach Christ out of selfish ambition, not sincerely, but intending to increase my suffering in my imprisonment.

Those who preach out of love are equated with those who understand that Paul is in prison "for the defense of the gospel." On the other hand, those who preach out of envy, rivalry, and partisanship do so to afflict Paul in his imprisonment. The logic of these verses indicates that Paul is connecting an interpretation of Paul's absence with partisanship.

In these verses Paul refers to a sense of division and sets up the dynamics of identification with allies and opposition to "enemies." Paul seeks to gain the good will of the audience in the *exordium*, not only by praising them but by referring to a sense of division within the Christian community. In 1:14, he writes that "most of the brothers and sisters" were made more confident, yet the implication is that some were not. Paul develops this observation in the verses that follow using the construction οἱ μεν / οἱ δε. Although all preach Christ, some are motivated by envy and rivalry and others from good will. Because these verses follow immediately after the reference to his imprisonment, they suggest that the division in the community is a result of Paul's imprisonment. Commentators interpret these verses to mean that this division to which Paul refers occurs in the city of his imprisonment and therefore does not accurately characterize the situation at Philippi.[34] Others note, however, that Paul's exhortations throughout the letter to Philippi to unity and selflessness are appropriate to address the situation of division he speaks of in 1:15–18.[35] Fee suggests that the situation Paul faces in Rome reminds him of the possible situation in Philippi.[36] These verses contribute to the problem of determining the character of the "opposition" to Paul both in the rhetorical and the historical situation.

Rhetorically these verses function as the first time in the letter when Paul sets up a negative example in contrast to a positive one. This contrast has the effect of increasing the good will of the audience toward Paul because the audience clearly is meant to identify themselves with those who preach from good will and out of love.

Paul returns to the subject of his future presence or absence from a different angle in 1:19–26 when he reflects upon whether he will live or die. Life or death could be "salvation" (σωτηρίαν). In the choice between living and dying, he prefers to be with Christ (1:23). However, he concludes his reflections by saying that "to remain in the flesh is more necessary for you" (τὸ δὲ ἐπιμένειν [ἐν] τῇ σαρκὶ ἀναγκαιότερον δι᾽ ὑμᾶς, 1:24). He says it is for this reason that he will remain with them. Paul raises his potential presence in the future in 1:25 ("I know that I will remain and continue with all of you") and in 1:27 ("whether I come to see you or am absent") in response to the sense of disunity of "some" and "others" (1:15–17). He promises his future presence, his return, and his coming in the flesh as having greater positive benefits for the progress and joy of the Philippians (1:25).[37]

---

[34]For example, Fee, *Philippians*, 8.

[35]For example, Garland, "Composition and Unity," 141–73.

[36]Fee (*Philippians*, 123) states: "It seems reasonable to suppose that some strife on the local scene has heightened his concern for the situation in Philippi. Thus with vv. 15–17, Paul anticipates the exhortations of 1:27–2:16 and 4:2–3."

[37]Robert W. Funk ("The Apostolic 'Parousia': Form and Significance," in William R. Farmer, C. F. D. Moule, and Richard R. Niebuhr, eds., *Christian History and Interpretation: Studies Presented to John Knox* [Cambridge: Cambridge University Press, 1967] 262) notes that the apostolic parousia, which is expressed finally in the passage about the sending of Timothy (2:19–24), is anticipated in Phil 1:8, 19–26, 27 and 2:12. According to Funk, the "apostolic parousia" is "the presence of apostolic authority and power" (p. 249). I observe how the reference to Paul's future presence operates in the rhetoric of the letter.

In addition to the association of Paul's presence with unity, the text works to build and to define a relationship between Paul and the Philippians through expressions about the passage of time from past to present to future. In the *exordium* in 1:5, Paul refers to his past relationship with those he addresses with the expression: "from the first day until now" (ἀπὸ τῆς πρώτης ἡμέρας ἄχρι τοῦ νῦν). This is the first of several times in the letter to the Philippians where Paul connects the present with the past and with the future. The expressions "now as always" (ὡς πάντοτε καὶ νῦν) in 1:20 and "as always" (καθὼς πάντοτε) in 2:12 are highly condensed ways of referring to the tension between past, present, and future, and thus of invoking Paul's presence in the past, his absence in the present, and his potential presence or absence in the future. By this construction of time, Paul strengthens his relationship with the community during the period of his absence. Their relationship with Paul in the past, portrayed positively in 1:5, is used as a prediction of the probability of its continuing in the present and the anticipation of reunion in the future.

In both 1:5 and 2:12, Paul refers to God being at work within time to bring something God began to completion. In 1:6, Paul expresses certainty "that the one who began a good work among you will bring it to completion by the day of Jesus Christ" (ὅτι ὁ ἐναρξάμενος ἐν ὑμῖν ἔργον ἀγαθὸν ἐπιτελέσει ἄχρι ἡμέρας Χριστοῦ Ἰησοῦ). With this construction of time Paul pairs his continuing relationship with the Philippians from past to present with God's continuing work, past to present. By describing his ongoing presence with the community as parallel to the description of God's activity with the Philippians, Paul indirectly responds to the problem of his imprisonment and his resulting absence from the Philippian community. The parallel that is built between God and Paul in the opening verses of the letter operates in Paul's exhortation in 2:12 where he refers to the Philippians' always having obeyed.

The *Narratio*: Phil 1:27–30

The adverb μόνον in 1:27 marks the shift to the *narratio*, the second element of the rhetorical arrangement. In 1:27–30, Paul states the main proposition, which he will develop in the rest of the letter. The rhetorical strategies that we have observed thus far in the letter operate in concert in these verses: Paul's association of his own presence with unity, assumption of the necessity of unity in the face of opposition from enemies, and identification of the congregation with Paul. The possibility of Paul's presence or absence is raised in Paul's exhortation in 1:27:

> Only, live your life in a manner worthy of the gospel of Christ, so that, whether I come and see you or am absent and hear about you, I will know that you are standing firm in one spirit, striving side by side with one mind for the faith of the gospel, and are in no way intimidated by your opponents.[38]

Whether he is present or absent, Paul wants to hear of their unity, their standing firm in one spirit and striving with one mind for the faith of the gospel. Paul's point that his absence is not necessary and at the same time that it is only temporary underscores the importance of Paul's presence. Drawing the parallel between his own continuing presence and God's ongoing activity implies that Paul's presence is even more important to the well-being of the community. Thus, relationship with Paul, Paul's absence, and unity in the face of others are all interrelated in these summary verses and in the opening chapter of the letter.

These verses suggest that Paul's absence makes the community especially vulnerable to not being unified, to seeking their own interests, and to being afraid of their enemies. The verb πολιτεύω ("live your life") will be touched on again in 3:20 with the reference to the τὸ πολίτευμα in heaven. The theme of Paul's presence or absence is an integral part of his exhortation to conduct worthy of the gospel.

The role of Christian suffering recurs in 3:10 where Paul describes himself as sharing Christ's suffering. Paul employs vocabulary associated with military and athletic contests: στέκω, συναθλέω, ὑπὸ τῶν ἀντικειμένων, and ἄγον. This language will be used again in 4:2–3 in Paul's description of Euodia and Syntyche as "coathletes" with himself. In 1:27–30, Paul conveys the necessity of unity in the face of opposition from enemies with the repetition of words for "one" (1:27). Paul uses

---

[38]Phil 1:27: Μόνον ἀξίως τοῦ εὐαγγελίου τοῦ Χριστοῦ πολιτεύεσθε, ἵνα εἴτε ἐλθὼν καὶ ἰδὼν ὑμᾶς εἴτε ἀπών, ἀκούω τὰ περὶ ὑμῶν, ὅτι στήκετε ἐν ἑνὶ πνεύματι, μιᾷ ψυχῇ συναθλοῦντες τῇ πίστει τοῦ εὐαγγελίου καὶ μὴ πτυρόμενοι ἐν μηδενὶ ὑπὸ τῶν ἀντικειμένων.

dualistic oppositional language to contrast the fates of "you" and your "opponents" (ἀντικείμενους): "For them this is evidence of their destruction, but of your salvation. And this is God's doing."[39]

The *Probatio*: Phil 2:1–3:21
Positive and Negative Examples of Behavior

In the *probatio*, or main body of proofs, Paul presents the positive examples of Christ, Timothy, Epaphroditus, and Paul in order to show how one should lead a life worthy of the gospel of Christ. Paul does not proceed by describing or criticizing any specific behavior of the members of the community. Rather, he urges them to behavior "worthy of the gospel of Christ" (1:27) in general terms. Throughout the letter Paul uses different words to describe and to refer to the desired behavior. The meanings of these words overlap, but each word has different connotations and associated contexts. With φρόνειν and its cognates, Paul exhorts his audience to "be of one mind."[40] In 3:17, Paul invokes the language of imitation. In 2:12, Paul draws on obedience language to summarize the behavior he has recommended beginning in 1:27 and continuing through 2:5. The word ὑπηκούσατε (2:12) alludes to the description of Christ in the previous verses (2:7–8) as "becoming obedient to the point of death" and as "taking the form of a slave." Paul chooses to emphasize the word ὑπήκοος from the narrative of Christ in Phil 2:6–11. By interpreting congregational behavior as obedience, Paul constructs his relationship with the congregation at Philippi in a particular way. Although it appears to be synonymous with φρόνειν and the other characteristics of self-denying behavior summarized in 2:1–4, the verb ὑπακούειν has different connotations because it is at home in a different symbolic universe. I shall illustrate the rhetorical effects of this choice in the discussion of Paul's adaptation of the early Christian tradition in the context of the letter to the Philippians.

Rather than telling his audience to do specific things or arguing with them about specific theological positions, Paul illustrates the kind of behavior that he encourages by presenting positive personal examples of those who behave in the manner that Paul endorses and by introduc-

---

[39]Phil 1:28b: ἥτις ἐστὶν αὐτοῖς ἔνδειξις ἀπωλείας, ὑμῶν δὲ σωτηρίας, καὶ τοῦτο ἀπὸ θεοῦ.
[40]Phil 1:7, 2:2 (twice), 2:5, 3:15 (twice), 4:2.

ing negative examples of those who do not. Likewise, Paul does not give concrete instructions except in 2:29 when he tells the audience to receive Epaphroditus and in 4:2 when he entreats Eudodia and Syntyche to agree in the Lord and asks the σύζυγος to help them (4:3). Both times that Paul gives *specific* instructions, he uses the names of members of the community who hold leadership roles.

Introduction to the First Proof: Phil 2:1–4

Paul's first example—that of Christ—begins with a restatement of the proposition (1:27–30) in the form of a conditional sentence. In Phil 2:1–4, Paul reiterates the exhortation to oneness referred to in 1:27. The first part of 2:3 states the motivation for behavior in negative terms: "nothing from selfish ambition or conceit" (μηδὲν κατ᾽ ἐριθεί αν μηδὲ κατὰ κενοδοξίαν), and then contrasts the positive motivation: "but in humility regard others as better than yourselves" (ἀλλὰ τῇ ταπεινοφροσύνῃ ἀλλήλους ἡγούμενοι ὑπερέχοντας ἑαυτῶν). The same word (ἐριθεία) appears in the negative statement as was used in 1:17 to describe some who preach Christ "from selfish ambition" (ἐξ ἐριθείας). The following verse employs the same pattern of stating the negative motivation in 2:4a and the positive in 2:4b. In 2:2, φρόνειν is used in two expressions connoting unity: "be of the same mind" (ἵνα τὸ αὐτο φρονῆτε) and "be of one mind" (τὸ ἓν φρονοῦντες). This is the language of moral exhortation in the context of friendship.[41] Paul introduces this first example of Christ by using the same verb—φρόνειν— in the imperative to exhort the audience to a certain kind of behavior (2:5).

The translation and interpretation of Phil 2:5 has been a subject of much dispute. Because the relative clause in 2:5b lacks a verb, one must supply a verb in translation and interpret the eliptical phrase "which also in Christ Jesus" (ὃ καὶ ἐν Χριστῷ Ἰησοῦ). If one reads the verse as a continuation of what precedes it, as indicated by the repetition of φρόνειν, then the logical translation is: "think/act this way among your- selves, the way Christ Jesus thinks/acts." In this case the verb supplied would be φρόνειν, parallel with the first clause. The problem with this translation is that the narrative that follows the phrase does not focus on Jesus' interior thinking or describe him in ethical terms. Ernst Käsemann

---

[41]Stowers, "Friends and Enemies," 109–10.

argues against this "imitative" interpretation of 2:5 when he suggests that ἐν Χριστῷ 'Ιησου should be translated "within the realm of Christ."[42] His argument for the translation of 2:5 is connected with his argument against the imitative interpretation of Phil 2:6–11. However, if one understands that Paul is quoting a tradition in 2:6–11 and incorporating it into his rhetoric, then one can see that Paul presents Christ as an example of a way of thinking/acting (φρόνειν), although the tradition he quotes understands the story of Jesus as a mythical drama with soteriological consequences. The summary verses that introduce the tradition (2:1–5) clearly show that Christ Jesus is used as an illustration of community unity, humility, and self-sacrifice. The verse that follows the tradition (2:12) draws an ethical conclusion from it.

Christ as the First Positive Example: Phil 2:6–11

Paul relates the story of Christ as his first positive example of community behavior. In both scholarly commentary and theological tradition, this description of the action of Christ in 2:6–11 has received a tremendous amount of interpretive attention. Because the exegesis of specific phrases such as "being in the form of God" and "emptied himself" has figured prominently in christological debates about preexistence and kenosis, debate over interpretation has been vigorous. For much of its history of interpretation, the importance of 2:6–11 has extended beyond its use in the letter to the Philippians. My major goal in commenting upon these verses is to employ a rhetorical perspective that considers *both* the way the narrative of Christ coheres with its context and the way it is in tension with it. A rhetorical reading can recognize tensions between the way an earlier tradition envisions or interprets Christ and the way Paul uses that tradition to serve his rhetorical purposes in his historical situation. When he quotes traditional material, Paul capitalizes upon certain features of the tradition and leaves others unexplored. A perspective that can recognize both the tension and the harmony between an early Christian tradition and its use by Paul is able to recover a sense of the diversity of early Christian language and imagery for interpreting Jesus' life and death.

The tension between the hymn and its context has long been recognized. Scholarly discussion about the interpretation of Phil 2:6–11

---

[42]Käsemann, "Critical Analysis," 84.

clusters around how to make sense of it in its context in Philippians. Käsemann's argument against an imitative understanding of the hymn attempts to deal with the tensions between the passage and its epistolary context.[43] He argues that the context, especially Phil 2:5 and 2:12, does not have an imitative meaning but a soteriological or kerygmatic one. Thus, he interprets Paul's introductory verses to the hymn as consistent with the hymn itself, which, as Käsemann argues correctly, is not primarily imitative. In his polemic against the imitative understanding of the hymn, Käsemann stresses the difference between the meaning of the hymn as primarily mythological and its interpretation by critics who claim that it is primarily ethical. His interpretation of the hymn becomes the hermeneutical key to the letter, and Käsemann interprets the rest of the letter in its light. However, other scholars emphasize the continuity between the narrative in 2:6–11 and its context in Philippians by pointing to vocabulary that occurs elsewhere in the letter and expressions that resemble images in 2:6–11, such as Phil 3:20–21. In recent work on Philippians, this emphasis has led to a claim by some scholars— against the widely held consensus that the hymn is a pre-Pauline tradition—that Paul composed Phil 2:6–11 for this location in Philippians.[44] With this approach, Paul's overall argument is the hermeneutical key to interpreting Phil 2:6–11. In addition, Paul's language in other letters and other rhetorical contexts is used to illuminate language in 2:6–11. This perspective results in an unmodulated harmony of the diverse traditions in evidence in the Pauline letters. A rhetorical perspective acknowledges the power of the author to shape the interpretation of earlier materials in an overall argument but also uses the insights of source criticism to identify earlier traditions from different community settings.

The weight of the evidence suggests that Phil 2:6–11 is an earlier Christian tradition adapted by Paul. The parallel hymnic structure, the unusual vocabulary, the introduction of the unit by the relative pronoun, and the similarity in thought and imagery to other New Testament christological hymns contribute to this view. Since Lohmeyer first

---

[43]Ibid., 45–88.

[44]This position is argued by Larry W. Hurtado, "Jesus as Lordly Example in Philippians 2:5–11," in Peter Richardson and John C. Hurd, eds., *From Jesus to Paul: Studies in Honour of Francis Wright Beare* (Waterloo: Wilfrid Laurier University Press, 1984) 113–26. It is adopted by Gordon Fee in his commentary (*Philippians*).

argued that the verses must be pre-Pauline, there has been a consensus that this text is an early Christian composition.[45] The majority of scholars regard the hymn as pre-Pauline [46] and understand it to have had some functional history in an early Christian community prior to its use by Paul in this letter. They do not consider the narrative of Christ in these verses to be an invention of Paul, but they attribute it to other early Christians whose tradition is adopted and adapted by Paul. Once in the letter to the Philippians, of course, it becomes part of the material of Paul's theology.[47]

Criteria for identifying early Christian traditions are based upon theology, imagery, language, and form. The Christ hymn contains rare vocabulary such as μορφή, καταχθόνιος, and ὑπερυψόω, which occur nowhere else in the New Testament, and οὐχ ἁρπαγμὸν ἡγήσατο, a *hapax legomenon* in the Greek Bible. The emphasis on exaltation rather than resurrection and the lack of reference to the death of Christ "for us" are unusual in Paul's discussions of the gospel.[48] The narrative in Phil 2:6–11 is a tradition that was used in a Christian community and was adapted by Paul for this context. Paul quotes an older tradition in a letter to an audience as part of his communicative strategy of appealing to the values of that community. As scholars argue that Rom 1:3–4 is an older confession of the community incorporated into the opening of the letter to the Romans,[49] so this christological hymn may have been known and used by the Philippian Christians. Before it was utilized by Paul in his letter to the Philippians, the early Christian hymn expressed the self-

---

[45]Ernst Lohmeyer, *Kyrios Jesus: Eine Untersuchung Zu Phil. 2, 5–11* (Heidelberg: Winter, 1928).

[46]For example, Ralph P. Martin (*Carmen Christi*) takes this position in his influential study of the Christ hymn in Philippians. As Lohmeyer, many consider 2:8c to be a Pauline gloss.

[47]Phil 2:6–11 plays a major role in scholarly constructions of Pauline theology. Even those scholars who understand it to be pre-Pauline insist that it dominates Paul's thinking in Philippians. For example, Pheme Perkins considers the Christ hymn to be the "governing metaphor" in the letter to the Philippians ("Philippians: Theology for the Heavenly Politeuma," in Bassler, *Pauline Theology*, 95–98). Käsemann depends heavily upon it for his discussion of free obedience.

[48]Martin, *Carmen Christi*, 49.

[49]For example, C. E. B. Cranfield, *A Critical and Exegetical Commentary on The Epistle to the Romans*, vol. 1: *Introduction and Commentary on Roman I–VIII* (ICC; Edinburgh: T. & T. Clark, 1975) 57.

understanding of an early Christian community. Both its vocabulary, unusual in other Pauline letters, and its position near the opening of the letter suggest that it may have been valued and preserved by the Christians in Philippi. Paul quotes a tradition valued by the Philippians in order to connect with the audience. By quoting it, he harnesses the positive associations that the audience has with the piece toward his rhetorical purposes in the letter. Quoting an authoritative tradition lends the author or speaker the authority of the tradition itself.[50]

In his argument up to this point, Paul has urged the audience in his absence to a certain kind of behavior, which he has characterized in 2:1–4 as unified and self denying. He uses the story of Christ to illustrate that behavior and draws a conclusion from it in 2:12. The language of obedience that occurs in 2:7 and 8 is reemphasized in 2:12 by the description of the behavior of the congregation as "obeying." Clearly, the rhetorical context points to obedience as an essential feature of the story of Christ narrated in Phil 2:6–11.

Jesus and Obedience in the Christological Hymn

The hymn is an early Christian interpretation of Jesus formed in the process of theological or mythical reflection. It adopts models and language from the surrounding culture to express its understanding of Jesus. Among the sources of language available was the system of kyriarchy in which the father and lord ruled slaves, wife, and children. The following reading of the hymn explores how the kyriarchal language of political and social rulership from the Hellenistic cultural milieu is used to proclaim the significance of Jesus' death.

Unlike its paraenetic context, in which Christ is a moral example, Phil 2:6–11 relates the story of Christ in primarily mythological rather than ethical terms. It is the narrative of a divine figure who becomes human, dies, and is exalted by God.[51] The story of Jesus is recounted not

---

[50]John W. Marshall calls this the development of "ethos through imported texts" ("Paul's Ethical Appeal in Philippians," in Stanley E. Porter and Thomas H. Olbricht, eds., *Rhetoric and the New Testament: Essays from the 1992 Heidelberg Conference* [JSNTSup 90; Sheffield: JSOT, 1993] 368–69).

[51]The position that the hymn is primarily mythological is upheld in an influential study by Ernst Käsemann ("Critical Analysis," 47–52), who argues vigorously against those scholars who claim that it refers not to Jesus' preexistence but to Jesus' earthly

as a historical narrative but as a drama that takes place on a cosmological plane. The christological drama of the hymn begins before the birth of Jesus, when he was "in the form of God" (ἐν μορφῇ θεοῦ) and narrates his incarnation, when he "took the form of a slave" (μορφὴν δούλου λαβών).[52] The story continues after Jesus' death on the cross to his exaltation by God and enthronement as ruler of the cosmos (2:9–11).

In the hymn, traditions about Jesus' life and death are interpreted in categories of contemporary mythology. Because it begins with the relative pronoun ὅς, and the text does not specify its subject until verse 11, the original subject of the hymn may not have been Jesus or Christ. The drama of descent and ascent and cosmic rulership may have praised other divine figures. In this hymn, elements resembling traditions found in the synoptic gospels (such as Jesus telling his disciples to be as "a slave of all," Mk 10:44 par.)[53] are radically reconceived and reexpressed. Early Christians reflected on the meaning of Jesus in the period between the death of Jesus and the letters of Paul.[54] Although traditions about Jesus' obedience, such as Gethsemane traditions, distantly may be related to the reference to Jesus as "obedient to the point of death" in 2:8, the mythological pattern of reversal of status dominates the interpretation of Jesus' death.

The drama of the hymn is built around the extreme contrast between God and slave, the major opposition in the first half of the hymn. The one who was in the form of God took the form of a slave. The language

---

life. Discussion of the hymn's mythical pattern has been furthered by Dieter Georgi, "Der vorpaulinische Hymnus Phil 2, 6–11," in Erich Dinkler, ed., *Zeit und Geschichte: Dankesgabe an R. Bultmann zum 80. Geburtstag* (Tübingen: Mohr/Siebeck, 1964) 263–94; Elisabeth Schüssler Fiorenza ("Wisdom Mythology and the Christological Hymns of the New Testament," in Robert L. Wilken, ed., *Aspects of Wisdom in Judaism and Early Christianity* [Notre Dame, IN: Notre Dame Press, 1975] 17–41) argues that the hymn speaks of Christ with the language of Wisdom and of Isis. See also idem, *Jesus: Miriam's Child, Sophia's Prophet* (New York: Continuum, 1994) 147–50.

[52]Scholars debate whether or not Jesus' preexistence is expressed in these lines. Although some have tried to argue that these lines refer only to the earthly Jesus, the phrase "in the form of God" best refers to Jesus before birth.

[53]See Larry W. Hurtado, "Jesus as Lordly Example in Philippians 2:5–11," in Peter Richardson and John C. Hurd, eds., *From Jesus to Paul: Studies in Honour of Francis Wright Beare* (Waterloo: Wilfrid Laurier University Press, 1984) 124.

[54]Schüssler Fiorenza describes this phenomenon as the development of a foundational Christian myth (*Jesus: Miriam's Child, Sophia's Prophet* [New York: Continuum, 1994] 148).

of the hymn is the language of status renunciation and elevation.[55] This observation about the major opposition in the opening of the hymn and the parallel phrases does not depend on any reconstruction of the precise arrangement of the lines into strophes. It notes only that Jesus' renunciation of status is narrated in 2:6–8 and his restoration to the ultimate position is related in 2:9–11. The drama concludes with the exaltation of the one who took slave form into a position of cosmic lord—the one to whom "every knee should bend and every tongue confess." Within this schema, the phrase that describes Jesus as "being obedient to the point of death" depends upon the participial phrase "taking the form of a slave" in 2:7. As shown in chapter two, the adjective "obedient" (ὑπήκοος) most often appears in the context of slavery, where being obedient is a conventional characteristic of slaves to masters. Obedience is demanded by the context of slavery. What might have been expressed as a contrast between God and human, the hymn expresses as a more radical contrast by using the social system of kyriarchy as an analogy and juxtaposing slave and God (lord). Although some commentators argue that the hymn—and Paul in general—equates human life with slavery, they do not recognize how the status language of the slave-lord dichotomy gives shape to the hymn.[56] Within this overall shape, Jesus' becoming obedient to the point of death is a feature of his slave form. In the drama of the hymn, exchanging the form of God for the form of a slave is the effective action that results in God's exaltation of Jesus. The central element is not "being obedient to God" as a moral virtue.

In the first half of the Christ hymn, Jesus is the subject, and his slavery is not specified as being to God, nor is his being obedient said to be "to God." The text does not speak of a command that Jesus obeyed or refer to the reason or motivation for the act of "emptying" and "humbling." This feature coincides with the telling of the story of humiliation and exaltation as a myth rather than as a psychological or ethical story. The lack of an expressed object for Jesus' obedience and the repetition of ἑαυτὸν in 2:7 and 8 ("emptied himself" and "humbled himself") has been cited as evidence for the fact that Jesus' obedience in these verses

---

[55]See Sheila Briggs, "Can an Enslaved God Liberate?" *Semeia* 47 (1989) 137–53.

[56]For example, Norman Petersen (*Rediscovering Paul*, 247) uses Romans 6 to argue that for Paul, human life is slavery. This interpretation accepts that there was no alternative to Paul's kyriarchal language.

is voluntary or free. The emphasis of 2:6–8 is not upon Jesus obeying God. In the lack of a master for the slave in 2:6–8 and the apparent choice involved in taking slave form, the hymn's use of the master-slave system breaks out of the conventional understanding of obedience in the context of slavery. Within the social context of slavery, renouncing the status of God and being obedient voluntarily would not make logical sense. By describing Jesus' taking slave form without emphasizing a master or a commander, the hymn transforms the commonplace understanding of the master-slave system.

In the second half of the hymn (2:9–11), God becomes the subject of the action in bestowing a name upon Jesus and putting him in the position of Lord of all (note the repetition of πᾶς in τὸ ὄνομα τὸ ὑπὲρ πᾶν ὄνομα, πᾶσα γλῶσσα, πᾶν γόνυ κάμψῃ). In language that alludes to Isa 45:23, the drama moves from abasement to exaltation. The hymn does not explain how or why, but simply proclaims that as a response to the action of self-emptying and self-humbling God raises Jesus to the position of God. The drama of the hymn works in the combined movement of descent and ascent. The emphasis lies on the second half of the hymn where Jesus Christ is proclaimed Lord. The last verses express the effects of what Jesus did in 2:6–8. The fact that Christians cannot imitate Jesus' action in 2:9–11 is one of Ernst Käsemann's reasons for arguing against an imitative context for the hymn. His insight points to the fact that in its original setting, outside of the epistolary context of Philippians, the crescendo of the hymn is 2:9–11. Like Col 2:13–15, the hymn in Phil 2:6–11 proclaims Christ's victory over the cosmic powers. In the hymn in Heb 1:2–4, the action of "making purification for sins" and "sitting at the right hand of the majesty on high" makes the "son" superior to the angels. In these three instances, the stress of the soteriological narrative lies on the results. The hymn itself does not address the problem that the whole world is *not* presently bending the knee before the Lord. The narrative makes the statement that that they do. For those who sang the hymn, the fact that Christ is ruler means that *Christ* rules, rather than those "in heaven and on earth and under the earth."

The christological tradition preserved in Phil 2:6–11 functions to proclaim a shift of rulership, a shift of power provoked by the drama of Jesus' action. Within this view, the significance of Jesus' obedience referred to in 2:8 and implied in 2:7 is not that he subordinated himself to his Father's will but that he exchanged the form of God for the form of a slave. This reversal of status caused a rearrangement of power; it transferred rulership from the powers of death to God and to Jesus as Lord. In the context of the hymn itself, Jesus' obedience as a moral virtue is not the essential feature of the story of Christ.

Previous interpreters read the significance of "becoming obedient" and "taking the form of a slave" differently, depending upon the background narrative that they identify behind the passage. The object, structure, and purpose of Jesus' obedience differs if Jesus' action is seen as modeled after the Servant of the Lord, Adam, or a righteous Jewish martyr The variety of proposals as to the background of the hymn results from the fact that the passage employs vocabulary and imagery that has no precise models in other ancient literature. The language that it does use, however, does not belong exclusively to any one tradition. For example, features of Adamic speculation, apocalyptic thought, and Hellenistic wisdom overlap in ancient texts.

Although there are multiple sources for the language of the hymn, this reading seeks to identify the main emphasis of the narrative. Commentators who identify one "background" for the hymn make the mistake of reading the tradition in light of Paul's use of it in Philippians or Paul's use of related concepts in other letters. For example, the fact that Paul interprets obedience in 2:12 as obedience to God, and therefore as something the congregation can imitate, does not mean that the hymn presents Jesus as an ethical example. Some of those who argue that the suffering servant from Isaiah is the major model for the hymn read Isaiah's father-son language and symbolism into the hymn, which in itself does not emphasize the father-son relationship between Jesus and God. Those who see the Adam-Christ comparison as the major dynamic of the hymn depend upon 1 Corinthians 15: 21–22, 45–49 and Rom 5:18–19 to support their view. Evidence that Adam is the model for Christ in the hymn is found not within the hymn but outside it.[57] In contrast to the approach that seeks to interpret one text in terms of another, rhetorical analysis

---

[57]The argument that obedience is the key feature of the hymn itself depends upon comparison with Rom 5:18–19, where Adam's disobedience is compared with Christ's obedience. In its context in Romans, Paul seems to be employing another pre-Pauline tradition in his argument. Clearly in the statement in Romans it is the obedience of Christ in contrast with Adam that has soteriological consequences. In the Philippians hymn, the emphasis of the hymn itself is not on Jesus' obedience but on his exchange of forms and the reversal of status that causes the overthrow of the powers.

allows one to see the major emphasis of a piece while highlighting how Paul transforms it by placing the emphasis differently.

The emphasis of the hymn upon the change of status of the actor, described in the language of humbling and exaltation or of descent and ascent, has been compared with the apocalyptic thought that has influenced Paul's language in other letters. The total reversal of position from God to slave causes a radical shift in the aeons, a shift in rulers, from the rule of the power of death to the rule of the exalted Lord. This apocalyptic feature of Phil 2:6–11 was explored by Ernst Käsemann and has been developed by David Seeley. In contrast to the reading presented here, which denies that obedience is essential to the drama of the hymn, Seeley points out that Christ's obedience is essential in causing this apocalyptic shift in rulers:

> These two features then, appear to be the most important for Paul with regard to the hymn: obedience and the two opposing spiritual realms.[58]

> Paul views Jesus as the only one who has died an obedient death. . . . This peculiarly Pauline move is placed in an apocalyptic framework according to which two mythic realms or aeons battle with each other. Reenacting Jesus' obedient death transfers a person from enslavement by an evil Lord, Sin, to the rule of a benign Lord, Jesus.[59]

Seeley's reconstruction depends upon reading Phil 2:6–11 in light of Rom 6:5–6 in which the necessity of reenactment is explicit within the text. If Phil 2:6–11 is interpreted as a pre-Pauline tradition with an earlier history in the Christian community, then proclamation, not reenactment, seems to be the stress of the text.

The shift of power from one realm to another and the narrative of descent and ascent has the same structure as the Hellenistic Jewish mythology about Divine Wisdom. Like Christ Jesus in Phil 2:6–11, Wisdom descended from her position with God:

> Wisdom could not find a place in which she could dwell, but a

---

[58]David Seeley, *The Noble Death: Graeco-Roman Martyrology and Paul's Concept of Salvation* (JSNTSup 28; Sheffield: JSOT Press, 1990) 57.
[59]Ibid., 110.

place was found (for her) in the heavens. Then Wisdom went out
to dwell with the children of the people, but she found no dwell-
ing place. (So) Wisdom returned to her place and she settle
permanently among the angels.[60]

Like the central figure in the Christ hymn, Wisdom returns to a heavenly status. The hymn interprets the historical Jesus who died on a
cross in mythological terms as one who surrenders divine status,
becomes human, dies, and is exalted to universal sovereignty over the
cosmos. Employing the pattern of descent and ascent, the hymn
describes Jesus' activity as causing a shift in rulers. Jesus' becoming
"obedient to the point of death" brings about that shift. In verse 8, the
first half of the hymn comes to its lowest point. The word ὑπήκοος
describes Jesus' self-humbling and submission to death.

The hymn emphasizes the universality of Christ's lordship. He is Lord
(κύριος) over the heavenly and earthly powers. Hellenistic texts show
that Isis was described with the image of cosmic ruler and queen (κύρια).
The Christ hymn draws on the categories used in praise of both Wisdom
and Isis in its proclamation of Christ' rulership.[61]

The mythological features of Phil 2:6–11 and the hymnic form of the
piece strongly suggest that the original purpose of the hymn was not
ethical instruction but proclamation. The hymn as a whole, from equivalence with God through abasement and death to exaltation to a position
where all powers bow to him, is a proclamation, an exclamation, and a
hymn of praise. Like other apocalyptic expressions, it asserts that God
is in charge: Jesus Christ is Lord. The significance of Jesus' obedience
was not that he was obedient *to* God but that he was obedient *as* God. In
its original setting, the purpose of the hymn was not to provide a model
for Christians but to proclaim that Jesus is Lord.

Deployment of the Hymn in Paul's Rhetoric: Phil 2:12

In his deployment of the hymn, Paul directs the audience's attention to
the first half of the hymn, especially 2:8, and leaves undeveloped the
proclamation of Christ's universal lordship. Käsemann points to the

---

[60] *1 Enoch* 42.1–2 (trans. E. Isaac, *OTP* 1. 33).

[61] Elisabeth Schüssler Fiorenza, "Wisdom Mythology and the Christological Hymns
of the New Testament," in Robert L. Wilken, ed., *Aspects of Wisdom in Judaism and
Early Christianity* (Notre Dame, IN: Notre Dame Press, 1975) 33–37.

second half of the hymn as evidence that the hymn did not present Jesus as a model to be imitated. Käsemann's insight points to the fact that Paul does not exploit the second half of the hymn in his rhetoric in the letter. The verse that follows the hymn functions as Paul's instruction as to how to interpret its significance:

> Therefore my beloved, just as you have always obeyed, not only in my presence, but much more now in my absence, work out your own salvation with fear and trembling.[62]

Here Paul exhorts the congregation after the quotation of the early Christian tradition in Phil 2:6–11. This exhortation should be interpreted in light of the constellation of elements set up in the opening of the letter: the community's relationship with Paul, unity, and the tension between past, present, and future. The congregation's "having obeyed" is expected to continue in Paul's absence.

In this verse Paul draws a conclusion from the narrative of Christ. The conjunction ὥστε indicates that the sentence that follows is a logical consequence of what precedes. He addresses his audience as "my loved ones" (ἀγαπητοί μου). This affectionate form of address introduces his description of the congregation as "obeying." The different rhetorical strategies that Paul has used in 1:1–2:5 come together in this sentence. The tension between Paul's presence and absence, the temporal tension of past, present, and future, and the parallel drawn between God's activity and Paul's are concentrated in this verse. The verb Paul chooses to describe the congregation's behavior in the past, which Paul expects to continue, is ὑπηκούσατε. This word alludes to the description of Christ in 2:8 as ὑπήκοος. To summarize the kind of behavior that constitutes being "of one mind," which Paul urged in 2:1–4, Paul uses the verb ὑπακούω.

Used without a direct object, ὑπηκούσατε has an implied object.[63] Commentators have been unclear as to whether the object of congregational obedience is God or Paul. Generally, they assume that the

---

[62]Phil 2:12: "Ωστε, ἀγαπητοί μου, καθὼς πάντοτε ὑπηκούσατε, μὴ ὡς ἐν τῇ παρουσίᾳ μου μόνον ἀλλὰ νῦν πολλῷ μᾶλλον ἐν τῇ ἀπουσίᾳ μου, μετὰ φόβου καὶ τρόμου τὴν ἑαυτῶν σωτηρίαν κατεργάζεσθε.

[63]English translations reflect the difficulty. While the RSV translates the verse "as you have always obeyed," the NRSV translates it "as you have always obeyed me."

ambiguity is natural: that obeying God and obeying Paul as authoritative apostle are equivalent.[64] The rhetorical analysis has shown how Paul's rhetoric makes the interpretation inevitable. Paul's reflections on his absence from the Philippians, the possibility of his impending death, and his choice to remain with them emphasize the importance of Paul's presence. Here in 2:12, the phrase "not only in my presence, but much more now in my absence" occupies a position where it can modify "you have obeyed" or "work out your own salvation."

The phrase "with fear and trembling" in the context of the verb ὑπηκούσατε indicates that the obedience of the Philippians is directed toward an object in a superior position, be it Paul or God.[65] In the other occurrence in Paul's letters where this phrase is used, it refers to an attitude of an inferior to a superior. In 2 Cor 7:15, it is joined with the noun ὑπακοή to describe the manner in which the Corinthians received Titus.[66] In a passage from the Pauline tradition, it refers to the way slaves are to obey their masters.[67]

In a divergence from the language of partnership and friendship that has characterized the letter up to this point, Paul interprets "being of the same mind" as "obeying" in 2:12. The language of obedience is not typical of the language of friendship. In describing "being of the same mind" and "regarding others as better than yourselves" as "obeying," and by leaving the object of the verb ambiguous, Paul implies that those who are not of one mind are not obeying. Further, he implies that they

---

[64]An example is Ralph Martin (*Carmen Christi*, 110) who cites 2 Cor 7:15, 10:6; 2 Thess 3:4; and Phlm 21 as other instances where Paul expects "a continuing obedience to his apostolic directives." See also Beare, *Philippians*, 89. Stephen Fowl (*Story of Christ*, 96) argues that Paul is the implied object of congregational obedience in this verse.

[65]See Fowl, *Story of Christ*, 96–97. See also Balz ("φοβέω," *TDNT* [1968] 217) who states: "If in contrast to Prv 24:21 a distinction is made between respect for the king and fear of God, in typical relationships of subordination, e.g., wives in 1 Pet 3:2; Eph 5:33, and slaves in 1 Pet 2:18; Eph 6:5; Col 3:22, fear can denote the obedience demanded by the superior authority of masters or husbands as lords."

[66]2 Cor 7:15: "And his heart goes out all the more to you, as he remembers the obedience of all of you, and how you welcomed him with fear and trembling" (καὶ τὰ σπλάγχνα αὐτοῦ περισσοτέρως εἰς ὑμᾶς ἐστιν ἀναμιμνῃσκομένου τὴν πάντων ὑμῶν ὑπακοήν, ὡς μετὰ φόβου καὶ τρόμου ἐδέξασθε αὐτόν).

[67]Eph 6:5: "Slaves obey your earthly masters with fear and trembling, in singleness of heart, as you obey Christ" (Οἱ δοῦλοι, ὑπακούετε τοῖς κατὰ σάρκα κυρίοις μετὰ φόβου καὶ τρόμου ἐν ἁπλότητι τῆς καρδίας ὑμῶν ὡς τῷ Χριστῷ).

are not obeying him. Paul simultaneously denies assertions of authority and independence that others might claim by constructing those others as (selfish) factions. Paul constructs a relationship of authority between himself and the congregation in which they obey—with fear and trembling—in his absence.

Thus, Paul employs the Christ hymn, whose primary purpose is proclamation and not moral instruction, into a new context of paraenesis. When he quotes the Christ hymn, Paul highlights one feature of the hymn—that Christ became "obedient to the point of death." He capitalizes and develops this feature by picking up on the adjective ὑπήκοος and using a cognate word ὑπηκούσατε to summarize the behavior of the congregation. The significance of Jesus' obedience within Phil 2:6–11, however, is that it is one feature of the reversal of status involved in "taking the form of a slave." Christ who is equal to God descends to human life and death in order to provoke a shift in power to God. By phrasing 2:12 the way that he does, and by placing the Christ hymn into the frame of 1:1–3:1, Paul leads his readers to the logical conclusion to be obedient like Jesus. But by employing the Christ "who became obedient" in Phil 2:6–11 as an ethical example, Paul has modified the structure and significance of obedience. In the epistolary context, the stress has shifted to the object toward which one is obedient, namely, God.[68] While within the hymn God and Christ are described in terms of equality and identity, in the context of the letter Christ and God are arranged as inferior and superior.

---

[68]In his discussion of mythological-christological narratives used by Paul in the context of paraenesis, Stephen Fowl notes that Paul capitalizes on particular features of the Philippians hymn and not others, and that the analogy between Christ in the hymn and members of the congregation in Philippi is not precise. Fowl employs the notion of "exemplar" to show how Paul focuses on the points of similarity between the Philippians' situation and the Christ hymn to urge a specific course of action, in this case, unity in the face of opposition (*Story of Christ*, 95). I find Fowl's analysis helpful in articulating how the analogy can work while remaining incomplete, but I want to point out how Paul's use of it shifts its interpretation. By employing the hymn as an "exemplar," Paul draws precisely upon an understanding of obedience that the hymn does not have, namely, the relationship of subordination between inferior and superior. Fowl's general conclusion that Paul uses this Christ-focused passage to argue for ethical positions coheres with my observation of his use of the Christ hymn in Philippians. Rhetorical criticism allows me to attribute this tension to a difference between Paul's redaction and the christology of the audience.

Timothy and Epaphroditus as the Second Positive Example: Phil 2:19–30

In 1:1–2:5, Paul has presented his absence from the community as part of the rhetorical problem of the letter. Among the different strategies Paul uses to respond to the problem of his absence is asserting that it has been beneficial (1:12–13), arguing that his surviving is important on the Philippians' account (1:24), emphasizing God's continuing activity in Paul's absence (2:12), and describing that activity as parallel to Paul's.[69]

Immediately following his exhortation to the Philippians to continue to obey in his absence, Paul continues the *probatio* by commending two friends, Timothy and Epaphroditus.[70] Both Timothy and Epaphroditus are described as having a special relationship with Paul: Timothy as child of a father and Epaphroditus as mirror image or double of Paul. Duane Watson identifies this section as a digression in the sense that the plans to send emissaries does not directly follow from Paul's ethical exhortation in the preceding verses.[71] But Timothy and Ephaphroditus serve a vital function within the argument. they are further examples of good conduct. Within the contrast Paul has constructed in the opening of the letter between those "friends" who are characterized by selflessness (for example, preaching the gospel from good will and not out of envy and rivalry) and those "enemies" who are selfish, Timothy and Epaphroditus represent friends.

Paul asserts Timothy's distinctiveness ("I have no one like him") and contrasts him positively with those who "seek their own interests" (2:21). In 2:4, Paul urges the addressees to "look not to your own interests but to the interests of others." Phil 2:22 elaborates upon Timothy's distinctive relationship with Paul: "like a son with a father he served with me

---

[69]Robert Funk ("The Apostolic 'Parousia': Form and Significance," in William R. Farmer, C. F. D. Moule, and Richard R. Neibuhr, eds., *Christian History and Interpretation: Studies Presented to John Knox* [Cambridge: Cambridge University Press, 1967] 248–68) has grouped Phil 1:25, 2:12, and 2:19–24 as functioning parts of the "apostolic parousia." Rather than seeing these features as part of one "form," my analysis has shown how they work together in the argument of the letter.

[70]Stanley Stowers ("Friends and Enemies," 114) notes that Timothy is portrayed as a "true friend" as opposed to "false friends." Meeks ("Man From Heaven," 334) says that "Paul heaps up friendship language in describing Timothy and Epaphroditus."

[71]Watson, "Rhetorical Analysis," 71–72.

in the work of the gospel" (ὅτι ὡς πατρὶ τέκνον σὺν ἐμοὶ ἐδούλευσεν εἰς τὸ εὐαγγέλιον). The familial metaphor of son and father both links Timothy to Paul in a unique way and subordinates him to Paul. In verse 23, Paul repeats his intention to send Timothy closely followed by Paul himself. Into the gap created by his own absence, Paul sends first his "son," and then himself.

Paul's commendation of Timothy here in Philippians may be helpfully compared with Timothy's appearance in 1 Cor 4:14–21. In that context of heightened conflict, Paul asserts his own distinctive relationship with the Corinthians as their "father." Sending Timothy, his "son," functions explicitly to remind them of Paul's ways in Christ. Paul does not threaten the Philippians with sending Timothy, but the situation of absence in which a representative is deemed necessary is similar. The mention of sending Timothy directly after the admonition to continue to obey in 2:12 supports the argument that the implied object of congregational obedience is Paul.

Paul then tells his plans to send Epaphroditus (2:25). According to 4:18, Epaphroditus was the messenger from Philippi sent with the monetary gifts from the Philippians. It is unclear whether Ephaphroditus-as-envoy is Paul's peer or subordinate. The words "brother," "coworker," and "fellow soldier" (τὸν ἀδελφὸν καὶ συνεργὸν καὶ συστρατιώτην μου) suggest that he is a peer. The similarities in the description of Epaphroditus with Paul suggest that Epaphroditus functions as a substitute for Paul in the symbolic universe of the letter. His being sent in Paul's absence is another way of Paul calling himself to mind with the Philippians. In x2:28, Paul claims that the Philippians should rejoice at seeing Epaphroditus again. Paul uses expressions of joy in 1:4 and throughout the letter to the Philippians.[72] Epaphroditus desired the Philippians (2:26) as Paul desired them (1:8). He was, like Paul, close to death (1:19–26). Like Paul, he was spared.[73] Paul concludes by asking the congregation to receive him.

The "Dogs" as Negative Example and Paul as Positive Example: Phil 3:1–21

Phil 3:1–21 constitutes the third stage of the *probatio* in which Paul

---

[72]Phil 1:4, 18, 2:2, 17, 3:1, 4:1, 4, 10. See Meeks, "Man From Heaven," 334.
[73]Wayne Meeks (ibid., 335) refers to Epaphroditus as a mediator.

develops a negative example of "enemies of the cross of Christ" (3:18), whom he contrasts sharply with himself. The description of the "dogs" occurs at the beginning (3:2) and the end (3:18–19) of the section. Although the language in these three verses is harsh, the emphasis of the proof is upon the positive example of Paul, which is developed between the references to enemies (3:3–17). While "they" have confidence in the flesh, Paul does not. Whatever gain Paul had, he considered loss for the sake of Christ. The unstated comparison here is between Jesus and Paul. As Christ renounced status (2:6–8), so Paul has lost status. In 3:10, Paul makes the comparison with Christ explicit. As he conforms himself to Christ's sufferings, he will replicate the process of death and resurrection. Language and imagery from earlier in the letter is reiterated here. The image of athletic contest in 1:27–30 recurs in 3:12–16. Exhortations using φρόνειν are repeated in 3:15: "Let those who are mature be of the same mind, and if you think differently about anything, this too God will reveal to you."[74] The contrast between destruction and salvation, which was brought up in 1:28, is reiterated in 3:19 and 3:20. The imagery of 3:21 reflects the last half of the narrative of Christ in 2:9–11.

The links between Phil 3:20–21 and the Christ hymn suggest that in these verses Paul may be referring back to 2:9–11. The verb πολιτεύω (1:27) seems to be mirrored by the expression τὸ πολίτευμα in 3:20. Commentators frequently try to interpret this verse in a way that makes its meaning consistent with 2:9–11. They explain, for instance, that in 3:20 Paul addresses the issue of why Christians are still suffering now that every creature is acknowledging Christ's lordship. However, distinct differences between the outlook of Phil 3:20–21 and Phil 2:9–11 should be acknowledged. First, in 2:9–11, God's exaltation of Christ is a completed fact and not something to be expected in the future as in 3:20. Transformation of the believer's body is something that will occur in the future in 3:20, while the proclamation of the Christ hymn in its pre-Pauline use was the liberation effected by Christ's action. In the context of the final part of Paul's presentation of the negative example of the "dogs" in 3:17–21, the operative contrast is between earth and heaven. To the "enemies" who focus on earthly things, Paul opposes the

---

[74]Phil 3:15: ὅσοι οὖν τέλειοι, τοῦτο φρονῶμεν καὶ εἴ τι ἑτέρως φρονεῖτε, καὶ τοῦτο ὁ θεὸς ὑμῖν ἀποκαλύψει.

spatial image of "in heaven." The contrast between earth and heaven is paralleled by the contrast between present and future; Paul is not "already perfect" but strives for "what lies ahead." This opposition between present and future does not operate within the hymn. Rather, the hymn expresses that salvation is accomplished. Although it seems to presume a descent from equality with God to an exaltation above, the hymn does not express the negative assessment of earth with respect to heaven that Phil 3:20–21 does. These differences suggest that when commenting upon the last two verses of the hymn in reference to "the enemies," Paul interprets the proclamation of the hymn to be an event that lies in the future.

The reference to "dogs," "evil-workers," and "those who mutilate the flesh" in 3:2 has led commentators to reconstruct the historical situation of the letter as one in which a threat of Judaizing missionaries endangered Paul's community.[75] In this rhetorical analysis, reconstruction of the *historical* situation will be postponed. However, the rhetorical analysis has shown how this third proof functions as a negative example providing a contrast with the positive example of the story of Paul. The author has referred to other negative examples in 1:15–17. Thus, Phil 3:1–21 has a significant function within the dynamics of identification and opposition that have been observed as a primary rhetorical strategy of the letter.

The *Peroratio*: Phil 4:1–23

The final section of the speech, the *peroratio,* recapitulates the arguments and creates a greater degree of pathos. Phil 4:1 recapitulates the injunction to stand firm first made in 1:27. The general injunctions to think the same thing—employing the expression φρόνειν (1:27–2:4)—become specific when Paul entreats (παρακαλῶ) two women "to be of the same mind in the Lord" (τὸ αὐτὸ φρονεῖν ἐν κυριῳ). Paul invokes himself again as a model in 4:9: "keep on doing the things that you have learned and received and heard and seen in me"[76] (ἃ καὶ ἐμάθετε

---

[75]Those who hold that Phil 3:2–21 is a fragment of another letter do not see the threat of "judaizing missionaries" as directly relevant to the situation of the rest of canonical Philippians.

[76]Elizabeth A. Castelli (*Imitating Paul: A Discourse of Power* [Louisville, KY: Westminster/ John Knox, 1991] 95–97) discusses Phil 3:17 as an example of Paul's discourse of *mimesis.*

καὶ παρελάβετε καὶ ἠκούσατε καὶ εἴδετε ἐν ἐμοί, ταῦτα πράσσετε). Phil 4:10–20 constitutes an emotional appeal (*adfectus*) in which Paul reemphasizes his relationship and history with the Philippians, including their financial relationship.

"I entreat Euodia and I entreat Syntyche": Phil 4:2–3

Many earlier studies of Philippians have not recognized Paul's address to Euodia and Syntyche in Phil 4:2–3 as playing a significant role in the rhetoric of the letter. One reason for this inattention is that when Philippians is read as an assembly of fragments, these verses come at a disputed and ambiguous position between the end of one fragment and the beginning of another.[77] However, rhetorical analysis of the whole argument indicates that the verses have an important position and are vitally interrelated with the operative rhetorical strategies. First, this instruction to the "true yokefellow" (γνήσιε σύζυγε, NRSV: "loyal companion") is one of only two specific instructions in the letter. The first is Paul's exhortation to receive Epaphroditus and to "honor such men [NRSV: people]" (2.29). Both specific instructions bear on the relationship of the congregation to particular individuals within it who appear to have a position of leadership. Second, in a text that operates by contrasting positive with negative examples, the status of Euodia and Syntyche is ambiguous. While they are named, as is the convention with "friends,"[78] they are instructed with the same verb that has been used to describe recommended behavior throughout the letter: φρόνειν. Paul's entreaty to them is one of the final instances of

---

[77]For example, in the partitions of the letter proposed by Francis Wright Beare, Jerome Murphy O'Connor, and Jean-François Collange, the verses are placed in "Letter B," while in the theories of N. Walter, P. Benoit, and Günther Bornkamm, they are attributed to "Letter C." See Beare, *Philippians*; Jerome Murphy O'Connor, "Philippiens (Epître aux)," *DBSup* 7 (1966) 1211–16; Jean-François Collange, *L'Epître de Saint Paul aux Philippiens* (CNT 10a; Neuchatel: Delachaux and Nestlé, 1973); N. Walter, "Die Philipper und das Leiden, aus den Anfängen einer heidenchristlichen Gemeinde," in Rudolf Schnackenburg, Joseph Ernst, and Joachim Wanke, eds., *Die Kirche des Anfangs: Für Heintz Schürmann* (Freiburg: Herder, 1978) 417–33; P. Benoit, *Les épîtres de saint Paul aux Philippiens, à Philemon, aux Colossiens, aux Ephésiens* (Paris: Cerf, 1959); Günther Bornkamm, *Der Philipperbrief als paulinische Briefsammlung* (NovTSup 6; Leiden: Brill, 1962).

[78]Peter Marshall (*Enmity at Corinth: Social Conventions in Paul's Relations with the Corinthians* [WUNT 23; Tübingen: Mohr, 1987] 35–67) describes the characteristic practice of naming friends and leaving enemies nameless.

φρόνειν-related words in the letter. The fact that this concrete instruction employs this language strongly suggests that it is the point to which the letter has been leading. Finally, the words addressed to Euodia and Syntyche occur immediately after Paul's attack on the "dogs," which begins at 3:2 and continues through 3:21. It is followed by the exhortation to rejoice, which is unambiguously positive in tone. The position of this reference immediately following a portrayal of a negative example indicates that the entreaty to Euodia and Syntyche takes part in the dynamics observed earlier in the analysis. The need for unity is juxtaposed with a threat from others. A similar juxtaposition occurs in the *narratio* in Phil 1:27–30. The harsh language of 3:2–21 against "enemies of the cross of Christ" not only sets up the need for unity but draws a contrast between dangerous "others" and those within the community.

The unusual multiplication of terms of endearment in 4:1 in the address to the community works within this dynamic as well: "Therefore, my brothers and sisters whom I love and long for, my joy and crown, stand firm in the Lord in this way, my beloved" ("Ωστε, ἀδελφοί μου ἀγαπητοὶ καὶ ἐπιπόθητοι, χαρὰ καὶ στέφανός μου, οὕτως στήκετε ἐν κυρίῳ, ἀγαπτοί). Phil 4:1 concludes the argument leading up to 3:21 and introduces the address to Euodia and Syntyche and the "true yokefellow." The expressions of longing and love recall the affectionate expressions in 1:7–8. The congregation is addressed twice: once at the beginning of the phrase as "brothers and sisters, beloved and longed for" and once at the end as "beloved." Beginning with the conjunction ὥστε and using the form of address ἀγαπητοί, this injunction resembles the verse that follows the Christ hymn and refers to the congregation as "obeying" (2:12). The many terms of positive regard in 4:1 sharply contrast with the invective of 3:18–19. The intensity of the harangue against the enemies is of the same degree as the effusive address to Paul's friends. This contrast is followed by the ambiguous reference to Euodia and Syntyche, named as friends, but described as having "to be of the same mind in the Lord" and assigned another member of the community to intervene with them. This text once again raises the difficulty, which has confounded commentators on Philippians, of determining the relationship between internal and external opposition. These verses cause one to question whether these categories of "inside" and "outside," which Paul's rhetoric constructs, refer to a historical situation in which there is outside opposition and internal friendship or whether the rhetoric of "us" and "them" might be a response to a different historical situation.

In 4:2, Paul repeats the first person singular verb παρακαλῶ once to Euodia and once to Syntyche and urges them to "be of the same mind in the Lord." He follows this statement by addressing another person, referred to as a "true yokefellow" to "help them" (συλλαμβάνου αὐταῖς). This address is unusual in Paul's letters and presents several problems of interpretation. Gordon Fee observes that it is unusual because Paul rarely names individuals in conflict settings.[79] Paul does name people in greetings and mentions coworkers and envoys. In Philippians Paul has already mentioned Ephaphroditus. Because Euodia and Syntyche are coworkers, mentioning their names is not unusual. What is unusual is that Euodia and Syntyche are both "inside" *and* participating in conflict of some kind. Thus, they are exceptions in the harmonious and unified picture of the Philippian community.

The singularity of these verses suggests that they are significant to the letter. Commentators have generally underplayed them, but recently some have come to see these verses as the major concern of the letter to which Paul has been leading.[80] Rhetorical analysis and attention to the use of obedience language in Philippians supports the argument that these verses are very significant in the letter and suggests that Euodia and Syntyche should be considered central to the rhetorical problem.

One question of interpretation is the strength of the verb παρακαλῶ in 4:1. The study of Carl J. Bjerkelund identifies sentences using παρακαλέω as denoting an authoritative word of an apostle but concludes that its use in Phil 4:1 was an exception and represented a personal appeal.[81] S. R. Llewelyn, however, finds that in other places where Paul uses παρακαλέω, the verb implies a person of superior status addressing

---

[79]Fee, *Philippians*, 389.

[80]See David E. Garland, "Composition and Unity," 172–73. In a paper presented at the 1995 AAR/SBL meeting and as far as I know unpublished, Caroline Whalen-Donaghey argues that Euodia and Syntyche's role was critical in the historical situation at Philippi. Her argument depends heavily on the verse as a culmination of φρόνειν language ("A Rhetorical Analysis of Philippians 4:2–3: Euodia and Syntyche Reconsidered" [paper read at the annual meeting of the Society of Biblical Literature, Philadelphia, PA, November 1995]).

[81]Carl J. Bjerkelund, *Parakalô: Form, Funktion und Sinn der parakelô-Sätz in den paulinischen Briefe* (Oslo: University Press, 1975).

another.[82] Because of the position of this appeal in the rhetorical structure of Philippians and its distinctiveness as a concrete instruction in the letter—parallel to the instruction to receive Epaphroditus—there is no reason not to assign it the same strength as such appeals in 1 Cor 1:10, 4:16, and 16:15. The verb παρακαλέω is a direct instruction, as it is in 1 Cor 1:10 and as it is in Phlm 8, despite Paul's implied contrast in Philemon between ἐπιτάσσω and παρακαλέω.

Rhetorical Genre: Philippians as Deliberative Rhetoric

Identifying the rhetorical genre is an effort to classify the rhetoric and to read the argument in terms of broad categories, but it does not answer all questions about a text or explain a text.[83] The preceding rhetorical analysis indicates that Philippians is best described as deliberative rhetoric,[84] which concerns how one should act in the future.[85] Paul is urging the Philippians to a certain course of behavior in the present and in the future.

Deliberative rhetoric urges the audience toward future action by encouraging them to confirm values that they already hold. Throughout Philippians, Paul refers to values that he and the Philippians share in common. He appeals to knowledge and beliefs acknowledged by the audience in order to persuade them to behave in a certain way. The "gospel" is the basis of the Philippians' relationship with Paul. Paul thanks the Philippians for their "partnership in the gospel" (1:5). He holds up the "gospel of Christ" as the standard of conduct in 1:27. In 4:3, Paul refers to the gospel in which Euodia and Syntyche have "struggled" beside him. The narrative of Christ's descent and exaltation, which Paul

---

[82]S. R. Llewelyn, *New Documents Illustrating Early Christianity: A Review of the Greek Inscriptions and Papyri* (vol. 6; North Ryde, NSW: Ancient History Documentary Research Centre, Macquarie University, 1989) 145–46.

[83]See Schüssler Fiorenza, *Revelation,* 23. See also Stephen Kraftchick, "Why Do the Rhetoricians Rage?" in Theodore W. Jennings, ed., *Text and Logos: The Humanistic Tradition of the New Testament* (Atlanta: Scholars Press, 1990) 55–79.

[84]See Watson, "Rhetorical Analysis," 57–88. In his rhetorical analysis, L. Gregory Bloomquist (*Function of Suffering,* 119–20) concludes that Philippians is best characterized as deliberative.

[85]See Schüssler Fiorenza, "Rhetorical Situation," 391. See also Mitchell, *Rhetoric of Reconcilation,* 24–25.

quotes in 2:6–11, is a piece of Christian tradition that is valued by the Philippians and that Paul draws on in his letter to them. Throughout the letter Paul appeals to the audience to strengthen the values that they hold. The language of Philippians suggests that partnership is one of the values of the Philippian audience.

In her discussion of 1 Corinthians as an example of deliberative rhetoric, Margaret Mitchell notes the following features of deliberative rhetoric: appeals to the common good, the treatment of specific topics such as factionalism, and the uses of examples as proofs.[86] These features occur in Philippians in a distinctive way. The appeals are not made with a "rational" argument, which explains why a point of view should be accepted, as in Paul's argument in 1 Cor 12:1–11 concerning the multiplicity of gifts being united by one Spirit and one Lord. Rather, the need for unity in the face of opposition is *assumed* as a value, as in 1:27–28:

> Only live your life in a manner worthy of the gospel of Christ, so that whether I come to see you or am absent, I may hear of you that you are standing firm in one spirit, striving side by side with one mind for the faith of the gospel, and are in no way intimidated by your opponents. For them this is evidence of their destruction, but of your salvation. And this is God's doing.[87]

By juxtaposing an exhortation to unity and the threat of opponents, Paul treats the need for unity as a fact. Paul's statement in 2:14–15 implies that the children of God are stars when they do not grumble or question. While in 1 Cor 1:11 Paul addresses the topic of factionalism directly, in Philippians he does not explicitly discuss factions as a problem that exists in the community. Rather, he alludes to division by the alternating expression of "some" and "others" in 1:15–17. In 2:21, Paul praises Epaphroditus by contrasting him with those who seek their own interests not those of Jesus Christ. His reference to the others would be recognized by the audience as a criticism of those others, but Paul does not name them or engage them directly.

---

[86]Ibid., 39–42, 60–64.

[87]Phil 1:27–28: Μόνον ἀξίως τοῦ εὐαγγελίου τοῦ Χριστοῦ πολιτεύεσθε, ἵνα εἴτε ἐλθὼν καὶ ἰδὼν ὑμᾶς εἴτε ἀπὼν ἀκούω τὰ περὶ ὑμῶν, ὅτι στήκετε ἐν ἑνὶ πνεύματι, μιᾷ ψυχῇ συναθλοῦντες τῇ πίστει τοῦ εὐαγγελίου καὶ μὴ πτυρόμενοι ἐν μηδενὶ ὑπὸ τῶν ἀντικειμέ νων, ἥτις ἐστὶν αὐτοῖς ἔνδειξις ἀπωλείας, ὑμῶν δὲ σωτηρίας, καὶ τοῦτο ἀπὸ θεοῦ.

The most developed feature of Philippians, in comparison with
1 Corinthians, is its use of examples as proofs.[88] Paul furthers his arguments about the Philippians' behavior by the use of positive and negative
examples. Paul uses as examples the narrative of Christ in 2:5–11, Timothy and Epaphroditus in 2:19–30, and himself in 3:4–21. Paul employs
his own life and situation as a positive model throughout the letter. His
imprisonment, his struggle (1:30), his decision to live and to remain
with the Philippians (1:19–26), his biography as a righteous Hebrew
(3:4–21), his loss of status, and his acceptance of all circumstances (4:10–
13), all illustrate how to conduct oneself. He describes the behavior he
is urging as "obeying" in 2:12 because Christ, the model in 2:6–11, is
described as "obedient to the point of death." Obedience, synonymous
with being of one mind, characterizes the community in contrast with
its adversaries. The negative examples are "opponents" in 1:28, "others" in 1:15–17, those who are contrasted with Timothy in 2:22, and the
"enemies" in 3:18. Euodia and Syntyche are told to do what the negative examples are described as not doing.

The three features of deliberative rhetoric—appeal to the common
good, argument against factionalism, and the use of examples as proofs—
are interrelated in Philippians. Unity is presented as necessary and
effective in the face of factionalism. The common good is equated with
unity. The positive examples portray those who consider others' needs
above their own and the negative examples portray those who are self-
seeking and not of the same mind.

Philippians as a Letter of Friendship

Recent work on Philippians places its language into the context of the
conventions of Greek friendship.[89] Scholars identify it as "a hortatory

---

[88]Margaret Mitchell (ibid., 49–60) argues that Paul's use of himself as an example
runs throughout 1 Corinthians. Paul uses this technique in Philippians as well, but its use
in Philippians it is even more striking because it is the *only* form of argument or proof.

[89]Abraham Malherbe (*Ancient Epistolary Theorists* [SBLSBS 19; Atlanta: Scholars
Press, 1988] 21, 31–41) categorizes Philippians as a letter of friendship. L. Michael
White ("Morality," 201–15) develops friendship as the Hellenistic moral paradigm that
Paul adapts in Philippians. Stanley K. Stowers ("Friends and Enemies," 105–21)
expands upon White's article. Gordon Fee (*Philippians*) takes up friendship as the key
to the interpretation of Philippians. J. Paul Sampley (*Pauline Partnership in Christ:*

letter of friendship." Classifying the letter in this way explains the rhetoric of "having all things in common" and "being of one mind" as relating to the social interactions of friendship.[90] Greek sources stress that friendship consists of agreement and equality.[91] L. Michael White argues that friendship is the moralizing context in which Paul adapts the pre-Pauline hymn in Phil 2:6–11:

> Thus Paul has grounded the fundamental ethical imperative of the Christians' social relationships within the community in the Greek ideal of virtue (friendship) exemplified in Christ's own actions. Christ then becomes a repository of virtue (much like Philo's logos) and thus, a divine source for Paul's exhortations to live in accord with the highest ideals of Greek culture.[92]

White suggests that the friendship with the Philippians may have been strained and needed to be reasserted. Thus, the purpose of the letter was to reassert the bonds of friendship.

In developing the topos of friendship in Philippians, Stanley Stowers uses the category of friendship to explain the rhetoric of friends and enemies in Philippians. He points out that Greek friendship was highly agonistic or competitive and that the definition of friendship depended dialectically upon the notion of enmity. Stowers identifies the language of Phil 1:15–18 as "typical vocabulary of friendship and enmity." He says that Paul's discourse of friendship must emphasize the common struggle against enmity. Thus, Stowers classifies Paul's construction of friends and enemies as typical of ancient rhetoric within the letter of friendship. Stowers's analysis of the rhetoric of the letter leads him to the conclusion that the so-called judaizers in 3:2–21 have no basis in historical fact: "Such paranetic features give little reason to think that the Philippians community was deeply divided or ravaged by 'false teachers.'"[93] Stowers uses his determination of the genre of Philippians

Christian Community and Commitment in Light of Roman Law [Philadelphia: Fortress, 1980]) uses the model of consensual *societas* as the category with which to analyze the letter.

[90]White, "Morality," 210–11.
[91]Stowers, "Friends and Enemies," 111.
[92]White, "Morality," 210.
[93]Stowers, "Friends and Enemies," 116.

to construct the historical situation in which Paul's relationship with the Philippians is unambiguously friendly, and the reference to "enemies" does not correspond with actual historical enemies.

The analyses of White and Stowers do not address the fact that Paul characterizes the behavior of the community in 2:12 as "obeying." These studies have not been able to explain how the rhetoric of obedience in 2:8 and 2:12 is consistent with that of friendship. The ambiguity of 2:12, which allows the interpretation of Paul as the object of congregational obedience, appears to contradict the ideal of friendship between partners that is expressed elsewhere in the letter. Many commentators deal with this contradiction by saying that in the context of friendship, one can be exhorted to obey.[94] Paul's move here in Philippians would then resemble the rhetoric in Phlm 8–9: "For this reason, though I am bold enough in Christ to command you to do your duty, yet I would rather appeal to you on the basis of love" (Διὸ, πολλὴν ἐν Χριστῷ παρρησίαν ἔχων ἐπιτάσσειν σοι τὸ ἀνῆκον διὰ τὴν ἀγάπην μᾶλλον παρακαλῶ). In this verse Paul simultaneously claims and denies the authority to command. This explanation, which tries to hold the language of friendship and obedience in tension within Philippians, does not attempt to explain why obedience is used if it is not a feature of the language of friendship. The appearance of obedience language in the midst of a letter of friendship is a contradiction that needs to be explored and understood in its significance for the whole letter.

The second problem that is not addressed in Stowers's analysis is the ambiguous status of Euodia and Syntyche. While they are members of the community, they are spoken of with language that has been used to characterize those who are "others." They are not named as enemies but are spoken of with words of partnership and friendship. However, they specifically are told to do what Paul has asked the congregation in general to do throughout the letter: to agree in the Lord. That Euodia and Syntyche do not fit neatly into the categories of friends and enemies as sketched out by Stowers is another indication of their significance to Paul's purpose in the letter.

---

[94]Gordon Fee (*Philippians*, 232) explains that Paul's expectation of their obedience is made in the context of a warm personal relationship with them.

Summary of the Rhetorical Situation

Unlike treatments of Philippians that assume identity between the position Paul articulates and that of his audience, the preceding rhetorical analysis reads Paul's letter as an argument presented to an audience. Observation of the argument has highlighted Paul's use of the dichotomizing language of "some" and "others," his adaptation of the language of obedience within the Christ hymn to emphasize subordination, the underlying equation of friendship with obedience, and his instruction to Euodia and Syntyche. These features lead to the following summary of the inscribed rhetorical situation. Paul has had a close relationship with the Philippians in the past in which they have supported him financially. From prison, Paul writes to encourage the community to behave in a way consistent with the values they share. Paul's rhetoric implies, but does not state directly or specifically, that in his absence some division has occurred within the community that must be corrected in the direction of unity. This community unity and "thinking the same" is all the more necessary in the face of threat from "dogs" and "evil-workers" who are in opposition to the community. This specific event is the rhetorical exigence or the situation that provokes utterance.

In responding, Paul appeals to the values of friendship and partnership held by the community and asserts the importance of unity and obedience. His main method of proof is the presentation of positive and negative examples. Of his positive examples, the most important are Christ and himself. In presenting Christ, he quotes an authoritative tradition valued by the Philippians that describes Jesus in the language of Wisdom who exchanged the form of God for the form of a slave and has been exalted as lord of the cosmos. While the hymn was valued by the Philippians, it is not the moral interpretation of Jesus as obedient to God that was central to the proclamation of the hymn in the Philippian community before it was quoted by Paul. The center of gravity in the hymn itself is the rule of the *kyrios* over the powers of the cosmos and the consequent liberation of those who have been enslaved to those powers. What Paul highlights from the hymn is the self-sacrificing obedience of Christ, which the Philippians are to read as a positive example of behavior.

After his injunction to the congregation to continue to obey, Paul commends Timothy and Ephaphroditus as those who represent him as son and surrogate in the community. The final specific instruction in the letter is his entreaty to Euodia and Syntyche to "be of one mind" and his appeal to the "true yokefellow" to intervene. He uses language of partnership in the gospel both at the beginning of the letter and at the end in order to appeal to the values of partnership that are held by the Philippians.

The dynamics of Paul's rhetoric, including his deployment of the early Christian tradition of the Christ hymn, and presenting himself as a positive example parallel to Christ and as an example to be imitated, work together to identify partnership as unity with himself and to reintroduce himself and the leaders who represent him to the audience at Philippi. In interpreting the language of obedience from the hymn in the context of superior and subordinate and of father and son in the letter to the Philippians, Paul is capitalizing upon rather than transforming the conventional language of obedience.

The rhetorical analysis of Philippians results in a more complex conclusion than the influential formulation presented by Meeks and Furnish. They accurately read the connection Paul makes between the obedience of Christ, expressed in Phil 2:8, and the obedience of the Christian in 2:12 in terms of imitation. They do not recognize, however, that by placing the mythical Christ hymn within the rhetorical and epistolary framework of "imitation of a model," Paul irrevocably shifts the interpretation of the hymn away from emphasis on reversal of status of slave and God and subsequent human liberation, toward obedience to God as a moral virtue. Because of the parallelism constructed in the letter between God's activity and Paul's presence, a shift toward obedience to God is also a shift toward greater authority for Paul within the community.

CHAPTER 4

Philippians:
From Rhetorical Analysis to Historical Situation

Previous studies of Philippians read Paul's references to those with whom he is allied and those with whom he is opposed as accurate reflections of the historical situation at Philippi. In general, they construct the situation in Philippi as one in which Paul is in harmony with the community but threatened by outside opposition. As I have noted, these reconstructions do not adequately account for the apparent references to internal opposition in Phil 1:15–17 or for the appeal to Euodia and Syntyche in 4:2–3. In this chapter I shall reconstruct a historical situation that makes sense of the observations of chapter three concerning the dynamics and strategies of Paul's rhetoric.

Elisabeth Schüssler Fiorenza has stressed that in contrast to formalist literary criticism, which remains within the rhetoric of the text and can only elucidate its androcentric perspectives and world view, rhetorical criticism must move beyond the author's rhetoric and attempt to reconstruct the historical situation.[1] Such a reconstruction of the historical situation requires reading Paul's rhetoric in light of other information from outside the text in order to gain a more accurate picture of the audience for the letter, their history and theological perspectives. Schüssler Fiorenza utilizes the categories from reader-response criticism and distinguishes between the inscribed audience and the historical audience. The inscribed audience is constructed by the writer of the text in relation to the inscribed author. The inscribed author, like the inscribed audience, is a construction of the author built

---

[1]Schüssler Fiorenza, "Rhetorical Situation," 386–403. See also idem, "Rhetoricity of Historical Knowledge," 447.

by rhetorical cues within the text. By keeping the inscribed audience distinct in analysis from the actual audience, an interpreter can use evidence from outside the text in dialogue with information provided by the author to begin to reconstruct the actual audience. The following analysis reconstructs the audience of the letter to the Philippians in light of both Paul's rhetoric in the letter and other sources beyond Philippians.

The Historical Audience

The rhetorical analysis of Philippians points out the tensions in the text that call into question Paul's inscription of the audience as unified and in harmony with him. First, that Phil 1:15–18 indicates "internal" Christian division must be taken into account. Second, the entreaty to Euodia and Syntyche to be "of the same mind" and the instructions to an intermediary to help them suggest that in this specific case, individuals were not of one mind. Finally, Paul's adaptation of the early Christian tradition in Phil 2:6–11 to emphasize congregational obedience, immediately before his recommendation of Timothy and Epaphroditus, suggests that his rhetoric may be addressing a situation that it does not directly describe.

Read together with indications from the rhetoric of the text itself, information from other sources beside the author can help to reconstruct a fuller picture of the historical audience than is possible by a description that uses only the clues provided by the author.

Philippi—Society and Language

In order to analyze how Paul writes in a specific social-historical situation, it is necessary to understand the contours of that unique situation. Certainly Paul refers to his own situation within the letter to the Philippians, and his words are essential to reconstruct the historical situation of the letter. But Paul's words alone cannot be read as accurate descriptions of the historical situation. They must be evaluated as rhetorically inscribed descriptions of the situation—that is, as the "rhetorical situation."[2] Evidence external to the letter to the Philippians must be used to fill in the picture of the audience to which Paul writes.

---

[2] See Schüssler Fiorenza, "Rhetorical Situation," 386–403.

Other letters of Paul, the Acts of the Apostles, and archeological and epigraphical evidence can contribute information about the city of Philippi that can be used to understand the social-historical situation of the letter.[3]

Social and economic diversity was a feature of the ancient city of Philippi, situated in Northern Greece at the border of East Macedonia and Thrace. The history of Philippi as a military colony suggests that the population of Philippi at the time of Paul's visit would have included Roman veterans and their descendants, Greeks descended from the inhabitants of earlier Hellenistic cities, and Greeks involved in trade who had migrated from Asia Minor. The city was administered by Roman law and influenced by Latin language and customs.[4] The social diversity of Philippi must be taken into account when evaluating Paul's calls for unity and "being of the same mind." Differences both in ethnic and religious background and social status would have affected the interpretation of the gospel by Christians in Philippi. The Christ hymn that Paul quotes provides evidence of a different language for and interpretation of Christ that had a liturgical life and history before Paul used it, and that may have been in current use within the community at Philippi. The diverse syncretistic culture of Philippi was a rich source for different models and languages to describe salvation.[5]

---

[3]It has long been accepted in the study of Paul that understanding the situation is necessary to understanding a "situational letter." However, there is great disagreement on how to interpret Acts of the Apostles as a historical source. The problems of interpreting archaeological evidence also are manifold. Nevertheless, given methodological caution, one can use these sources to supplement the critical reading of the inscribed rhetorical situation.

[4]Holland L. Hendrix, "Philippi," *ABD* 5 (1992) 313–17; Lilian Portefaix, *Sisters Rejoice: Paul's Letter to the Philippians and Luke-Acts as Seen by First-century Philippian Women* (Coniectanea Biblica New Testament Series 20; Uppsala: Almquist & Wiksell, 1988); Valerie Abrahamsen, "Women at Philippi: The Pagan and Christian Evidence," *JFSR* 3 (1987) 17–30. See also Carolyn Osiek, "Philippians," in Schüssler Fiorenza, *Searching the Scriptures*, 237–49.

[5]For example, Lilian Portefaix (*Sisters Rejoice: Paul's Letter to the Philippians and Luke-Acts as Seen by First-century Philippian Women* [Coniectanea Biblica New Testament Series 20; Uppsala: Almquist & Wiksell, 1988] 147) describes the language of cosmic ruler as applied to Isis in the Isis aretologies. Although Portefiax reads Philippians against the background of the pagan culture of Philippi, with Philippians as the privileged text, her appreciation of the diversity of the historical audience for Philippians and her understanding of the interplay between mythological and "Christian" language helps to refocus on the community as the source for language rather than on Paul alone.

In contrast to historical reconstructions that follow the directions of the androcentric text and assume the marginality of women, reconstruction of the audience of Philippians must assume women to be active members of the community. Recent studies of literary and inscriptional evidence highlight the active participation of women in social and religious life. Valerie Abrahamsen's study of the Diana sanctuary at Philippi discusses the evidence for the popularity of the goddess cults of Diana and Isis among Philippian women in the late second and early third centuries.[6] The story of the conversion of Lydia told by Luke in Acts 16:11–15 describes Lydia, a merchant of purple cloth, as the first to be baptized among the group of women to whom Paul preaches.[7] Polycarp's letter to Philippi from the middle of the second century generally addresses Christian wives and widows concerning Christian virtue.[8] The fact that Polycarp singles out women as a group for his exhortations and mentions asceticism in 5.3 suggests that Polycarp may have viewed female asceticism as a problem. The *Acts of Paul and Thecla* deals explicitly with celibate women and seems as a whole to be encouraging asceticism. The apocryphal Acts contain one fragment set in Philippi in which the main character, Frontina, converts to a celibate life, is killed, and raised.[9] The literary evidence from different time periods that asso-

---

[6]Valerie Abrahamsen, "The Rock Reliefs and the Cult of Diana at Philippi" (Th.D. diss., Harvard University, 1986; Ann Arbor, MI: UMI, 1986); idem, *Women and Worship at Philippi: Diana/Artemis and Other Cults in the Early Christian Era* (Portland, ME: Astarte Shell Press, 1995).

[7]The historical value of the Acts of the Apostles as a source for Christian history remains disputed. For comparative rhetorical analysis of the conversion stories of women, see Shelly Matthews, "High Standing Women and Mission and Conversion" (Th.D. diss., Harvard University, 1997).

[8]"Next to teach our wives to remain in the faith given to them, and in love and purity, tenderly loving their husbands in all truth, and loving all others equally in all chastity, and to educate their children in the fear of God. Let us teach the widows to be discreet in the faith of the Lord, praying ceaselessly for all men, being far from all slander, evil speaking, false witness, love of money, and all evil, knowing that they are an altar of God, and that all offerings are tested, and that nothing escapes him of reasoning or thoughts, or of 'the secret things of the heart'" (Polycarp *Phil.* 4.2–3 [*The Apostolic Fathers* (trans. Kirsopp Lake; LCL; 2 vols.; Cambridge, MA: Harvard University Press, 1912) 2. 287–89]).

[9]Valerie Abrahamsen, "Women at Philippi: The Pagan and Christian Evidence," *JFSR* 3 (1987) 17–30. For an older review and evaluation of the evidence, see W. Derek Thomas, "The Place of Women in the Church at Philippi," *ExpTim* 83 (1972) 117–20. Francis X. Malinowsky ("The Brave Women at Philippi," *BTB* 15 [1985] 60–64) argues that Euodia and Syntyche were

ciates the city of Philippi with the ministry of women should be considered significant for reconstruction of the historical situation to which Paul responds in Philippians. Paul's construction of himself as father to Timothy and model to be imitated is read differently if one highlights the activity of Christian women in Philippi than if one assumes women to be absent from early Christian communities.

Euodia and Syntyche

It is in the context of the ongoing participation of women in the Christian community at Philippi that we may reevaluate an early piece of evidence for women's participation in the Christian congregation at Philippi: the reference to Euodia and Syntyche in Phil 4:2. This injunction is linked with the opening of the letter by the coincidence of standing firm (1:27), unity (2:2) and opposition, and by the reference to "be of the same mind" (2:2).

The historical situation behind Paul's injunction to Euodia and Syntyche has most commonly been read as a disagreement between the two women.[10] The phrase τὸ αὐτὸ φρονεῖν has been interpreted as meaning "to be of the same mind with each other." However, the dynamics of Paul's rhetoric show that the phrase may indicate a historical situation in which Euodia and Syntyche were not of the same mind as Paul.

Paul's rhetorical response in the letter to the Philippians can give clues to the historical situation behind the letter. The rhetorical dynamics that have been observed in the letter operate in Paul's instruction to Euodia and Syntyche and make the reading of disharmony with Paul a plausible one. First, throughout Philippians Paul has closely identified his own situation with the community as a whole. For example, in 1:17 he identifies preaching Christ "out of selfish ambition" with "intending to increase my suffering in my imprisonment." Solidarity with Paul has

---

not "fellow preachers or presiders," but were described as they are in Phil 4:2–3 because they provided financial support and shared in Paul's suffering.

[10]The evaluation of the significance of their disagreement within the letter has been disputed. David E. Garland ("Composition and Unity," 141–73) argues that it is the focus of "disunity" within the church. Caroline Whelan-Donaghey ("A Rhetorical Analysis of Philippians 4:2–3: Euodia and Syntyche Reconsidered" [paper read at the annual meeting of the Society of Biblical Literature, Philadelphia, PA, November 1995]) argues that it is this "internal" dispute that Paul has in mind throughout the letter.

been constructed as unity within the community. In 3:15, "our thinking" is contrasted with those "who think otherwise." The constellation of Paul's absence, internal "unity," and threat from "opponents," which operates in the context of the narrative of Christ in 2:6–11—leading up to the injunction to continue to obey in 2:12—may be explained as an adequate response to the challenge of independent leaders within the congregation.

My analysis has traced the way the verb φρονεῖν is used in various ways throughout the letter to the Philippians to describe an attitude or way of conduct.[11] The particular expression τὸ αὐτὸ φρονεῖν is used in Phil 2:2. Here it is emphasized by the synonymous expression τὸ ἓν φρονοῦντες. Elsewhere in the letter the verb means "to think." This thinking is not simply cognitive but has a behavioral component, although that behavior is not described concretely. The "thinking" is modified as in 2:5: "think this way among yourselves which was in Christ Jesus" (τοῦτο φρονεῖτε ἐν ὑμῖν ὃ καὶ ἐν Χριστῷ Ἰησοῦ) and in 3:15 where "we" who think thus (τοῦτο φρονῶμεν) are contrasted with those who think differently (τι ἑτέρως φρονεῖτε). In Greco-Roman literature the conventional context of expressions involving φρονεῖν is the letter of friendship in which friends are urged to "think alike." The phrase τὸ αὐτὸ φρονεῖν is used in political rhetoric as a variation of ταῦτα λεγεῖν to denote a state of unity.[12]

In 4:3, Paul addresses someone else in the second person and instructs that person to become involved with both women: "And I ask you also, true yokefellow [NRSV: loyal companion], help these ones" (ναὶ ἐρωτῶ καὶ σέ, γνήσιε σύζυγε συλλαμβάνου αὐταῖς). This move, unique in Paul's letters, signals the seriousness of the situation of Euodia and Syntyche. In distinction to παρακαλέω, the verb ἐρατάω implies an equal relationship between the one who asks and the one who is asked.[13] The precise identity of γνήσιε σύζυγε has been the focus of much scholarly speculation. The assumption has been that it is either someone very well known

---

[11]Phil 1:2 (twice), 2:5, 3:15 (twice), 3:19, 4:2, 10.

[12]Mitchell, *Rhetoric of Reconciliation*, 69–70. Pointing to its use in Aristides, Mitchell reads the rhetoric of Paul from the point of view of the author. She not does highlight the power dynamics of Paul's rhetoric of unity.

[13]S. R. Llewelyn, *New Documents Illustrating Early Christianity: A Review of the Greek Inscriptions and Papyri* (vol. 6; North Ryde, NSW: Ancient History Documentary Research Centre, Macquarie University, 1989) 145–46.

to Paul (Timothy, Epaphroditus, Luke, Silas) or possibly a person with a proper name of Syzygos.[14] The theory that Syzygos is a proper name is undercut by the fact that no examples of the name have been found in antiquity. The significance of the word may be symbolic rather than literal. In order to explain why Paul would name the people in dispute, but refer to the person he asks to intervene by means of a descriptive phrase, one must focus on the meaning of the name. In contrast with Euodia and Syntyche, the former coworkers of Paul who are not of the same mind and who therefore are no longer truly yoked with him, Paul calls upon the *true* yokefellow. By using this oblique reference and not using his real name, Paul draws attention to the relationship of the person with Paul himself. The following subordinate clause, which describes why the σύζυγε should intervene, supports this reading. Paul presents the fact that the women have co-contested with Paul in the past as a reason for them to continue in relationship as partners with Paul now. According to this reading, Paul's reference to "Clement and the rest of my coworkers whose names are in the book of life" functions to reinforce his relationship with other coworkers and to place Euodia and Syntyche within that wider group.

These indications in the text that Paul may be responding to a perceived lack of same-mindedness with himself may be combined with evidence from other New Testament texts that refer to pairs of women. Three pairs of women are mentioned in the New Testament: Euodia and Syntyche, Tryphaena and Tryphosa, and Martha and Mary. In her analysis of these three pairs of women, Mary Rose D'Angelo argues that Euodia and Syntyche should be interpreted as missionary partners who work together.[15]

Like Tryphaena and Tryphosa in Rom 16:2, who are among the important individuals in the Roman church greeted by Paul and who are described as those "who have labored in the Lord," Euodia and Syntyche are described by Paul as those who "struggled beside me in the work of the gospel." Both pairs of women fit the pattern of missionary couples such as Prisca and Aquila (Rom 16:3), Andronicus and Junia (Rom 16:7),

[14]For a summary of the proposals, see Fee, *Philippians*, 393–94.

[15]Mary Rose D'Angelo ("Women Partners in the New Testament," *JFSR* 6 [1990] 65–86) argues that the partnership of women missionaries may have had a sexual dimension. In my reconstruction of the historical situation behind Paul's rhetoric, I build upon her claim that they were partners. Their sexual orientation is not essential to my reconstruction.

Philologus and Julia (Rom 16:15), and Nereas and his "sister" (Rom 16:15). D'Angelo notes that Paul himself is always accompanied, often by Timothy, whom he refers to as "brother." By interpreting Euodia and Syntyche in the company of other missionary pairs, D'Angelo views them not as tangential individuals in Philippi but as those who fill a specific leadership role. In addition, seeing them as a *pair* who may, like Apollos, be independent of Paul, adds to the possibility that their disagreement may not be with one another. The prescript of the letter in which Paul refers to "all the saints at Philippi in Christ Jesus, with the bishops and deacons" signals that Paul distinguished among members of the congregation at Philippi. Euodia and Syntyche may be among the bishops and deacons to whom the letter is addressed.

D'Angelo hypothesizes that the historical situation in Philippi is one in which Paul attempts to settle a disagreement, not between the two women themselves but between himself and the women partners. My reading of the rhetorical context in Philippians adds support to this theory. Paul's insistence on the unimportance of his absence functions to underscore its importance. By commending Epaphroditus and Timothy, who resemble himself in important ways, by setting them up as implied contrasts to Euodia and Syntyche, and by using the word "obeying" to describe the Philippians' behavior, Paul may be responding to the challenge of the independent missionary pair, Euodia and Syntyche.

The Rhetoric of Obedience in
Paul's Letter to the Philippians

The rhetorical analysis and consideration of information from outside the text has led to an alternate reconstruction of the historical situation of the letter. Paul writes from prison to a diverse community of Christians with different backgrounds and histories. Among that group are women and men who themselves may have sung the hymn about God taking the form of a slave and being exalted to the position of God. The churches at Philippi have had an ongoing history with leaders, *episkopoi* and *diakonoi*, some of whom may be named Euodia, Syntyche, Epaphroditus, and Clement. The community shares the value of partnership with each other. Their financial gift to Paul in the past expressed that partnership in concrete terms. The model of partnership formed their symbolic universe. The kyriarchal language of the ruler who becomes a slave and who is exalted to ruler expressed their liberation from the other rulers and enabled them to be in *koinonia* with each other. In response to a challenge he perceived to his unique relationship with the church at Philippi, Paul writes a letter that both affirms the value of partnership and emphasizes that the partnership is defined in a particular way—as being of the same mind, as obeying and as imitating him. What Paul constructs as a threat to unity on the part of Euodia and Syntyche, which has traditionally been read as a disagreement between them, may be a disagreement with Paul. From prison, Paul responds to the independent activity of the women partners in the gospel by constructing a model of voluntary renunciation of status, obedience to a superior, and imitation of himself as authoritative model.

Paul's rhetoric in the letter is able to address this historical situation without directly attacking members of the church, taking on a theological dispute, or criticizing specific behavior. Paul's construction of friends and enemies in the letter and the ambiguity of his reference to Euodia and Syntyche indicate that leadership is an indirect concern of the letter. By describing Euodia and Syntyche with the language that he does, Paul points to them as the problem. The letter is not addressed to them but to other members of the community whom he might influence. Whatever is the specific case, disagreement or independence or a divergent understanding of partnership, Paul's adaptation of the obedience language from the Christ hymn effectively counters the symbolic values of Euodia and Syntyche.

Within this historical reconstruction, Paul's adaptation of the early Christian hymn valued by the Philippian church is very significant in the struggle over symbols. The hymn envisions Christ's obedience as one feature of his exchanging the form of God for the form of a slave, which frees human beings from bondage to cosmic powers. In his rhetorical use of the hymn in the context of Philippians, Paul highlights the relational aspect of obedience language in which the inferior obeys the superior: the congregation obeys God and Paul. His interpretation of obedience language works within the overall rhetoric of the text to highlight the importance of Paul's presence in the community. The master-slave structure is in harmony with the father-child structure that Paul calls on in his recommendation of Timothy and the original-copy structure that underlies his sending of Epaphroditus.

Paul's emphasis or reiteration of a symbolic universe in which obedience operates meets the rhetorical challenge presented by Euodia and

Syntyche's leadership in Philippi. Both their partnership with each other and their gender as women clash with the symbolic universe that Paul's rhetoric constructs. They do not "fit" with the hierarchical father-child relationship that Paul has constructed with Timothy. Nor do they fit with the "double" relationship that Paul has built with Epaphroditus. As leaders whose primary identification is with each other and not with Paul, they are also excluded by the ideal of partnership with Paul which the friendship language of the letter and the techniques of identification have so strongly emphasized. Partnership with Paul—defined as being of one mind and of one soul and of agreeing in the Lord—is defined so as to exclude both internal division *and* internal alliances within the community. The congregation at Philippi is constructed as those who must continue to obey in Paul's absence.

This reconstruction of the historical situation of Philippians solves two key problems of interpretation of Philippians, that is, the character of the "opposition" to Paul in Philippians (the relationship between 1:15–18, 1:28, and 3:2–21) and the discontinuity between the language of friendship and the language of obedience in the letter to the Philippians.

The emphasis of scholars upon Phil 2:6–12 as the key text employing obedience language in Paul and their reading of the hymn in light of Paul's exhortatory conclusion in Phil 2:12, are testimony to the effectiveness of Paul's rhetoric. By quoting the rhetorically powerful hymn, Paul harnesses its power to serve the paraenetical goals in his appeal for unity and harmony in the community. By interpreting the significance of Jesus' exchange of form from God to slave and his exaltation to ruler primarily as a model of virtuous behavior, Paul—followed by the majority of his commentators—eclipses the theology of the hymn and its community. The achievement of Paul's rhetoric, that is, the limitation of the meaning of partnership to partnership with Paul and the male leaders who are identified with him, has been accepted as natural throughout the interpretive tradition.

CHAPTER 5

The Letter to the Ephesians:
Rhetorical Analysis and Rhetorical Situation

It is a common hermeneutical feature of earlier scholarly treatments of obedience to draw a distinction between obedience in Paul's genuine letters and subordination in the later Pauline tradition. While the former is considered free, the latter is closely bound up with the social system in which inferior obeys superior. As Bultmann expressed it, in the early church obedience became "a work." In Käsemann's language, the focus of the text on Christ becomes domesticated with its interest in the church. Using a cultural-anthropological method, Wayne Meeks describes the shift from the letters of Paul to later Pauline tradition in such letters as Ephesians and Colossians as accommodation to the surrounding culture. The exploration of the words for obedience in Greek authors in chapter two illustrates that both ὑπακούειν and ὑποτάσσεσθαι customarily appear in the hierarchical contexts of political subjugation, slavery, and marriage, and thus the distinction between obedience and subordination cannot be made on the basis of different vocabulary. Rather, the claim that Paul used the language of obedience outside of the conventional social contexts must be reexamined by analysis of his letters themselves. That analysis began in chapters three and four with the study of Philippians, an undisputed letter of Paul. The analysis focuses on Paul's rhetorical adaptation of early christological traditions and the dynamics of opposition and identification within the letter. Obedience language in Philippians constructs relationships of authority and a symbolic universe that makes some conclusions inevitable and others implausible. For example, the possibilities of independence and partnership are limited by the language of obedience and the symbolic universe it constructs. The next step of the analysis will be to explore the language of obedience in a letter that all the exegetes discussed in chapter one agree is from the later Pauline tradition: the letter to the Ephesians.

Obedience in Ephesians is most often contrasted with the so-called free obedience of Paul's genuine letters. Ephesians presents explicit ethical instructions based upon obedience language. Those injunctions to maintain a particular social order rest on claims about Christ and God. The rhetorical analysis of Ephesians traces how the author constructs this symbolic universe and seeks clues with which to reconstruct the historical situation of the letter. Some commentators argue that the author of Ephesians, as well as Paul, transforms the language of obedience by equating obedience and love. Therefore, the rhetorical analysis attends to the language of love in Ephesians in order to see how it relates to the language of obedience. In reconstructing a historical situation for the letter to the Ephesians, some exegetes reconstruct a problem to which the author applies the household code. As with the study of Philippians, this theory is evaluated in light of the language of opposition within the letter.

This investigation of the rhetoric of obedience in the letter to the Ephesians proceeds as did that of Philippians. By analyzing the rhetoric of the letter as a whole and the symbolic universe it constructs, it is possible to describe the inscribed rhetorical situation. Attention is given to the persona of the inscribed author, the construction of the audience, and the language of opposition. The next chapter examines the rhetorical situation in light of information from outside the letter to the Ephesians in order to reconstruct a possible historical situation for the letter. This chapter shares the perspective articulated in the introduction: the letter is read as a rhetorical discourse designed to persuade an audience in the midst of competing understandings. Therefore, tensions within the rhetoric of the letter can be read as clues to different early Christian languages and interpretation.

Ephesians's position in the canon along with other earlier letters written by Paul has worked very much against this critical perspective. First, the letter's rhetoric of obedience and submission has been used to interpret earlier letters of Paul with the result that the differences between them have been obscured. The dynamic of harmonization works both among the Pauline letters and within individual letters. In the case of Philippians, interpreters read earlier traditions within the letters according to the directions that Paul's rhetoric provides. This approach minimizes diversity and blurs distinctions among points of view. In the case of Ephesians, a further dynamic is at work to discourage seeing Ephesians as a rhetorical argument in the context of debate. Scholars who understand Ephesians within the category of "early catholicism" assume that all controversial questions had been settled at the time of the writing of Ephesians as the church was "on its way to becoming an institution."[1] Thus, the developments in the language of Ephesians are considered inevitable. This assumption makes evidence to the contrary invisible.[2]

The opposite of this tendency towards harmonization has also operated in the study of Ephesians, particularly among Protestant scholars who want to hold Paul's genuine letters as the authoritative standard against "later" developments. Attempts to hold apart the genuine letters and the later ones are made by the distinction in vocabulary and by the separation of the language into "religious" and "social" categories. Using a perspective that neither harmonizes differences on the basis of Pauline authorship nor constructs a preconceived dichotomy between Ephesians and Paul's earlier letters based on non-Pauline authorship, this chapter explores how the rhetoric of obedience and submission functions in Ephesians. The exploration of the language of obedience in two distinct rhetorical and historical contexts—Philippians and Ephesians—enables a comparison between them.

Authorship and Pseudonymity

Any attempt to understand the rhetorical and historical situation must take seriously the fact that Ephesians is written as a letter from Paul. While much scholarly debate has circulated around whether Ephesians

---

[1]Dennis C. Duling and Norman Perrin, *The New Testament: Proclamation and Parenesis, Myth and History* (3d ed.; Fort Worth, TX: Harcourt Brace, 1994) 279–82.

[2]For an analysis of the history of interpretation of Ephesians and Colossians, see Schüssler Fiorenza, *Bread Not Stone*, 65–92. See also idem, *In Memory of Her*, 251–84. For a survey of various feminist approaches to the Pauline tradition, see Cynthia Briggs Kittredge, "Pauline Texts," in Letty M. Russell and J. Shannon Clarkson, eds., *Dictionary of Feminist Theologies* (Louisville, KY: Westminster/John Knox, 1996) 207–9. A recent work that tries to reconceive Paul outside the perspective of Paul in the New Testament canon is Neil Elliott, *Liberating Paul: The Justice of God and the Politics of the Apostle* (Maryknoll, NY: Orbis, 1994). Elliott argues that the genuine Paul was egalitarian with respect to slavery and women and that it is the presence of Ephesians and Colossians in the canon that biases later interpreters.

is written by Paul or is pseudonymous—and therefore whether it should contribute to or be excluded from Pauline theology—I understand that the author of Ephesians, by claiming the name of Paul, is positioning the argument squarely and self-consciously in the Pauline tradition.[3] Therefore, after exploring how the rhetoric of obedience functions in Philippians, an undisputed letter of Paul, it is valuable to investigate how that language operates in Ephesians, a letter in which an author claims the name and authority of Paul, in order to understand the Pauline tradition. A comparison between the use of the rhetoric of obedience in two letters from different points in the tradition may result in previously unnoticed points of similarity and difference.

Ephesians is a letter written to persuade an audience and can be understood as argument. Both its character as a letter and its reputed audience have been called into question. It has been described as a "meditation" or a "prayer" rather than a letter, and its techniques of assertion and exhortation may not appear to be an argument in the same way as Romans or 1 Corinthians.[4] Because the author does not describe specific aspects of the rhetorical situation or name any coworkers known from other letters, scholars have found it difficult to determine a precise historical situation for the work. However, a rhetorical perspective understands that Ephesians is provoked by some rhetorical exigence or problem, which the rhetoric seeks to respond to and overcome. Even if the audience is conceived very broadly, the letter was written to be persuasive to a certain audience. The lack of a precise description of the audience may itself be part of the rhetorical strategy. The letter claims to be a letter from Paul. While they are not rational arguments, the various kinds of language within the letter—prayer, hymn, doxology—have a powerful rhetorical dimension within the argument. The purpose of the rhetorical analysis is to trace the movement of the argument, to identify the kind of proofs employed, and to locate the argument's center of gravity. It describes the symbolic universe that the letter constructs and

---

[3]See, for example, Johan Christiaan Beker, *Heirs of Paul: Paul's Legacy in the New Testament and in the Church Today* (Minneapolis: Fortress, 1991); James D. G. Dunn, "The Problem of Pseudonymity," in idem, *The Living Word* (London: SCM, 1987) 65–85. See also the literature cited in Lincoln, *Ephesians*, lix–lx.

[4]For example, Schnackenburg (*Ephesians*, 21–24) characterizes Ephesians as a "meditation." Joachim Gnilka (*Der Epheserbrief: Auslegung* [HThKNT 33; Freiburg: Herder, 1971] 29–33) calls it a "homily."

identifies the tensions or contradictions within that symbolic universe. It attempts to show how earlier traditions are utilized and provides the evidence for a description of the rhetorical situation.

The problem of the literary relationship between Ephesians, Colossians, and other letters of Paul complicates attempts to interpret Ephesians. The rhetorical analysis first focuses on the movement of the argument of Ephesians itself without explaining features of the text by reference to other letters. Initially, no particular theory of literary relationship with Colossians will be used to read Ephesians. I explore the relationship of Ephesians with Colossians in chapter six, where I discuss the historical situation.

In this rhetorical analysis of Ephesians, I do not use the terms *haustafel* or "household code" to describe Eph 5:21–6:9, nor do I discuss the issue of its form or source at this point. Rather, I focus on the way the address to members of the community, wives, husbands, children, fathers, slaves, and masters functions in the author's argument and relates to the author's major concerns in the letter. Focus on the household code as a unit draws attention away from how it functions in the letter as a whole. In addition, certain assumptions are built into the category of "household code": first, that it is primarily about internal relationships within the private household; second, that it was something that a reader would recognize and expect; and third, that its place at the end of a letter was conventional and necessary. This perspective centers around how the author adapts or Christianizes a code that he inherits. This analysis will assume that the author of Ephesians uses various traditions in his address to the audience and harnesses them for his rhetorical purposes.

Rhetorical Arrangement

The language of obedience and submission is concentrated near the end of Ephesians in 5:21–6:9, the portion that modern scholarship calls the "household code." The result of the focus on the form of this passage as having its origin and background in another setting besides Ephesians and being imported into its context has been to treat the obedience language in the passage in isolation from the rest of the letter to the Ephesians. The language of obedience, therefore, is ascribed to the tradition of the household code and not to the author of Ephesians. In contrast, my rhetorical analysis attempts to understand where Eph 5:21–6:9 fits and how it functions in the argument of the letter as a whole. I explore how the symbolic universe that this passage assumes and constructs coheres with the symbolic universe that the letter has been building to this point. The position of this passage in the arrangement of the argument can reveal information about the rhetorical situation of the letter to the Ephesians.

The argument of the letter falls into the broad categories of rhetorical arrangement: Eph 1:1–23 is the *exordium*; 2:1–3:21 forms the *narratio*; a passage that is either a *digressio* or a part of the *narratio* runs from 3:2 to 3:21; and an *exhortatio*—which replaces the usual *argumentio*—runs from 4:1– 6:9. The *peroratio* is 6:10–20.[5] The *exordium* introduces the main topics of the letter and builds a relationship with the audience. The *narratio* describes events on which the argument is based. The *exhortatio/argumentio* presents proofs, and the *peroratio* summarizes and recapitulates the argument.

The Construction of the Symbolic Universe

Affirmation and Appeal

Ephesians appears to lack what rhetorical critics call an *argumentio* and what epistolary theorists call the body of the letter. Many scholars divide Ephesians into two main sections: 1:1–3:21 and 4:1– 6:23.[6] They categorize the first section as "affirmations" and the second as "appeals." It has been frequently pointed out that this division corresponds to the two typical divisions of Pauline letters into what Bultmann labeled the "indicative" and the "imperative." In general, affirmations do provide the basis for ethical appeals in Ephesians. Andrew Lincoln identifies 4:1– 6:9 as *exhortatio* rather than *argumentio* and argues that

---

[5]Ephesians has been interpreted by several scholars who employ rhetorical criticism. Andrew Lincoln's commentary on Ephesians uses the categories of rhetorical criticism and attempts to read it as an argument with a specific rhetorical purpose (Lincoln, *Ephesians*). He analyzes Eph 6:10–20 as a *peroratio* in Lincoln, "Stand Therefore," 99–114. See also Mouton, "Reading Ephesians Ethically," 359–77. I have benefited from discussions with Ann Holmes Redding whose forthcoming doctoral dissertation ("Together, Not Equal: The Rhetoric of Hierarchy and Unity in Ephesians," Union Theological Seminary) includes rhetorical analysis of Ephesians.

[6]This division is widely accepted. See Lincoln, *Ephesians*, xxxvi.

the *exhortatio* draws out the implications of the earlier chapters of the letter.[7] However, the division of the letter into affirmation and appeal does not completely explain the movement of the argument. Rather, throughout the letter to the Ephesians, narration of divine events is combined with ethical appeal. For example, in the section of affirmations reference is made to ethical purity (2:3–5) and to good works (2:10). There is narration of divine events throughout the paraenetic section (4:4–6, 18–21, 5:2, 23–32). In other letters of Paul, such as 1 Corinthians, Philemon, and Philippians, ethical appeal and argument work together in the rhetoric of the letter. None of these letters falls neatly into distinct sections of affirmation and appeal. The symbolic universe is constructed not just through the author's rhetoric in Eph 1:1–3:21 but also in the paraenesis in 4:1–6:24.[8]

The recognition of the interplay between affirmation and ethical exhortation has implications for the interpretation of the obedience language in Eph 5:21–6:9. This passage, which instructs wives and husbands, parents and children, and slaves and masters about their roles in relation to one another, is not simply a logical drawing out "in the sphere of every day life" of the affirmations about the relationship between God, Christ, and the community in 1:1–3:21. Rather, the exhortations and their supporting explanations contribute to the construction of a symbolic universe that begins in Eph 1:1. These instructions both are based on and build upon what the author has established as the symbolic universe within the letter. These exhortations develop and modify earlier affirmations by delineating hierarchical relationships within the community. The obedience language of Eph 5:21–6:9 builds a picture of *ekklesia*, which has been a focus throughout the rhetoric of the letter. Rhetorical analysis can trace how the author builds his arguments with reference to the values and traditions of the audience.

Self-Reference and Prayer

The movement of an argument may be discerned by noting elements that run through the letter as a whole and are repeated and elaborated

[7] Ibid., xliii–xliv.

[8] Following Nils Dahl, J. Paul Sampley argues that the pattern of the entire letter alternates between reference to the readers, christological development, and return to the situation of the readers. This pattern occurs throughout both sections of the letter (Sampley, *One Flesh*, 11–12).

in the course of the argument. An important structural element of this letter is the three points where the author refers to himself. Each of these self-references is connected with prayer. The first is in the opening verse of the letter in which Paul identifies himself as "apostle of Christ Jesus by the will of God." The prescript is followed immediately by a doxology and thanksgiving. The second is in 3:1, the beginning of an extensive explication of Paul's history and role, which is followed by a prayer in 3:14–21. The third is in 6:19, when the author asks the congregation to pray for him. These repeated occurrences throughout the letter indicate that the author's presentation of himself is an important feature of the argument of the letter.[9]

This presentation is not done by referring to specific details of the author's present situation, such as where he is and whom he knows.[10] Rather, the self-presentation is done by using shorthand references that point to a well-known situation, such as "apostle" or "prisoner," which then serve as titles for the author. That prayer is linked to these references contributes to the author's self-presentation because it expresses his theological outlook, his relationship with God, and his vision of how things are. Thus, the author's presentation of himself is intertwined with the identity of the audience (as he constructs it). As in all rhetorical works, that presentation contributes to the persuasiveness of the argument.[11]

Unity

Throughout the letter, the author uses different language and imagery to address the theme of unity or oneness. The first reference uses the difficult word ἀνακεφαλαιώσασθαι ("to gather up") in the opening blessing of the *exordium* (1:10). The second occurs in the *narratio* in 2:13–18 with a concentration of unity language: "he has made us both one" (2:14), "that he might create in himself one new person in the place of two" (2:15), "might reconcile us both to God in one body through the cross" (2:16), "we both have access to one Spirit" (2:18).

---

[9]See Martinus C. de Boer, "Images of Paul in the Post-Apostolic Period," *CBQ* 42 (1980) 359–80.

[10]See Rom 16:1–23; 1 Cor 16:5–20.

[11]Andrew Lincoln (*Ephesians*, xlii) points out how the "ornamentative thanksgiving and prayer of Eph 1:3 is an effective rhetorical strategy." Lincoln does not explore the results of this strategy in the letter as a whole.

The author employs unity language again at the opening of the *exhortatio* in 4:1–6. The final occurrence of unity language comes in the author's discussion of marriage in which Genesis 2 is quoted: "and the two shall become one flesh." The construction of a symbolic universe in which unity is a critical feature is a major concern of the argument of Ephesians.[12]

An overview of the argument of the letter shows the interplay of narration of divine events with ethical instruction, which contributes to the construction of a symbolic universe. Unity and the author's identity and authority are elements to which the author repeatedly returns throughout the letter. By tracing the movement of the argument more closely, one can discern how these emphases relate and discover the role of the language of obedience in 5:21–6:9 within the overall argument.

The *Exordium*: Eph 1:1–23

The letter begins with the naming of the sender, "Paul," and a phrase to describe him, "apostle of Christ Jesus by the will of God" (ἀπόστολος Χριστοῦ Ἰησοῦ διὰ θελήματος θεοῦ). The addressees are named: "the saints who are also faithful in Christ Jesus" (τοῖς ἁγίοις τοῖς οὖσιν καὶ πιστοῖς ἐν Χριστῷ Ἰησοῦ). The phrase "in Ephesus" (ἐν Ἐφέσῳ) is not found in the earliest manuscripts and is not considered part of the original letter.[13] Unlike other Pauline letters, the author does not name any coauthors. This detail is consistent with the author's emphasis on his unique role as the apostle to the Gentiles, which he presents in Eph 3:1–13.[14]

In the *exordium* the author establishes good will by referring to, describing, and constructing a relationship with the audience. The

[12]Among many scholars, Wayne Meeks ("In One Body," 214) notes that unity is the dominant theme of the letter. I argue that a rhetorical analysis illustrates the successive development and modification of that notion of unity. This development is explained, not by understanding the thought of the author as consistent throughout all passages in the letter but by seeing the variety and tension as evidence of places where the view of the audience was in tension with that of the author.

[13]For a review of the discussion of the textual problems surrounding this verse, see Josef Schmid, *Der Epheserbrief des Apostels Paulus* (Freiburg: Herder, 1928) 37–129; and Ernest Best, "Ephesians i. 1," in idem and R. McL. Wilson, eds., *Text and Interpretation* (Cambridge: Cambridge University Press, 1979) 29–41.

[14]Lincoln, *Ephesians*, 5. See also Martinus C. de Boer, "Images of Paul in the Post-Apostolic Period," *CBQ* 42 (1980) 363–66.

author constructs this relationship not by referring to the facts of past association, such as the last time Paul visited, or by citing concrete details of the relationship, but by retelling the story of divine election and redemption, which took place "before the foundation of the world" (1:4). The retelling serves to ground the relationship with the audience not in recent but in primordial divine history. The author retells the story through the blessing in 1:3–14 and the prayer in 1:15–23, both elements of the *exordium*. Both the blessing of God and the following modifying phrase provide the occasion for describing God in 1:3. In the opening description of God's choosing of "us," the phrase ἐν ἀγάπῃ is used. God bestows grace "on us in the beloved" (ἐν τῷ ἠγαπημένῳ). This is the first time that love is mentioned in the letter. It recurs again in 1:15 with reference to the audience's "love toward all the saints." The relative clause describes the relationship of "us" with God and "our" history with God.

The blessing is the first of several times in Ephesians when the author tells a story of salvation. The narration of this story, told in Eph 1:4–10, 11–14, 18–19, 2:1, 4–7, 11–13, 5:2, 24, is the primary means by which this author establishes the identity of the audience, his identity, and their relationship with him. He relates a story that takes place on a cosmic plane, before history, in which the main actors are God, Christ, and the community whom God has chosen. Ann Holmes Redding describes the five interrelated moments of the "story" of the letter as a whole: 1) the bestowal of extraordinary benefits by God on the elect (Ephesians 1); 2) the formation of the cosmic hierarchy under Christ as head (Ephesians 1); 3) the movement from enmity to unity between Jews and Gentiles accomplished through Christ's death (Ephesians 2); 4) the commissioning of Paul as apostle to the Gentiles (Ephesians 3); 5) the unveiling of the plan of salvation, the mystery of God described both as the "summing up of all things in the headship of Christ" (1:10) and as the change in status for Gentiles to being "co-inheritors and co-members of the body and co-sharers of the promise in Jesus Christ through the gospel" (3:6).[15] This opening effectively grounds the author's identity and his appeals in the story of the origin of the community and their relationship with God. The story is told in liturgical language. Although

---

[15]Ann Holmes Redding, "What Price Unity?" (paper presented at the annual meeting of the Society of Biblical Literature, Chicago, IL, November 1994).

not itself a hymn,[16] the rhythmic language of the eulogy of 1:3–14 encourages audience assent to and participation in its symbolic universe.[17] The language of prayer that opens the letter also serves to contribute to the construction of the author as a person of prayer. Insights about the structure of reality or about the narration of divine events expressed in the language of prayer are linked with divine revelation, a theme that gains importance throughout the letter.

The strongly positive terms in which the author describes the story and its position in the *exordium* suggest that the outlines of the story are accepted by the audience. In other words, this symbolic universe, in which the identity of the community is established, is shared by the author and audience. The author refers to it at the opening to confirm their common ground and to provide the basis for the rest of the letter.[18]

The blessing expresses a sense of accomplishment or fulfillment— that everything has already been given. What has been made known to "us," the audience with whom the author identifies, is the "mystery of his will" (τὸ μυστήριον τοῦ θελήματος αὐτοῦ, 1:9). It is significant that τὸ μυστήριόν is mentioned in the context of prayer. In two places in Paul's letters, Rom 11:25–26 and 1 Cor 15:51–57, an announcement of a "mystery" is followed by an acclamation of God's greatness or a "shout of thanks" to God. In Ephesians, the author's presentation of the "mystery" is made in a letter in which the author uses prayer to express his understanding of divine events and of the identity of the audience. The use of prayer contributes to the authority of the author's interpretation of the "mystery."[19]

In the prayer in 1:17, the author prays that God "may give you a spirit of wisdom and revelation as you come to know him" (δώῃ ὑμῖν πνεῦμα σοφίας καὶ ἀποκαλύψεως ἐν ἐπιγνώσει αὐτοῦ). The repetition of the words "wisdom" and "revelation" in the prayer and throughout the letter indicates that they are disputed terms and suggests that their proper interpretation is going to be part of the purpose of the letter. "Mys-

---

[16]Lincoln (*Ephesians*, 13–15) provides a history of research on this question. See J. T. Sanders, "Hymnic Elements in Ephesians 1–3," *ZNW* 56 (1965) 214–32.

[17]Lincoln, *Ephesians*, 18.

[18]Lincoln (ibid., 44) points out the way the eulogy works in the rhetoric of the letter: "In this way the eulogy has an epistolary function as a prelude and a rhetorical function as an exordium."

[19]Wire, *Corinthian Women*, 141.

tery" and "wisdom" are explicitly addressed further in the letter, both in the elaborate self-presentation of the author in 3:1–21 and in the explication of marriage as the analogy between Christ and the Church in 5:32. In 1:10, the "mystery" is defined as God's plan "to gather up all things in Christ" (ἀνακεφαλαιώσασθαι τὰ πάντα ἐν τῷ Χριστῷ). The meaning of the verb ἀνακεφαλαιώσασθαι is ambiguous and disputed. This verb, whose root is κεφάλαιον meaning "summary,"[20] is customarily used to describe the summation of a rhetorical argument.[21] The main question in its interpretation here is whether the notion of "subjection" within "headship" already operates within this verb. Some commentators claim that the imagery of headship, which appears later in the letter, does not operate in this section.[22] But others claim that one must interpret the statement in which this verb occurs and the meaning of the verb in a way consistent with other passages in Ephesians involving the word or the image, "head."[23] Jennifer Berenson Maclean argues that the most common meaning of the verb in its time was "to summarize an argument." She argues that the phrase that follows is best understood as a Stoic doxological formula and that the conventional meaning is appropriate here.[24] The ambiguity of the word's meaning in the initial statement of God's purpose in Christ—at the first point at which the author presents a picture of unity or unification—functions in the development of the author's symbolic universe in the letter. The immediate context in which the author places the word gives it a new meaning in the construction of a symbolic universe beyond its conventional meaning as a rhetorical term. If the images developed later in the argument of the letter are read back into this one, then the verb is interpreted as implying subjection. If one reads the argument as progressing from beginning to conclusion, then the ambiguity of the verb here at the beginning is resolved by the picture of head and body and subjection within the church that is presented in the exhortation to wives and husbands in Eph 5:21–33.

Some of the language in the eulogy has a close connection with baptism ("chose us," "sonship," "good pleasure," "beloved," and "marked

---

[20]Compare Acts 22:28; Heb 8:1.

[21]Quintilian *Inst. Orat.* 6.1; Aristotle *Frag.* 133; Rom 13:9.

[22]Lincoln (*Ephesians*, 33) stresses the meaning of "summing up" rather than "subordinating."

[23]See Heinrich Schlier, "κεφαλή, ἀνακεφαλαιόομαι," *TDNT* 3 (1965) 681–82

[24]Maclean, "Ephesians," 51–60.

with the seal of the promised holy Spirit"). The baptismal language is projected back in time and described in terms of God's past choice and future plan. If the language of this eulogy reflects an earlier tradition that was known by the audience, then the audience would have recognized the baptismal language. They may have understood their baptism primarily in terms of their election and change of identity as a community.[25] Along with the author, they may have understood the goal of God's work in Christ to be "uniting" all things in some sense. The argument of the letter to the Ephesians presents a picture of what that "summing up all things" looks like. Both the blessing and the prayer focus on the community— who they are and what God has done for them—but no specific word has been used to designate that community. This specific word is introduced in 1:22, in the prayer that concludes the *exordium*, in the phrase τῇ ἐκκλησίᾳ. The word *ekklesia* occurs when the author refers to what God did in Christ. With the word *ekklesia*, the author introduces another major issue in the argument of the letter: the identity, role, and structure of the *ekklesia* in the symbolic universe set up by the author. Again the narrative of salvation contributes to the construction of a symbolic universe.

In order to understand the role of Eph 1:19–23 in the argument of the letter, it is important to note the emphasis on power (both the power of God and the power "in us who believe"), the relationship of Christ to the powers, and how the author connects that with the church. Up until this point, there has been no sense of conflict or of enemies in the letter. In these verses the stress is on the position of Christ above the powers. Eph 1:20 refers to Psalm 110 to describe God making Christ sit at his right hand. Using four synonyms for power (ἀρχῆς καὶ ἐξουσίας καὶ δυνάμεως καὶ κυριότητος), verse 21 describes all the powers above which Christ is. Verse 22 quotes Ps 8:7—using ὑποτάσσω in the active voice— in the same version used in 1 Cor 15:27 (καὶ πάντα ὑπέταξεν ὑπὸ τοὺς πόδας αὐτοῦ). In 1 Corinthians, Paul uses the psalm to say that this complete subjection will be finished only in the future and that when it happens, Christ will be subjected to God. The eschatological perspective of these verses in Ephesians is that the subjection has already

---

[25]Nils A. Dahl, ("Adresse und Proömium des Epheserbriefes," *TZ* 7 [1951] 263–64) argues that the blessing was modeled on prayers before baptism. See also J. Coutts, "Ephesians 1:3–14 and 1 Peter 1:3–12," *NTS* 3 (1956–57) 115–27.

occurred.[26] In Ephesians, this subjection is described as "making him head over all things for the church." The dative τῇ ἐκκλησίᾳ means that the subjection is done on behalf of the church. The author does not say that Christ is head *over* the church.[27] The church is then identified with "his body" (τὸ σῶμα αὐτοῦ), "the fullness of him who fills all in all" (τὸ πλήρωμα τοῦ τὰ πάντα ἐν πᾶσιν πληρουμένου). The image of the church as the fullness of Christ, the entity which fills the cosmos, is more consistent with the image of Christ over all things "on behalf of the church" than it is with Christ as head over the church.

Commentators on this verse, as on Eph 1:10, have interpreted the meaning of this statement and the spatial picture it creates in light of the author's later statements in the letter about Christ as head of the body. The ambiguity of earlier statements about the church and unity in Ephesians is clarified by later statements in the letter.[28] This approach does not allow one to see how the author leads the audience from one step to another, each time modifying and concretizing the relationship between church, head, and body. Reading the letter as a rhetorical argument can explain such a progression as part of the author's strategy. Rather than present the full-fledged picture of hierarchy from the beginning, to which the audience might object, the author seeks to gain audience acceptance of each successive detail of the symbolic universe until it is finally completed in Eph 5:21– 6:9.

[26]Lincoln (*Ephesians*, 66) observes the difference in eschatological perspective from Paul's use of Psalm 8 in 1 Cor 15:27. He argues that this difference does not weigh decisively against Paul as the author because elsewhere Paul describes the cosmos as already subjected. Lincoln cites Phil 2:10, 11, 3:21b, and Col 2:15 as support. In chapter three, I explore Paul's use of the Christ hymn (Phil 2:6–11) and his modification of its eschatological perspective in Phil 3:21. In the following chapter I compare Col 2:15 with its interpretation in Ephesians. A method that acknowledges diverse perspectives within the Pauline letters allows for a different understanding than one that attempts to systematize Paul's language.

[27]Noting that the author does not say this explicitly, Lincoln (*Ephesians*, 68) suggests that Christ being "head" over the church "is the clear implication." My analysis shows that the author's ambiguity about the position of Christ and its consequences for roles within the church is gradually resolved in the course of the letter. The slow development is part of the rhetorical strategy and may indicate that the symbolic universe that the author constructs is not shared by the audience. This problem is discussed in G. Howard, "The Head/ Body Metaphors of Ephesians," *NTS* 20 (1974) 350–56.

[28]An example of this tendency is found in Schnackenburg, *Ephesians*, 79–80. In discussing the various ways to interpret the "two in a way contrary thoughts—that God forces the powers of evil under Christ's feet and gives him to the Church as the one who fills her

The *Narratio*: Eph 2:1–21

Eph 2:1–21 constitutes a two-part *narratio,* which contrasts the pre-Christian past of the Gentile addressees with their Christian present. The section begins and ends with the contrast between "you who were dead" and "you who are alive" (2:1 and 5). The author interprets the contrast of dead and alive in terms of sin: "And once you/we were dead through your trespasses and sins" (καὶ ὑμᾶς ὄντας νεκροὺς τοῖς παραπτώμασιν καὶ ταῖς ἁμαρτίαις ὑμῶν). The section begins and ends with the reference to "walking" (περιεπατήσατε, 2:2, 10; NRSV: "living"). Since "making alive" through baptism has implications for behavior, Schnackenburg has characterized both passages of the *narratio* as baptismal catechesis.[29] Here the past and present are vividly contrasted in order to increase pathos by making the audience more aware of the difference between their past and their present. It identifies them closely in the church by the shift to "we."

The language of opposition appears in 2:2 where the author refers to the "ruler of the power of the air," "the spirit that is now at work in the sons of disobedience [NRSV: those who are disobedient]." In the blessing and prayer in the first chapter, there is no threat of enemies or conflict but rather a sense of everything being finished. In the verses just before 1:20–23, the author has described Christ as having everything under his feet and as head of all things. Yet here the present threat is indicated. The sense of threat is conveyed in Eph 3:10, 4:14, 5:6, 6:11, and 6:12. The necessity of fighting this threat recurs in the final call to battle in the *peroratio* of the letter in 6:10–20. Clinton Arnold argues that the frequent mention of the "powers" in Ephesians indicates that the audience of the letter had a keen sense of the power of magic beings. Therefore, the letter to the Ephesians is Paul's pastoral response in which he outlines where Christ and believers stand in terms of the powers.[30] I

---

with his power to bless," Schnackenburg concludes: "In view of the later passages where Christ is named as the head of the Church (4.15f.; 5.23) and of the statement which immediately follows—that she is his Body—we must recognize as the main emphasis the fact that Christ is given to the Church as Head."

[29] Ibid., 102–8.

[30] Clinton Arnold, *Ephesians: Power and Magic: The Concept of Power in Ephesians in Light of its Historical Setting* (SNTSMS 63; Cambridge: Cambridge University Press, 1989) 69.

shall postpone discussion of the historical situation until a later point, but it is important to note that here and at the end of the letter the author constructs the presence of powers outside subjection by Christ, who continue to be a threat to the audience. God, who is described as acting "out of the great love with which he loved us," "made us alive together with Christ" (Eph 2:4, 5).

Eph 2:11–21 begins with μνημονεύετε ("remember") followed by ὅτι indicating that a tradition follows. Schnackenburg characterizes this procedure of admonition and exposition as anamnesis.[31] As in the previous section of the *narratio*, the contrast is expressed in temporal terms, between "once" and "now." This contrast increases pathos, and this "reminding" has the effect of making the audience grateful and well-disposed to the paraenesis that follows.[32] The language of this passage, which is associated with baptism, is the contrast between past and present, of becoming one (2:14–18), and of incorporation and reconciliation. The incorporation and becoming one is not described as if it were happening to an individual believer but as if it were happening between two peoples: Jews and Gentiles. Unlike the baptismal language in Rom 6:3 and Col 2:12, the text of Ephesians does not explicitly use the verb "baptize" or the noun "baptism."

This passage is important to the developing image of unity, which we have observed running through the argument of Ephesians. Here the situation of Gentile and Jew in the community is described as "two becoming one" (ὁ ποιήσας τὰ ἀμφότερα ἓν) and as "making in himself one new man in place of the two" (ἵνα τοὺς δύο κτίσῃ ἐν αὐτῷ εἰς ἕνα καινὸν ἄνθρωπον). The language of oneness is concentrated in 2:14–18, where expressions using "one" occur four times. Oneness is described with the language of reunification of two separated beings. Making two into one is described as "reconciling us both to God in one body" (καὶ ἀποκαταλλάξῃ τοὺς ἀμφοτέρους ἐν ἑνὶ σώματι τῷ θεῷ).[33] Eph 2:14–18 is preceded by a description of the Gentiles before Christ, drawing on

---

[31]Schnackenburg, *Ephesians*, 102–3. This passage as "baptismal anamnesis" is developed by Meeks, "In One Body," 209–21.

[32]Lincoln (*Ephesians*, 132) comments on the rhetorical purpose of this passage in this position.

[33]Schnackenburg (*Ephesians*, 105–8), as others, divides the passage into three main sections: 12–13 using the image of coming close; 14–16 using the image of union; 17–18 returning to the imagery of near and far; 19–22 the "conclusion for the ecclesial status of the addressees."

imagery of separation, alienation, and hopelessness. Using Isa 57:19, the Gentiles are described as being brought near from far off. The language of Isaiah returns in 2:17 to refer to Christ preaching peace to both the far off and the near. Then the language of oneness returns.

Scholars have discussed whether a hymn lies behind all or part of Eph 2:1–20. The repeated emphasis on oneness, which stands out from its context, the shift from "you" in verse 13 to "we" in verse 14 and back to "you" in verse 19, the christological emphasis, the parallel style, and the relative pronoun "who" in verse 14 all contribute to the evidence that traditional hymnic material lies behind these verses.[34] The hymn shares the cosmological concerns of Hellenistic Judaism.[35] It refers to the reconciliation within the cosmos of separated spheres. The close relationship of the view of Christ of Eph 2:14–18 and Col 1:20 indicates that a similar tradition lies behind both or that Ephesians depends upon these verses in Colossians. I shall postpone the comparison of the two passages until the discussion of the historical situation of Ephesians. At this point it is sufficient to recognize that Col 1:20 and Eph 2:14–18 share common elements of the idea of cosmic reconciliation. In Ephesians this reconciliation or cosmic unity is applied to the human unity of Jew and Gentile.[36]

Behind the passage lies a mythical and cosmic notion of reconciliation. The repetition of images of oneness belies a tradition that Wayne Meeks has discussed as "the baptismal reunification formula" in which the hallmark of the new human was unity. Variations on that formula include Gal 3:28, 1 Cor 12:13, Col 3:11, and Ignatius *Smyrn.* 1.2.[37]

The most complete form of the formula is preserved in Gal 3:28:

> There is no longer Jew or Greek, there is no longer slave or free, there is no longer male or female, for all of you are one in Christ Jesus.

> οὐκ ἔνι Ἰουδαῖος οὐδὲ Ἕλλην, οὐκ ἔνι δοῦλος οὐδὲ ἐλεύθερος, οὐκ ἔνι ἄρσεν καὶ θῆλυ· πάντες γὰρ ὑμεῖς εἷς ἐστε ἐν Χριστῷ Ἰησοῦ.

---

[34]Lincoln, *Ephesians*, 127.
[35]Lohse, *Colossians*, 46–55.
[36]Lincoln, *Ephesians*, 132.
[37]Meeks, "Androgyne," 165–208.

Eph 2:14–18 may reflect a liturgical elaboration of the first element of Galatians 3:28: "For there is no longer Jew nor Greek." Like Gal 3:27–28, Eph 2:14–18 emphasizes oneness. Gal 6:15 speaks of "a new creation" (καινὴ κτίσις) and Eph 2:15 speaks of "one new man [NRSV: humanity]" (εἰς ἕνα καινὸν ἄνθρωπον).

The creation of "one new man," which is part of the mythological language behind the hymn, recalls Genesis 1 and 2. The terms κτίζω and ἄνθρωπος link Eph 2:15 with Genesis 1. The language is akin to pre-Pauline Adam speculation in which the second Adam is no longer male and female, no longer two but one.[38]

The author of Ephesians describes the unification of Gentiles and Jews within the church with this image of unity. Wayne Meeks interprets this passage by saying that the author of Ephesians is "historicizing" this myth by seeing the inclusion of the Gentiles as the primary manifestation of God's plan. The key paradigm for reconciliation is the inclusion of Gentiles into the people of God.[39] The author of Ephesians utilizes this hymn to support the equality of Jew and Gentile in the church. This unity does not construct hierarchy between them or the necessity of subordination of one to the other. The author's argument demonstrates that in accomplishing the unity of Jew and Gentile, Christ transcended one of the fundamental divisions in the first-century world.[40] Eph 2:18 asserts that the old categories of Jew and Greek are transcended, and "both of us have access in one Spirit to the Father." The symbolic universe that these verses assume and that these verses simultaneously construct is of reunification, of joining two into one without hierarchical differentiation. This symbolic universe is not identical with that to which the author refers in 1:10 as "to gather up all things in Christ" or in 1:22–23 as "making him head over all things for the church which is his body."

The imagery of these verses contrasts with the picture of the church presented in 5:21–6:9 in which obedience and subordination, not join-

---

[38]For the discussion of Jewish texts showing the last Adam as God's intention for human existence, see Robin Scroggs, *The Last Adam* (Philadelphia: Fortress, 1966); and Miletic, *One Flesh*, 59–60.

[39]Meeks, "In One Body," 210–15. Elisabeth Schüssler Fiorenza argues that a baptismal formula lies behind Eph 2:11–20 (*In Memory of Her*, 267). See also Lincoln, *Ephesians*, 129.

[40]See Lincoln, *Ephesians*, 114. Lincoln does not note the contradiction between this claim and the exhortation to gender hierarchy.

ing of two into one, is the distinguishing characteristic of the church. There are both links and contradictions between 5:21–23 and 2:14–16. The author of Ephesians uses this powerful passage in this critical position in the letter. Eph 5:21–6:9 and 2:14–16 form the most extensive presentation of the church in the letter. Yet there is considerable tension between them.

The word "church" does not occur in this section of the *narratio*, but a picture of the community is conveyed. Those who were formerly "strangers and aliens" (ξένοι καὶ πάροικοι) are now "citizens with the saints and members of the household of God" (συμπολῖται τῶν ἁγίων καὶ οἰκεῖοι τοῦ θεοῦ). The image is one of *inclusion* in which the Gentiles receive privileges of membership in the household of God. The final picture of the household of God, consistent with the passage in which it occurs, emphasizes inclusion as equals and not hierarchical differentiation. The picture of the household of God is described in terms of a building. It is significant in the context of the author's argument that the temple is "built upon the foundation of the apostles and prophets." The author claims in Eph 1:1 to be "apostle of Christ Jesus." In the next passage, the mystery of Christ is said to be revealed "to his holy apostles and prophets by the Spirit" (3:5). The author claims to be both apostle and prophet, explicitly with his use of the title of apostle for himself in 1:1 and in the language of prayer he employs throughout the letter.

Scholars have often discussed this passage together with Eph 5:21–33.[41] Sampley suggests that the author argues for the continuity of Christ with Yahweh's promises to Israel in Eph 2:11–20 in order to prepare the groundwork for his introduction of marriage between Yahweh and Israel as the model for the relationship of Christ and the church. He points out the connection between the image of "one new man" in 2:15 with "one flesh" in 5:31 and says that the first is unity of Jew and Gentile in a more general sense and the second is unity of husband and wife in a more specific sense. However, his explanation does not account for the tension between the two passages. Stephen Francis Miletic argues that in the first passage the author is reflecting on the death of Jesus in terms of Christ as the New Adam and in the second the author is encouraging the audience to read the Christ-church relationship in terms of

---

[41]Sampley, *One Flesh,* 152–53, 161. See also Miletic, *One Flesh,* 45, 57.

New Adam and New Eve. He explains how subordination and mutuality can be held together by noting that the author is "quite comfortable mixing metaphors."[42]

Miletic's argument does not take into account that the author employs a traditional formulation in these verses, and therefore he attributes the reflection on Genesis 1 to the author of Ephesians. A rhetorical reading that notices the tensions in the text as indications of points of tension between author and audience can account for the contradiction by attributing the traditions of reflection on Genesis 1 that equate oneness with equality to the audience. The emphasis that the author gives these verses, their critical location in the argument of the letter, and their tension with the symbolic universe at the end of the *exhortatio* may be explained by understanding the relationship of the author of Ephesians to his audience. The audience valued the tradition about unity resulting from baptism. Perhaps they applied this idea of oneness to their own situation as Gentile Christians who conceived their history of inclusion into the people of God as the reunification of two previously fractured peoples into one community. Or perhaps the author of Ephesians elaborated upon this interpretation. This passage celebrates the experience and the value of that unity. The author refers to this tradition here in order to gain the audience's assent as the argument progresses and to prepare them for his modification and critique of that notion in the latter part of the letter.

The *Digressio*: Eph 3:1–21

In a rhetorical argument the *digressio* is associated with the *narratio*. Its purpose is to treat a theme relevant but not logically necessary to the case being made.[43] In the transition between *narratio* and *exhortatio*, the author retells the story of his own role. The designation *digressio* should not imply that the self-presentation of the author at this point in the letter is parenthetical. Rather, the position of this passage between the *narratio* and the ethical admonitions is emphatic and linked both to what precedes and what follows. Here the author links his own role as minister of the gospel with the reconciliation of Jews and Gentiles

---

[42]Ibid., 49.
[43]Quintilian 4.3.1, 14. Lincoln, *Ephesians*, 171.

established in the previous passage. The author emphasizes his apostolic role, which will give authority to the instructions that follow in the letter.

In this self-presentation the author claims a distinctive role in making the audience see (φωτίσαι) or enlightening them about God's revelation. He positions himself, as διάκονος, directly amidst the issues and contested terms that he has set up in the letter thus far: "mystery," "revelation," "wisdom," and the "church." The word τὸ μυστήριον is used three times (3:3, 3:4, and 3:9). The first time, the author says that the readers have heard "how the mystery was made know to me by revelation." He reiterates "you have heard" and mentions a link with past tradition. The second time refers to the "mystery of Christ" evident when reading this letter, and the third describes Paul's appointed role "to make everyone see what is the plan of the mystery hidden for the ages." The repetition of "you know," "you have heard," and "you accept" indicates that the author is linking his authority with God's plan of the inclusion of the Gentiles. The passage takes the author's argument about *ekklesia* a step further when it says in 3:10 that "through the church the wisdom of God in its rich variety might now be made known" (ἵνα γνωρισθῇ νῦν ταῖς ἀρχαῖς καὶ ταῖς ἐξουσίαις ἐν τοῖς ἐπουρανίοις διὰ τῆς ἐκκλησί ας ἡ πολυποίκιλος σοφία τοῦ θεοῦ). As the author of the letter, "Paul" presents himself as the interpreter of a mystery that God has revealed to him. This digression has the effect of grounding the ethical exhortations that follow in the mystery of God's plan of salvation and in Paul's special role as their interpreter. He establishes his role as interpreter of τὸ μυστήριον, and he will call upon that role later in the letter (5:32).[44]

In 3:10, the phrase "to the rulers and authorities" describes to whom the mystery will be made known. As in 2:2, the author mentions the present existence of enemy powers. Establishing the presence of

---

[44]Schnackenburg (*Ephesians*, 130) states: "This also makes more concrete the author's pragmatic objective. In the self-portrayal of Paul as the Apostle to the Gentiles called according to God's plan, to whom a special insight into the Mystery of Christ was given, the addressees are made vividly aware of his God-given, irrevocable competence and authority. This emphasis is perhaps connected with the situation of the congregations after the Apostle's death or with the dying out of the old 'apostolic' generation of preachers in general. The congregations should preserve the continuity with the apostolic tradition. The metaphor of the Apostle captive and suffering for his congregation is suited to strengthen their relationship to him."

enemies in opposition to the audience prepares them for the call to battle that ends the letter and is one of the ways that the author gives a sense of urgency and purpose to his ethical instructions.

Eph 3:14–21 is a lengthy prayer asking for the general qualities of strength, comprehension, power, and love. Love is both a virtue of the one addressed: "being rooted and grounded in love" (3:17), and of Christ: "to know the love of Christ" (3:19). The use of language of family, "from whom every family in heaven and earth takes its name" (ἐξ οὗ πᾶσα πατριὰ ἐν οὐρανοῖς καὶ ἐπὶ γῆς ὀνομάζεται), is similar to the language of the household of God in 2:19. The phrase emphasizes inclusion but does not specify any ranking within that household. The author's use of the language of prayer serves to strengthen his self-presentation as an interpreter with knowledge of God's plan. In addition, the language of prayer contributes to the construction of a symbolic universe without asking the audience to do anything.

The *Exhortatio*: Eph 4:1–6:9

We have discussed above the misleading distinction between affirmation and appeal in Ephesians that has affected interpretation of the *exhortatio*. Scholars argue that this section of Ephesians employs primarily ethical materials, while the first section uses liturgical ones.[45] Much attention has been given to what forms the author has adapted and how he has adapted them. Rather than focus on the "source" of this language, this rhetorical analysis first examines how obedience language works within the overall argument of the letter.

The Position of Eph 5:21–6:9 in the Exhortatio

The long section of exhortation seems to have no obvious principle of organization. It includes exhortations about not living like the Gentiles (4:17–24), not lying and stealing (4:25–32), making the most of time, not being foolish, and not getting drunk (5:15–18). Love is mentioned several times (4:2, 15, 16). The random quality of this series of rules and maxims indicates that this is a collection of conventional materials that the author has collected here and given his own theo-

---

[45]See, for example, Victor Furnish, "Ephesians, Epistle to the," *ABD* 2 (1992) 535–42.

logical elaboration. Scholars have attempted to identify an organizing principle for this exhortation that might explain the function of Eph 5:21–6:9. The obedience language is concentrated in a passage that deals with relationships among members of the household: wives and husbands, children and parents, slaves and masters. Eph 5:21–6:9, therefore, is often considered an extension in the author's ethical exhortations in the area of family relationships.[46] Reading the argument of Ephesians as a whole, however, one can see that unity is addressed both at the beginning (4:1–5) and near the end of the *exhortatio* (5:31–32). In addition, both the beginning discussion of the various gifts in the community (4:7–16) and the final injunctions to wives and husbands refer to the corporate life of the community. Rather than labeling the subject of this section as "daily life," a more appropriate heading would be "relationships within the *ekklesia*."[47]

The author opens the exhortation with the verb παρακαλῶ and the an appositive phrase "the prisoner for/in the Lord." The term "prisoner" links the verse with the previous section, explicitly with 3:1—where the author refers to himself as ὁ δέσμιος—and with the reference to suffering in 3:13. A call to unity heads the exhortation.[48] The repetitive phrases and strophic pattern of these verses may reflect traditional material about oneness. The phrase "the unity of the spirit in the bond of peace" (4:3) recalls 2:14 ("he is our peace") and 2:18 ("both of us have access in one spirit"). The value of unity is not linked explicitly to Jew and Gentile but is made in general terms. Unity is connected explicitly with baptism in 4:5 and with the oneness of God. In 4:7–12, it is qualified by the discussion of the various gifts.

The hymnic confession of one body, one faith, one baptism is followed by an explanation of gifts. The "unity of faith" (4:13) is developed in 4:15 into a picture of a differentiated body in which Christ is the "head" (κεφαλή, 4:15). With this statement, the author introduces a nuance into the symbolic universe established thus far in the letter. In

---

[46]Lincoln (Ephesians, 350) titles the section "Household Relationships." See also Mouton ("Reading Ephesians Ethically," 366), who says that 4:17–6:9 contains "exhortations and conclusions about the principle of new life on a more personal level."

[47]Schnackenburg (*Ephesians*, 6) puts Eph 5:15–6:9 under the heading, "The Life of the Christian Congregation."

[48]As in Phil 1:27, oneness is expressed as a value.

1:10, the author spoke of "gathering up" all things in Christ. Next, Christ is called "head over all things for the church, which is his body" (1:22). In 4:15, the author introduces Christ "who is the head" (ὅς ἐστιν ἡ κεφαλή, Χριστός).

The author will refer to this expanded image of the body of Christ again at the end of this exhortation in his presentation of the analogy of husband and wife and Christ and the church. The second half of the letter modifies what the first half has established about unity. It shifts attention away from the focus on Jew and Gentile to a different understanding of unity in the marriage relationship. The various images and understandings of unity have been observed by scholars and explained in different ways. For example, Sarah Tanzer argues that the household code in Eph 5:22–6:9 was not originally part of Ephesians. She suggests that without 5:22–6:9, Eph 5:21 through 6:10 makes "a more cohesive, logically ordered set of short exhortations." As other commentators, she notes that the imagery of light and darkness does not occur in the passage but does occur before it (4:18 and 5:8–14) and after it (6:12).[49] She observes the contradiction that the earlier chapters of Ephesians advocate an equality of Jew and Gentile in Christ, while 5:22–6:9 does not concern equals but hierarchy within marriage and the family. Earlier commentators have noted the difference between the understanding of key concepts—such as κεφαλή, σῶμα, and ἐκκλησία—in this passage and in other places in Ephesians. Schlier points to the difficulty of making sense of figurative language that characterizes the "body" in the epistle as actually a "torso," and Christ as both the κεφαλή alone and the σῶμα and κεφαλή of the ἄνθρωπος and the ἐκκλησία.[50] Winsome Munro uses these differences to build her case for a literary stratum added to Ephesians and Colossians by a later interpolater.[51]

In contrast to a source-critical approach, a rhetorical reading of Ephesians seeks to make sense of the entire document as an argument

[49]Sarah J. Tanzer, "Ephesians," in Schüssler Fiorenza, Searching the Scriptures, 340–42.

[50]Heinrich Schlier, Christus und die Kirche im Epheserbrief (Tübingen: Mohr/Siebeck, 1930) 38.

[51]Winsome Munro, "Col III. 18–IV.1 and Eph.V. 21–VI.9: Evidences of a Later Literary Stratum?" NTS 18 (1972) 434–47. See also Winsome Munro, Authority in Paul and Peter: The Identification of a Pastoral Stratum in the Pauline Corpus and 1 Peter (SNTSMS 45; Cambridge: Cambridge University Press, 1983) 27–37.

designed to be persuasive to its audience. Clearly the author of Ephesians incorporated much traditional material into his letter, and many of the differences between passages can be attributed to the different language of the sources. But a rhetorical reading asks how the quotation and adaptation of sources contributes to the author's rhetorical argument. The contradictions between different understandings of terms such as "head," "body," and "unity" within a single letter may be interpreted as evidence that the author appeals to different understandings of the audience.

Arguing for a literary history of the text in which some material in the text was added later is one way to explain the difference between the way oneness is interpreted and expressed in 2:11–20 and 5:21–6:9. This rhetorical analysis interprets the difference as part of the author's strategy in building his argument. He secures the audience's agreement with him by adaptation of familiar traditions of oneness, particularly related to the relationship between Jews and Gentiles. In the course of his argument, he seeks to move the audience to a different position by the further details he provides in his construction of a symbolic universe of *ekklesia* and by his interpretation of "mystery" and "wisdom."

The author's emphasis on unity and on *ekklesia* holds the *exhortatio* together and indeed builds the argument from 4:1 to 6:9. The injunction to members of the household includes the disputed words *ekklesia* and *mysterion*, and the image of oneness occurs in 5:32 in the quotation of "the two shall become one flesh." The mention of the identity of the author occurs in Eph 5:32 with the words ἐγὼ δὲ λέγω in the midst of an assertion about the mystery of Christ and the church.

Although Eph 5:21–6:9 occurs in the hortatory section of the letter, the passage about the obedience and subjection of wives, children, and slaves—like the rest of the letter—combines ethical instructions with reference to a symbolic universe that justifies those instructions. The passage has its significance in the context of Christian community and Christian worship. The address to wives and husbands (Eph 5:21–32) employs the constellation of loaded terms and concepts that have been the ongoing concern of the letter: κεφαλή, ἐκκλησία, μυστήριον, "oneness," and the self-reference of the author. This passage is critical to the argument of the author, whatever its source or background.[52]

---

[52]In his study of Eph 5:21–33, J. Paul Sampley (*One Flesh*) treats the passage as

Reading Eph 5:21–6:9 within the argument of Ephesians

In Eph 5:21–6:9, the author attempts to move the audience from their understanding of unity in the church to a more nuanced and differentiated picture of the church as body, and to a particular definition of unity. In 2:11–20, the author cites a tradition known by the audience about the unity of Jew and Gentile in the community in order to gain their agreement about the value of unity. In this passage, the author uses the same strategy as he does in the rest of the letter to construct a symbolic universe—he refers to the narrative of salvation. The disputed terms "mystery" and "church" and an image of oneness occur in the part of the *exhortatio* that addresses wives and husbands. Both the length of the instruction to wives and husbands and the appearance of key words within it suggest that the wife-husband relationship and the church-Christ analogy with which it is linked is the primary concern of the author of Ephesians.

The opening verse of this section enjoins the congregation to mutual submission, "be subject to one another out of fear [NRSV: reverence] of Christ" (ὑποτασσόμενοι ἀλλήλοις ἐν φόβῳ Χριστοῦ, 5:21). However, the verses that follow the instruction to "be subject" or "be obedient" are directed solely at wives, children, and slaves. This contradiction has led to the theory that 5:22–6:9 was not originally part of Ephesians. However, the repetition of the root of the verb "to fear" (φοβέω) forms an inclusion between verse 5:21 (φόβος) and 5:33 (φοβέω). In addition slaves are told to serve their masters "with fear and trembling" (μετὰ φόβου καὶ τρόμου, 6:5).

Others argue that 5:21 and 5:33 provide a rubric of mutuality for the household code instructions as a whole.[53] Tension still exists, even within 5:21–6:9, between the exhortations that imply mutuality and those that prescribe obedience.[54] When one looks at the letter as a whole, however, one sees that the author's "correction" of the symbolic universe in Eph 5:21–6:9 is strongly in the direction of subordination. When the author

---

integral to the argument of the author and explores how the author utilizes traditions within it. This presentation seeks to look at the way the passage is used by the author before determining the author's sources.

[53]For example, Sampley argues that the author does not agree with the code he adopts (*One Flesh*, 117). See also Mouton, "Reading Ephesians Ethically," 367.

[54]Against other commentators, Lincoln argues that both operate and do not cancel each other out (*Ephesians*, 66).

urges mutuality within the structure of the relationship, he reinforces the structure itself.

In 5:22, the author opens the address to wives with the implied verb carried over from the previous verse: "[be subject] to your husbands as you are to the Lord" (αἱ γυναῖκες τοῖς ἰδίοις ἀνδράσιν ὡς τῷ κυρίῳ). In other words, "your husband" parallels "lord/master." This is the logic of the Colossians exhortation to slaves (Col 3:22–25). In Eph 5:23 and 24, in two parallel statements, the author provides the justification for this exhortation "to be subject." It is an argument based on analogy to the structure of reality:

> For the husband is the head of the wife just as Christ is the head of the church, the body of which he is the savior. Just as the church is subject to Christ, so also wives ought to be, in everything, to their husbands.[55]

> ὅτι ἀνήρ ἐστιν κεφαλὴ τῆς γυναικὸς ὡς καὶ ὁ Χριστὸς κεφαλὴ τῆς ἐκκλησίας, αὐτὸς σωτὴρ τοῦ σώματος ἀλλὰ ὡς ἡ ἐκκλησία ὑποτάσσεται τῷ Χριστῷ, οὕτως καὶ αἱ γυναῖκες τοῖς ἀνδράσιν ἐν παντί.

The phrase ἐν παντί may be a reflection on the other uses of τὰ πάντα in 1:10 and 1:22. If Christ is head of all things, wives should submit in all things. In other words, the church-to-Christ structure of subordination justifies the wife-to-husband structure.

The verb ὑποτάσσεσθαι, which occurs in 5:21 and which is implied in 5:22, is the same verb describing God subjecting everything to Christ in Eph 1:22. Used in the middle voice, the verb is conventional in discussions of the roles of wife and husband from Josephus and Philo and other Hellenistic moralists.[56] Scholars have discussed whether the source of the verb is the household code tradition or the tradition in Paul of the quotation of Ps 8:7.[57] Many argue that the source is the household code. However, making the distinction between two sources is less helpful

---

[55]Antoinette Wire (*Corinthian Women*, 35–38) categorizes some of Paul's arguments in 1 Corinthians as those "establishing the structure of reality."

[56]See the discussion of Philo and Josephus in chapter two. The exploration of Greek authors shows that the verb customarily was used in contexts of political subjugation as well as in marriage.

[57]Lincoln, *Ephesians*, 373.

than noting the significance of the coincidence of the same word in both contexts. In 1 Cor 14:34–35, Paul argues that Christ will be subordinated to God in order to support his imperative, "let them be subject" (ὑποτασσέσθωσαν).[58] Here in Ephesians, there is tension between the passages where ὑποτάσσω appears in the active voice, as in Eph 1:22, and where it is introduced in the middle/passive voice to apply to wives. In the first passage, the emphasis is on God subjecting "all things" to Christ. In Eph 5:22, it is specifically wives who are to be subject to Christ.

This assertion in 5:22 introduces "new" information into the context of the letter. It is information for which the groundwork has been laid, but it is a development beyond its foundation. As yet in the letter, the author has not established that Christ is the head of the church. He has asserted that "God has made him head over all things *for the church*, which is his body, the fullness of him who fills all in all" (1:22). He has stated that Christ is "head" in 4:15: "we are to grow up in every way into him who is the head, into Christ." The major statement about the community in 2:11–20 has been that the *ekklesia* is characterized by the unity of Jew and Gentile as fellow citizens in the household of God. In the unfolding rhetoric of the letter, the author makes a hierarchical modification of the symbolic universe constructed in the letter thus far. He does this by the analogy between Christ and the church and husband and wife.

When one follows the argument of the letter as a whole and notices the tensions within it without harmonizing distinct statements with one another, one recognizes that the focus of the letter throughout has been the *ekklesia*. Although the author does give instructions to husbands and wives, the primary rhetorical purpose of 5:21–6:9 is not to describe how the Christ-church relationship should manifest itself in marriage but to describe *ekklesia* by analogy with marriage. By his elaboration of the relationship between wives and husbands and his justification of wifely submission on the basis of analogy with Christ and the church, the author models the Christ-church relationship upon expectations of submission of wife to husband. Kyriarchal structures are thus theologized and concretized.[59]

The widespread reading of this exhortation as a request for "voluntary" submission or "free obedience" must be questioned. The author's

[58]Wire, *Corinthian Women*, 165–66.
[59]Schüssler Fiorenza, *In Memory of Her*, 269.

argument has constructed the structure of reality so that the submission of wife to husband is the only way to evidence the unity of the church, which is so important to this audience. By constructing submission as the natural relationship of wife to husband and justifying it by analogy to Christ and the church, the author has made obedience to husbands a requirement for wives.

A reading of the rhetoric of Ephesians in which the contradictions between the understanding of unity in 2:11–20 and 5:31–32 are explained not by the history of composition of the text (original and interpolation) or by importation of a foreign element (household code), but as a rhetorical strategy of moving the audience from one position to another, allows us to ask how the audience might have heard Eph 5:23–24. The author's argument builds to this point. Even though the imagery of ἡ κεφαλή and ὑποτάσσεσθαι occurs in Paul's letters, especially 1 Cor 11:3–16 and 1 Cor 14:33b–36, the audience would not necessarily have taken these images for granted, accepted them without question, or recognized them as Pauline. In Ephesians the author has put together the pieces that will lead him to this conclusion and this symbolic universe built upon the principle of submission and obedience. The traditional interpretation of this passage is that subordination of wife to husband is a consequence of unity; subordination is the way they are to exhibit their unity. This is the conclusion to which the arrangement of the argument points. However, this analysis has shown how the author modifies a picture of unity as equality of Jew and Gentile with imagery of subordination.[60]

In 5:25, the instruction to husbands is not to submit but to love. This half of the exhortation takes seven verses (5:25–32) and presents a series of arguments and analogies to justify the instructions. In order to accept this extension of the analogy, the reader would have had to agree with the premise stated in 5:23 and 24. The first justification is an analogy introduced with καθὼς: "as Christ loved the church and gave himself up for her" (καὶ ὁ Χριστὸς ἠγάπησεν τὴν ἐκκλησίαν καὶ ἑαυτὸν παρέ

---

[60]Ann Holmes Redding ("What Price Unity?" [paper presented at the annual meeting of the Society of Biblical Literature, Chicago, IL, November 1994]) argues that the author of Ephesians "uses unity as a rhetorical mask for the hierarchy of the household code." Nils Dahl ("Anamnesis," ST 1 [1947] 69–95) and Wayne Meeks ("In One Body," 209–10) observe that unity is the focus of the letter. I argue that the unity the author uses in the first part of the letter is a value held by the audience to which the author appeals.

δωκεν ὑπὲρ αὐτῆς). The vocabulary of love has been used earlier in the letter to speak of God's love (2:4), Christ's love (3:18), and the love of members of the community (4:2, 15, 16). Similar language appears in the exhortation in 5:2: "walk in love as Christ loved us and gave himself for us a fragrant offering and sacrifice to God." In those lines, however, Christ's loving and giving of himself are things to be imitated by the community and are for the benefit of the community. The result of the reuse of this language in the context of 5:25 is that the community, the church, is equated with the female wife, who is loved by her husband, and not with the community as a whole. Christ is compared with the male husband.

In 5:26, the phrase "by cleansing her with the washing of water by the word" is a reference to baptism.[61] The husband's loving and giving up operates for the sanctification of the church. In the next verse, the imagery of the cleansing of the church is extended to describe the holiness and purity of the bride for her husband (5:27). Wayne Meeks argues that in this verse the author takes an earlier tradition in which baptism is identified with the purification of the bride for her husband and connects it with the household code.[62] Meeks questions how the marriage of Christ and the church could simultaneously be understood as a prototype of baptism and of marriage. This problem may be explained by the previous observation that in this passage *ekklesia* is being defined by analogy with marriage. If this is the case, then by incorporating baptism language into the marriage metaphor and interpreting baptism as cleansing a bride for her husband, the author is once again making the marriage model primary. A very similar interpretation of oneness in association with baptism also happens at the end of this argument in 5:31–32.

In verse 28, the author returns to the statement that husbands should love their wives as their own bodies. This verse shifts from the strong "be subject" language in 5:22–24 by recommending that the husband be identified with the wife. If the church is the body of Christ and Christ loves the church, then husband must love his own body. Verses 28, 29, and 30 are all maxims or truisms called upon to support this argument for love.

[61]Sampley, *One Flesh,* 132–33. See also Heinrich Schlier, *Der Brief an die Epheser* (Düsseldorf: Patmos-Verlag, 1957) 257.

[62]Meeks, "Androgyne," 205.

The author quotes Gen 2:24—a verse from the Hebrew Bible which traditionally provided the justification and explanation for marriage. The verse is attributed to Jesus by the synoptic gospel authors Mark and Matthew (Mk 10:2–12; Matt 19:3–12). In both places the quotation of Gen 2:24 is combined with Gen 1:27. In Ephesians, the author quotes Gen 2:24, which expresses the idea of making one out of two, and applies it pointedly to the union of Christ and the church.[63]

In his analysis of these verses, Paul Sampley relates this quotation to a widespread pattern in the New Testament in which a statement that women should be submissive is supported by a reference to Torah.[64] Sampley shows that the author chooses a passage that refers to the relationship of Adam and Eve and presents that primordial marriage pattern as "prototypically true in an eschatological way of the relationship that does and should exist between Christ and his church."[65] He suggests that the recipients of Ephesians may have drawn different conclusions from Gen 2:24 about the relationship of husband and wife.[66] The fact that this quotation contains the image of two becoming one— which was used so prominently in Eph 2:14–16 to describe the unity of Jew and Gentile in Christ—adds support to Sampley's suggestion. If the understanding of unity-as-reunification is attributed to the audience, then the author's quotation of the verse and his sharp delimitation of it in the next verse makes sense. Eph 5:32 makes a strong statement of the author's own interpretation. He says explicitly that "mystery" refers to Christ and the church, by which he means their marriage relationship.

The concluding section of the *exhortatio*, that is, the exhortation to wives and husbands, children and parents, and slaves and masters operates to critique the notion of oneness characterized by equality and not subordination. The address to wives and husbands, in which the metaphor of marriage is the guiding principle, circumscribes the interpretation of unity as it applies to gender and to slavery. In his work on Ephesians, Wayne Meeks notes how the baptismal traditions of reunification are

---

[63]Piet Farla, "'The two shall become one flesh': Gen. 1.27 and 2.24 in the New Testament Marriage Texts," in Sipke Draisma, ed., *Intertextuality in Biblical Writings: Essays in Honour of Bas van Iersel* (Kampen: Kok, 1989) 67–82.

[64]Sampley, *One Flesh,* 97–100. He cites 2 Cor 11:2; 1 Tim 2:8; 1 Cor 14:33b–34; and 1 Peter 3:1–6.

[65]Ibid., 101.

[66]Ibid., 100 n. 2.

clearly expressed in Eph 2:11–22 but are eclipsed in the second half of the letter:

> In the later developments in the Pauline school the peculiar eschatological and social tensions that characterize Paul's position in the Corinthian correspondence tend to dissolve. On the one hand, the "realized eschatology" of the baptismal traditions, expressed in the language of cosmic myth, is far less restrained. On the other hand, the mythical language is linked up with a prosaic ethic of community order, upon which it has apparently little effect.[67]

Therefore he concludes that in Ephesians:

> For our present purposes, it is sufficient to observe that the baptismal reunification formula's "no more male and female" has not produced a radical reassessment of the social roles of men and women in the congregation.[68]

This exploration of the way the author builds his argument gives clues to the strange distance between the traditions in the early parts of the letter and the exhortations at the end. While such baptismal understandings are present—and may be provoking a reassessment of social roles in the community that the author addresses—the author of Ephesians seeks to persuade the audience differently.[69]

In the logic of the passage, the author begins with a statement to wives to submit. He extends the church-Christ and wife-husband analogy by enjoining husbands to love. The equivalence of husband and wife is supported by a quotation from Gen 2:24 about man and woman becoming one. Then the author completes his argument by an unambiguous statement that the mystery of marriage refers to Christ and the church. Thus, the author not only makes the shift to greater differentiation of the structure of the body of the church by distinguishing distinct

---

[67]Meeks, "Androgyne," 205.

[68]Ibid., 206.

[69]Meeks understands Ephesians and Colossians to be in essential agreement. They share the quality of having a baptismal eschatology that does not affect the paraenesis. The discussion of this disjunction will be continued in chapter six.

roles for wives and husbands within it, but in the culmination of his argument, he quotes a well-known tradition about oneness (Gen 2:24), which the rhetorical reading of the argument of Eph 2:11–20 suggests was associated, by the audience, with the unity and equality of Jew and Gentile. The rhetoric of this passage identifies that unity with marriage, then with "mystery" (5:32), and with Christ and the church. By this series of steps the author has limited the meaning of oneness to marriage, which the previous verses define as patriarchal marriage. By strongly asserting that the contested term "mystery," which the audience associates with the unity of Jew and Gentile, really refers to the union of Christ and the church, the author shifts the interpretation of unity and mystery from one of equality and oneness to a hierarchically structured unity patterned on the patriarchal marriage relationship between wife and husband.

The "mystery" of marriage is interpreted asymmetrically beginning at verse 22. Subordination is thus a necessary feature of that union. The author's final assignment of duties in 5:33—to each husband to love his wife and each wife to fear her husband—reinforces the inequality of the relationship.

The Address to Children, Fathers, Slaves and Masters: Eph 6:1–9

Arguments about the structure of the church do not play into the author's reasoning in the next two injunctions. However, the kyriarchal system that has been reiterated and reinforced by the elaborate instructions to wives and husbands plays itself out in these instructions. The author does not justify the instruction to children and to parents with any arguments by analogy to the structure of reality but simply states that it is right and quotes a commandment. He instructs fathers not to provoke children to anger but to bring them up in the "discipline and instruction of the Lord." The author does not modify or elaborate upon these well-known injunctions to children and fathers because they are not as relevant to his rhetorical purposes.

The injunction to slaves operates on the implicit analogy between earthly masters and the Lord Jesus. The slaves must be "slaves of Christ" (6:6), serving the Lord and not men. Verses 5 and 6 identify earthly masters with Christ. Verse 7 distinguishes and contrasts the two. Verse 8 and 9 work on the principle that either slave or free will receive fair treatment from the Lord. The final phrase of 6:8 reflects the baptismal formula in Gal 3:28, but it has been placed in a context that reinforces the social difference between slave and free rather than eliminating it.[70] Although the final verse enjoins the masters to behavior equivalent to the slaves, the repetition of the words οἱ κύριοι and ὁ κύριος serves to reinforce the hierarchical structure of slave and master.

The decision to bracket the question of the source, form, and intention of Eph 5:21–6:9 and to avoid the term "household code" in the rhetorical analysis of Ephesians results in several key interpretive shifts. First, it shows that in the argument of the letter the author's primary concern is with *ekklesia*. The exhortations to family members shape the view of *ekklesia*. The author's view of marriage, although of great interest to commentators, is secondary to the author's purpose of defining *ekklesia* by analogy with marriage. The presentation of the argument of Eph 5:21–6:9 is not a paraenetic epilogue to the soteriological affirmations in 1:1–3:21, but the point to which the argument is leading. It represents the introduction of new information, especially the Christ-church analogy, to which the author wants the audience to agree. Focusing on the role of Eph 5:21–6:9 in the argument shifts the major interpretive question from "how does the author change an existing code?" to "why and to what effect does the author bring in marriage at this point in the argument?"

The *Peroratio*: Eph 6:10–20

The argument concludes with the *peroratio* in Eph 6:10–20.[71] Here, the language of opposition is expanded and exaggerated. The fact that evil continues to exist in the present is mentioned in 2:2–3, 4:14, 17–20, and 5:6–8. In 2:2–3, the evil is supernatural evil: "the ruler of the power of the air, the spirit that is now at work in the sons of disobedience." In the paraenesis in chapters 4 and 5, the evil opposition is described as "people's trickery" (4:14) or as "the Gentiles" (4:17–20). Now the author asserts that the opposition is supernatural, and he suggests that its presence requires arming for battle. This section recapitulates the major themes of the argument in an extended call to stand firm in

---

[70]Schüssler Fiorenza, *In Memory of Her*, 268. See also Meeks, "In One Body," 216.
[71]Lincoln, "Stand Therefore," 99–114.

spiritual battle. Several aspects of the *peroratio* link it with the preceding parts of the letter. First, throughout the letter the readers have been reminded of their role in God's plan for the cosmos. In 6:12, the phrase "in the heavenly places" occurs for the final time in the letter. The language of opposition is intensified by the repetition of πρός and multiple synonyms. The exhortation conveys that the believers have a vital role in the cosmic struggle between the forces of good and evil. The three words for "strength" in verse 6:10 emphasize that the audience has access to the power of God (3:7, 16, 20). The special role of the audience as members of the church is rephrased here as soldiers of Christ. The various items of armor that they are called to put on recall vocabulary from earlier parts of the letter: truth (4:15, 25, 5:9), righteousness (4:24, 5:9) and peace (2:14–18, 4:3). The final call to prayer in 6:18 reiterates the importance of prayer in the letter as a whole. The author's request for the audience to pray for him is the final appearance of the device of pseudonymity, which has played such an important role throughout the letter. Once again it reiterates Paul's role "to proclaim the mystery of the gospel." It serves to increase pathos by reference to Paul's imprisonment in 6:20. The *peroratio* directs the readers' attention away from their relationships with one another and outward to the battle they must fight. This call to battle, modeled on the speeches of generals before battle,[72] focuses the readers on the opposition and their role in that conflict. Unity, structured as subordination, is necessary for the battle against the "rulers against the authorities, against the cosmic rulers of this present darkness, against the spiritual forces of evil in the heavenly places" (6:12).

The letter concludes with the author informing the audience that he has sent Tychicus, "a beloved brother and a faithful minister in the Lord." This ending follows the convention of other letters of Paul. It is consistent with the rest of the letter in that Tychicus's purpose is to inform the audience about the author, "to let you know how we are" (6:22).

Rhetorical Genre

The preceding discussion leads to the conclusion that Ephesians is best characterized as deliberative rhetoric. The author's argument tries to

---

[72]Ibid., 100.

encourage the audience to make a decision based upon values they share. The identification of the letter as a "letter of congratulation"[73] is based upon the interpretation that there is no tension between the author's view and the views of the audience. Classification of the letter as epideictic is based on the praise of the audience in the first three chapters, which provides the basis for appeal in the remaining chapters.[74] Lincoln calls the first part epideictic and the second deliberative. However, the previous analysis shows that the letter provides evidence of the tension between two different views of unity, how that unity is related to the head and the body, and how that unity plays itself out in *ekklesia*. This tension has led some commentators to postulate a history of composition of Ephesians in which the view of unity as making one out of two was original and the other view of unity-as-hierarchy was inserted in the letter at a later stage of composition. Rather than merely affirming the status and views of the audience, however, Ephesians congratulates the audience in order to lay the groundwork for a redrawing of the picture of *ekklesia*. This makes clear that the unity of Jew and Gentile, which makes them "fellow citizens with the saints in the household of God," does not apply either to the relationship of male and female nor to the relationship of slave and master.

The Rhetorical Situation

A summary of the rhetorical situation of the letter to the Ephesians can now be made. In the letter to the Christian community, the author writes in the name of Paul, with a claim of authority based on his role as apostle to the Gentiles and of special insight into the mystery of God's plan. His primary purpose is to persuade the audience to correct their view of *ekklesia* in favor of another view that is built upon the model of the kyriarchal family. He needs to make this correction in a way that builds upon and does not appear to directly contradict the audience's views about the value of unity nor deny the role of baptism in accomplishing that unity. Most importantly, he needs to reframe and redefine unity in baptism away from the model of "making two one"

---

[73]Nils Dahl, "Interpreting Ephesians: Then and Now," *TD* 25 (1977) 314.

[74]Lincoln (*Ephesians*, xlii) argues that the letter mixes epideictic and deliberative rhetoric.

to a model in which unity is defined as relationships between subordinate and superordinate operating harmoniously.

The author meets this rhetorical problem with a variety of interrelated strategies. First, using the language of doxology, blessing, and prayer, he retells again and again the story of the election of the community by God and their role in God's plan. Specifically, he uses language that recalls implicitly or explicitly their baptism and the imagery of coming to life from death and of two becoming one. He sharply contrasts their former life in sin with their present life. Quoting a well-known tradition about unity, he presents their past life—characterized by alienation and separation—and their present life of inclusion and incorporation (Eph 2:11–20). This contrast is expressed in traditional liturgical language that evokes gratitude and praise. Finally, he seeks to persuade the audience of his view of unity by gradually constructing a symbolic universe through statements about God and Christ. The culmination of this progressive construction is the passage at the end of the *exhortatio*, Eph 5:21–6:9, in which the language of obedience is concentrated. In the argument of these verses, the author tries to achieve all these purposes at once: redefine unity, interpret baptism, and reframe the church. The language of obedience, which is a typical feature of wife-husband and slave-master relationships and which appears throughout the exhortations to subordinate members of the family in Hellenistic Judaism, becomes the defining feature of the church-Christ relationship. By using the language of obedience, conventional in the context of the kyriarchal family, the author is able to correct the view of unity and *ekklesia* held within the community. The slow and careful development of the argument indicates that such an argument may not have been fully accepted if presented all at once.

The inscribed audience is described very generally, and the author never criticizes their behavior. The lack of definitive references to the readers leads scholars to describe the rhetorical situation as one that lacks urgency. For example, Andrew Lincoln describes the rhetorical situation "as one in which its implied readers are not as aware as they should be of some key elements of their Christian identity, and consequently are falling short in displaying the conduct appropriate to such an identity."[75] However, the fact that this letter is written with an

---

[75]Lincoln, "Stand Therefore," 112. See also Mouton ("Reading Ephesians Ethi-

emphasis on the author as the chosen and authoritative revealer/inter-preter of the mystery, combined with the careful manner in which the author builds his argument to reach the exhortation in 5:21–6:9, suggest that the author considered the rhetorical problem to be very significant and worth his persuasive efforts.

Conclusions

Attention to the development of the argument in the letter to the Ephesians shows that the language of obedience in the injunctions to wives to submit to their husbands, children to obey parents, and slaves to obey their masters in Eph 5:21–6:9 plays a critical role in the author's per-suasive strategy to modify a notion of unity imagined as the reconciliation of opposites. The author seeks to move the audience toward a notion of unity constructed as a hierarchy in which inferior is linked to supe-rior by the expectation of obedience. The language of obedience and the symbolic universe of marriage and slavery in which it convention-ally operates is employed to define and to structure the symbolic universe of the *ekklesia*. This strategy is supported further by the dynamics of the language of opposition in which "enemies"—in Ephesians, "the spiritual forces of evil in the heavenly places"—are constructed as posing an ongoing threat to unity. To this opponent, unity-as-hierar-chy is presented as an effective response.

The author constructs a symbolic universe built hierarchically, with Christ as the head of church and husband as the head of wife. He inter-prets the subjection of all things as a chain of command in which not only is Christ head of all things, but "all things" are arranged hierar-chically beneath him along the model of the kyriarchal system. This interpretation represents a shift from the emphasis on Christ's subjec-tion of the powers as liberation from oppression. The center of gravity of Phil 2:6–11 and Col 2:13–15—that Christ now rules what once ruled human beings—shifts to an emphasis upon a hierarchy among crea-tures created by that subjection. This interpretive shift makes possible the image of the body of Christ as a hierarchically ordered social sys-tem to which the author's argument directs the audience.

---

cally," 372), who states: "I suggest that its exigence be investigated as an imperfection concerning the implied readers' self-awareness."

Within the argument of Ephesians, the language of love and self-sacrifice (5:2) is not equivalent to the language of obedience. The author of Ephesians has prepared for the instruction to the husband in his description of God and Christ earlier in the argument. The instruction to husbands to love their wives attempts to mediate between the notion of male and female in marriage as an undifferentiated unity ("the two shall become one flesh") and the hierarchical notion of marriage as wife obeying and husband ruling. However, the emphasis on love symbolically strengthens the analogy between husband and Christ rather than making mutual the relationship between husband and wife.

CHAPTER 6

Ephesians: From Rhetorical Analysis to Historical Situation

A n author's rhetoric cannot be read as a mirror of the historical situation of a text but must be read critically along with other clues from outside the text in order to recover its historical audience. This chapter addresses the association of baptism, unity, marriage, and women's authority in Ephesians in order to understand the letter's audience, which the author does not directly describe. I shall delineate those who might have valued unity effected in baptism and to whom the author's argument in Eph 5:21–32 might have been directed. Next, the author's interpretation of Colossians shall be explored in order to show that evidence of the author's adaptation of material from Colossians may help to reconstruct the historical situation in the interval between the two letters.

Previous research on the household code has centered around its ori gin and function in early Christianity.[1] Taking an approach that focuses on the author, his materials and how he adapts them, and the reconstruction of the situation as it is inscribed by the author has led many commentators to explain why the household code was nec essary.[2] Explanations of such necessity may be literary: the author was obliged to use a household code that he inherited. Because he was critical of it, he modified it.[3] They also may be sociological: in order for the church to

---

[1]Crouch, *Origin*; Balch, *Let Wives Be Submissive*.

[2]For a detailed analysis of the history of frameworks of interpretation of the household codes, see Elisabeth Schüssler Fiorenza,"Discipleship and Patriarchy: Toward a Feminist Evaluative Hermeneutics," in idem, *Bread Not Stone,* 65–92.

[3]See, for example, Sampley, *One Flesh,* 117.

survive, it had to conform to the conventions of the society of the time. One influential explanation for its appearance is that the author developed and used the household code as a response to a problem in the community. Crouch's analysis exemplifies this position. In his discussion of the purpose of the household code in Colossians, Crouch argues that it served to oppose the excesses of women and slaves who were involved in an enthusiastic-pneumatic movement.[4] The arguments for the necessity of the codes, even by those who argue that Paul is not the author, are based upon an assumption of the orthodoxy of the author and an apologetic approach to the material. If the injunction to be subordinate is there in the canon and written in Paul's name, it must be "necessary." However, if the emphasis is not on reconstructing the author's position but on reclaiming the voices within early Christianity, then the passages advocating subordination on the model of the household may be read as a strategy to prescribe certain roles and foreclose other possibilities. Rather than reconstructing a historical situation that isolates and marginalizes those who represent some problem, this approach attempts to reconstruct communities, visions, and languages with which the author of a canonical letter such as Ephesians was in dialogue.

Unity, Baptism, Marriage

The rhetorical analysis of Ephesians in chapter five has shown that the author presents an argument about how unity is to be interpreted. To those who envision unity as "making two one"—as the elimination of privilege between previously unequal groups—the author argues for another vision of unity by means of the analogy between the church and marriage. With this analogy, unity is defined as the subordination of wives to husbands and by extension of inferior to superior, child to parent and slave to master. The author does not describe explicitly the position of those with whom he argues. Therefore, the only access to their position is through the traditions transmitted in the letter and the clues to their position in the author's rhetoric. In order to identify who the members of the audience of Ephesians might be, it is necessary to examine the evidence within the New Testament of early Christians

[4]Crouch, *Origin*, 139.

who valued unity and for whom "becoming one" meant the abolition of traditional privilege between social groups.

The language of "becoming one" is found three times in the New Testament in Gal 3:28, 1 Cor 12:13, and Col 3:11. In two cases the context explicitly refers to baptism (Gal 3:28 and 1 Cor 12:13). In Col 2:12, believers' resurrection is associated with baptism. In each case two or more pairs of opposites are listed followed by the statement that "all are one in Christ" or "Christ is all in all." The fact that each verse stands out from its context in the Pauline letter in which it appears further argues that a traditional baptismal formula lies behind these verses.[5] The phrase "no male and female," which occurs only in Gal 3:28, is considered part of the original formula because the pair is not relevant to the context of Paul's argument in Galatians. That the phrase does not occur in the other two citations indicates that, although original, its status was tenuous.[6]

The formula can be attributed to the pre-Pauline missionary movement. The many attempts to interpret this saying as referring to equality on a symbolic level and not a social level testifies to the effectiveness of the interpretation presented by the authors of Ephesians and Colossians.[7] There is indirect evidence that early Christians interpreted this abolition of status distinctions as having concrete results on the social level. The letter of Pliny to Trajan from the early second century states that women servants were ministers in the church of Bithynia.[8] The letter from Ignatius to Polycarp exhorts the recipient not to set free either male or female slaves at the expense of the church.[9] The ministry of Paul centered around the erasure or cancellation of religious differences between Jew and Greek, not only in their status before God but in their social status and function.[10]

---

[5]Meeks, "Androgyne," 180–81; Hans Dieter Betz, *Galatians* (Hermeneia; Philadelphia: Fortress, 1979) 181–201; Schüssler Fiorenza, *In Memory of Her*, 208.

[6]Wire, *Corinthian Women*, 136–38.

[7]Schüssler Fiorenza, *In Memory of Her*, 205–7. This is also the argument of Neil Elliott, *Liberating Paul: The Justice of God and the Politics of the Apostle* (Maryknoll, NY: Orbis, 1994). He argues that the presence of Ephesians and Colossians in the canon has indelibly affected the interpretation of Paul's genuine letters.

[8]Pliny, *Ep.* 10.96.

[9]Ignatius *Poly.* 4.3: "Let them not desire to be set free at the Church's expense, that they be not found the slaves of lust" (μὴ ἐράτωσαν ἀπὸ τοῦ κοινοῦ ἐλευθεροῦσθαι, ἵνα μὴ δοῦλοι εὑρεθῶσιν ἐπιθυμίας).

[10]Rom 3:22, 10:12.

In Gal 3:28, "male and female" is not expressed as opposites as in "Jew or Greek, slave or free" but as "male *and* female." This is a quotation of Gen 1:27 where the creation of "male and female" in the image of God introduces the theme of procreation. Elsewhere in the New Testament the quotation of this verse is used to explain the origin of marriage. In the saying of Jesus in Mark 10:6, the quotation of Gen 1:27 is combined with the quotation of Gen 2:24.[11] Therefore, the appearance of the phrase "no male and female" in the baptismal formula suggests that it refers to freedom from marriage. The making one of male and female in Gal 3:28 does not describe return to an original androgynous form but the abolition of social privileges based in patriarchal marriage.[12]

Research on women in early Christianity has pushed scholars to reevaluate the conventional view of the exhortations in Colossians, Ephesians, and in the Pastoral Epistles as descriptive of the historical situation in the Pauline churches. The texts are now generally read as prescriptive rather than descriptive, and interpreters recognize their perspectival nature. Women mentioned within Paul's letters: Junia, Prisca, Phoebe, and others have been studied with renewed interest, and the history of their androcentric interpretation has been traced. The presence and leadership of women as deacons and apostles has been well demonstrated. The fact that these individuals are not named in reference to their husbands suggests that they were unmarried. This evidence contributes to the reconstruction of the history of women in early Christianity beyond Paul's statements about women. The participation and leadership of women within the Christian missionary movement is the context within which to reconstruct the audience for Ephesians.[13]

---

[11]Piet Farla, "'The two shall become one flesh': Gen 1.27 and 2.24 in the New Testament Marriage Texts," in Sipke Draisma, ed., *Intertextuality in Biblical Writings: Essays in Honour of Bas van Iersel* (Kampen: Kok, 1989) 67–82. See also Dennis Ronald MacDonald, *There is No Male and Female: The Fate of a Dominical Saying in Paul and Gnosticism* (HDR 20; Philadelphia: Fortress, 1987).

[12]Elisabeth Schüssler Fiorenza and Antoinette Wire argue that the purpose of the final pair expressed not androgyny but, parallel with the other two pairs, proclaimed freedom from a hierarchical relationship of marriage. On the other hand, Meeks argues that return to original androgyny was the intention of the myth of reunification that lies behind Gal 3:28 (Meeks, "Androgyne"). See also Dennis Ronald MacDonald, *There is No Male and Female: The Fate of a Dominical Saying in Paul and Gnosticism* (HDR 20; Philadelphia: Fortress, 1987).

[13]Note the work of Elisabeth Schüssler Fiorenza, "Missionaries, Apostles, Cowork-

Evidence that women used the third element of the pre-Pauline baptismal formula to claim authority to preach and prophesy within the *ekklesia* surfaces through a reading of Paul's rhetoric in 1 Corinthians. Antoinette Wire argues that when Paul asserts in 1 Cor 11:2–16 that "woman is the glory of man," he is contesting the Corinthians' claim to be in God's image through Christ.[14] The baptismal formula reflected in Gal 3:28, 1 Cor 12:13, and Col 3:11 is a reworking of Gen 1:27–28 and Gen 5:1b–2. The baptismal formula developed as a new creation story in which God's claim in Genesis to create humankind "in the image of God, male and female he made them" is reversed to become "not male and female." The women prophets in Corinth confessed a new creation that reversed the old creation and in which male and female was now *not* male and female just as the formula proclaimed "not Jew or Greek" and "not slave or free." Their being in the image of God through Christ as a result of their baptism gave them authority to pray and to prophesy and to experience the resurrection-life in the present.

The various points in 1 Corinthians where Paul distances himself from baptism—his protest that he baptized only Crispus, Gaius, and the household of Stephanus (1 Cor 1:14–16) and his assertion that Christ did not call him to baptize but to proclaim the gospel (1 Cor 1:17)—indicate that he may have been trying to underplay the importance of baptism held by some in his audience. When he quotes the baptismal formula in 1 Cor 12:13, it does not contain the phrase "male and female." By not quoting this part of the tradition, Paul disputes the Corinthian prophets' interpretation of the new creation.

In Corinth, the women prophets attributed their authority to pray and prophesy to being in the image of God in Christ through baptism. They interpreted the resurrection to be a present reality. Paul's argument begin-

ers: Romans 16 and the Reconstruction of Women's Early Christian History," *Word and World* 6 (1986) 420–33. See also Bernadette Brooten, "Junia . . . Outstanding among the Apostles (Romans 16:7)," in Leonard S. Swidler and Arlene Swidler, eds., *Women Priests* (New York: Paulist, 1977) 141–44; Bernadette Brooten, "Early Christian Women and their Cultural Context: Issues of Method in Historical Reconstruction," in Adela Yarbro Collins, ed., *Feminist Perspectives on Biblical Scholarship* (Chico, CA: Scholars Press, 1985) 65–91; and Ross Shepard Kraemer, *Her Share of the Blessings: Women's Religions Among Pagans, Jews, and Christians in the Greco-Roman World* (New York: Oxford, 1992).

[14]Wire, *Corinthian Women*, 123.

ning in 1 Cor 15:12 about those who deny the resurrection of the dead can be understood as addressing those who claim to experience the resurrection of the living.[15]

In his arguments against fornication and for marriage in 1 Corinthians, Paul's rhetoric suggests that for some women prophets expression of the new creation motivated them to withdraw from sexual relations within marriage. Paul's arguments about the husband having authority over the wife's body opposes their position. The asceticism of the prophets in Corinth represents a problem for Paul to which he responds with the arguments about mutuality of obligation between wife and husband (1 Cor 7:2–5).

The language of the prophets in Corinth is that of "wisdom." The terms "wise" and "wisdom" appear in the first four chapters of 1 Corinthians and reflect the terminology of the audience.[16] To their claim to be "spiritual" and "wise," Paul presents Christ as "the wisdom of God and the power of God" (1 Cor 1:22–24).

Antoinette Wire's reconstruction of Paul's audience in 1 Corinthians rejects the scholarly characterization of the "opponents" of Paul in Corinth as "enthusiastic" or "heretical" and reconstructs their self-understanding from Paul's rhetoric and from other evidence in early Christian and contemporary literature. As a result, her analysis of the prophets in Corinth gives a more complete picture of early Christians who associated baptism, prophecy, and Christ as the wisdom of God. Their experience of the Spirit led them to pray and prophesy and to experience Christ's resurrection as the conquest of the forces of bondage and the powers that enslaved them. They used the language of freedom and of "not being enslaved" to describe their experience of the resurrection. Paul's arguments for the futurity of the resurrection and the necessity for God to achieve a final victory in the future in 1 Corinthians 15 function to critique the Corinthians' view of the resurrection.

A fuller description of the prophets in Corinth provides important information to read alongside the rhetorical situation of Ephesians. First, it shows Christians for whom baptism rewrites the story of creation told in Gen 2:24. In the culmination of his discussion about wives and husbands, the author of Ephesians quotes Gen 2:24 and reinforces its meaning as a marriage text and not an anti-marriage text. The author's

---

[15]Ibid., 163–68.
[16]Ibid., 52.

description of marriage and the union of Christ and the church as a "mystery," combined with the author's claim to be the chosen revealer of that mystery, suggests that those he is in dialogue with may also claim authority on this basis. If Christians who shared such a perspective were part of the audience of the letter to the Ephesians, they would draw the picture of *ekklesia* differently than the author of Ephesians. The author writes to persuade them of a different view of "two becoming one." When the author concludes his argument with the Christ-church analogy, which structures *ekklesia* on the model of patriarchal marriage, he challenges the foundations of their understanding.

The association of prophecy and leadership in Corinth may be understood within the whole continuum of women's religious leadership in Asia Minor.[17] The role of women in Greco-Roman religious offices is documented in inscriptional evidence. The revival of prophecy in the Montanist movement led by Priscilla and Maximilla demonstrates the ongoing dispute over revelation and prophecy in Asia Minor.[18] That the author argues in the name of Paul, the single apostle, to interpret the mystery and that he communicates with the language of prayer, must be interpreted within the struggles over prophecy, revelation, and writing that took place during the late first and second centuries CE. By putting the exhortation to obey within the rhetorical setting of revelation, the author of Ephesians seeks to persuade his audience by appealing to authorities that they would acknowledge.

---

[17]Although the phrase "in Ephesus" was not part of the original text of Ephesians, other strands of evidence link the letter to western Asia Minor. The author's use of Colossians, in which Hieropolis and Laodicea are linked with Colossae (Col 4:13), and the recommendation of Tychicus, who is associated with Asia Minor in Col 4:7–8, suggest that the audience for both letters may have been in Asia Minor. See the discussion in Lincoln, *Ephesians*, lxxxi–lxxxv.

[18]For a summary of the evidence for women's religious leadership in Asia Minor, see Schüssler Fiorenza, *In Memory of Her*, 245–50. See also, Ross Shepard Kraemer, *Her Share of the Blessings: Women's Religions Among Pagans, Jews, and Christians in the Greco-Roman World* (New York: Oxford, 1992) 84–88. For a discussion of the Montanist movement in Phrygia, see Susanna Elm, "Montanist Oracles," in Schüssler Fiorenza, *Searching the Scriptures*, 131–38. See also Steven J. Friesen, "Provincial Highpriesthoods," in idem, *Twice Neokorus* (Leiden: Brill, 1993) 76–113; and idem, "Women in Religious Offices in Western Asia Minor: First Century Developments" (paper presented at the annual meeting of the Society of Biblical Literature, Philadelphia, PA, November 1995).

When the rhetoric of the author of Ephesians is placed within the wider picture of an early Christianity in which women hold leadership positions and interpret baptism to abolish the conventional privilege of patriarchal marriage, then the possible historical audience and the motivation for the rhetoric of obedience in Ephesians comes into sharper relief. To those women for whom "all are one in Christ Jesus" meant "not male and female" and whose positions of leadership and authority within the *ekklesia* was thereby legitimated, the author of Ephesians gives voice to the imagery of oneness. But he also restricts that imagery to the relationship between the historic communities of Jew and Gentile (Eph 2:11–20). With the introduction of the metaphor of marriage as the foundation of reality for Christ and the church, the author combats the view of those for whom the marriage metaphor is typical of the old creation overcome in Christ. He does so in a way that does not deny the value of the dramatic shift achieved in baptism but that specifies its inapplicability to men and women. Thus, the marriage relationship—as interpreted in Gen 2:24—remains in effect.

In the interpretation of Ephesians, the common assumption is that the "problems" in Corinth were no longer problems. Whatever the understanding of social relationships in the pre-Pauline and Pauline churches had been, it was replaced by a social arrangement conforming to the conventions of Greco-Roman morality. However, reconstructing the audience of Ephesians through rhetorical analysis suggests an alternative picture. Paul's rhetoric in 1 Corinthians did not succeed in silencing Christian women or curtailing their leadership. However, his rhetoric did succeed in labeling as Other those who held that their baptism had effected concrete changes in their status. The author of Ephesians chooses not to inscribe his audience too specifically as a rhetorical strategy. He describes them very generally, not because there was no conflict but in order to address that conflict in a way that would not inflame it. By writing in the name of Paul, and presenting an argument that claimed the kyriarchal family as normative for the definition of *ekklesia*, the author of Ephesians attempts to subordinate the imagery of baptism with that of marriage and to interpret women as wives who were subject to their husbands as the church is subject to Christ.

Relationship between Ephesians and Colossians

The discussion of Ephesians as a whole gives analytical priority to the rhetoric of the argument rather than to explaining it by its use of a source. The rhetorical analysis of Ephesians has shown how the letter exhibits an argument in which the disputed terms *mysterion* and *ekklesia* are developed as themes. That argument culminates with the presentation of the exhortations to submission in Eph 5:21–6:9.

Injunctions to submission also occur at the end of the letter to the Colossians. In addition, the content of the Ephesians passage overlaps substantially with that of Colossians. At this point, it is useful to compare Ephesians and Colossians and to focus on how the exhortations to wives, husbands, children, fathers, slaves, and masters at the end of Colossians functions in its argument. The purpose of this comparison is to explore whether Ephesians's use of Colossians may be read in conjunction with the rhetorical analysis in order to shed light on the historical situation of Ephesians. A comparison between Ephesians and Colossians may help to answer why an author who knew Colossians would write another very similar letter in Paul's name.

The letter to the Ephesians has a close literary relationship with Colossians.[19] The extensive parallels between Ephesians and Colossians and the similarity of their literary style are well known. The overall structure and sequence of the letters is also similar.[20] In addition to parallels in blocks of material between the two letters, some material of Colossians appears to be developed in different positions in Ephesians. An example is the hymnic material about Christ from Col 1:15–20, which has similarities with the statement about Christ's relationship with the church in Eph 1:20–23. Many theories have been proposed for the relationship between the two letters in order to account for these similarities. One is that both letters are dependent upon a third letter.[21] Another is

---

[19]For early history of interpretation of the relation between Ephesians and Colossians, see A. Van Roon, *The Authenticity of Ephesians* (NovTSup 39; Leiden: Brill, 1974) 4–6; C. Leslie Mitton, *The Epistle to the Ephesians: Its Authorship, Origin and Purpose* (Oxford: Clarendon, 1951).

[20]See discussion of the parallels in Lincoln, *Ephesians,* xlvii–lviii.

[21]A. Van Roon, *The Authenticity of Ephesians* (NovTSup 39; Leiden: Brill, 1974) 426.

that they are both dependent on early Christian oral tradition.[22] The best and most widely held explanation is that the author of Ephesians utilized Colossians in some way in his composition of Ephesians. I will not provide a detailed analysis of how the author of Ephesians used his sources.[23] Rather, evidence of general tendencies in the author's reworking of Colossians provides indications of the situation that may have developed between the writing of the two letters and suggests an explanation for the writing of one pseudonymous letter that repeats so much of another letter in the name of Paul.

Despite the repetition of its language in Ephesians, a reading of Colossians shows a great difference in emphasis between the two letters. The emphasis on unity and oneness that runs through Ephesians, particularly in Eph 2:11–20 and 4:1–16, is not present in Colossians. The word "mystery" appears in Colossians (Col 1:26, 27, 2:2, and 4:3) but it does not appear to be a term under dispute as in Ephesians. It is not repeated so frequently throughout the letter, and the word μυστήριον does not appear in Colossians in the exhortation to submit.

Colossians emphasizes the supremacy of Christ. The letter contains a hymn to Christ (Col 1:15–20) in which Christ is described in terms similar to Wisdom. His role in creation is emphasized in 1:16–17. The repetition of "all" in the hymn is consistent with the phrase in the version of the baptismal formula in Col 3:11 ("but Christ is all in all"). Christ both has a role in creation and pervades all things. Col 2:2 specifies that Christ is the content of God's mystery.

The imagery of head and body, which are elaborated more and more specifically in the unfolding argument of Ephesians, is present in Colossians in connection with the church. The word *ekklesia* appears in Colossians, first in connection with the head and body in the Christ hymn in Col 1:18: "He is the head of the body, the church." A similar connection is made in Col 1:24 in reference to Paul's suffering and his ministry

---

[22]Nils Alstrup Dahl, "Der Epheserbrief und der verlorene, erste Brief des Paulus and die Korinther," in Otto Betz, Martin Hengel, and Peter Schmidt, eds., *Abraham unser Vater. Juden und Christen in Gespräch über die Bibel. FS O. Michel* (Leiden: Brill, 1963) 71–72.

[23]The standard work of comparison is C. Leslie Mitton, *The Epistle to the Ephesians: Its Authorship, Origin and Purpose* (Oxford: Clarendon, 1951). Andrew Lincoln discusses the relationship of the two letters in *Ephesians*, xlvii–lvi. In a recent dissertation ("Ephesians"), Jennifer Berenson Maclean examines in detail the technical redactional practices applied by the author of Ephesians to his use of Colossians and other Pauline letters.

"for the sake of his body, that is, the church." This hymn describes Christ with the attributes of Wisdom. He is "the image of the invisible God" and the "beginning." Both these phrases are used to describe Sophia in Hellenistic Wisdom texts.[24] According to this Hellenistic conception, the body over which Christ is head is the cosmos as a whole. Käsemann argues that the phrase in verse 18a (τῆς ἐκκλησίας) is an addition to the hymn. Lohse argues that the addition was made by the author of Colossians. The hymn would have been familiar to the Christian communities in Asia Minor.[25] The interpretive phrase τῆς ἐκκλησίας, added to the hymn, has the effect of shifting the object of which Christ is head. A mythological statement about Christ as head of the cosmos is defined by the historical entity of the church.[26] The author of Ephesians takes up Colossians's modification of the idea of Christ as head over the body-as-cosmos and further elaborates it to Christ as head of the body-as-church. With the Christ-church analogy and with the marriage of wife and husband, the author of Ephesians builds a substructure to undergird the image of head and body that is found in nascent form in Colossians.

The author of Colossians uses the notions of head and body together again in Col 2:19 in his warning against "those who take you captive through philosophy and empty deceit" (2:8): "and not holding fast to the head, from whom the whole body, nourished and held together by its ligaments and sinews, grows with a growth that is from God" (καὶ οὐ κρατῶν τὴν κεφαλήν, ἐξ οὗ πᾶν τὸ σῶμα διὰ τῶν ἁφῶν καὶ συνδέσμων ἐπιχορηγούμενον καὶ συμβιβαζόμενον αὔξει τὴν αὔξησιν τοῦ θεοῦ). "Holding fast to the head" is contrasted with being ruled by spirits of the universe (2:20). Because Christ is "head of every ruler and authority" (2:10), one who holds to Christ as the head is not ruled by others. When the author of Ephesians uses a similar formulation in Eph 4:16, he specifies that the head is Christ: "we must grow up in every way into him who is the head, into Christ, from whom the whole body, joined and knit

---

[24]D'Angelo, "Colossians," 317–18. Of the voluminous commentaries on the hymn in Col 1:15–20, see especially Ernst Käsemann, "A Primitive Christian Baptismal Liturgy," in idem, *Essays on New Testament Themes* (trans. W. J. Montague; Napierville, IL: Allenson, 1964) 149–68; James M. Robinson, "A Formal Analysis of Colossians 1:15–20," *JBL* 76 (1957) 270–87; Lohse, *Colossians*, 41–61.

[25]Ibid., 46.

[26]Ibid., 55.

together by every ligament with which it is equipped, as each part is working properly, promotes the body's growth in building itself up in love." The author of Colossians specifies that the head, left implied or ambiguous in the hymn, is Christ. This lays the groundwork for the author of Ephesians to further develop the analogy of the church and Christ later in the letter. In Ephesians, this image appears in the early part of the paraenetic section of the letter where it can be more closely associated with the exhortations about unity and the church. The warnings against false teachers, which play a central role in Colossians, appear to be of no further interest to the author of Ephesians. Instead the author of Ephesians uses oppositional language to refer to the power of supernatural evil in the present.

The two other instances of the word *ekklesia* in Colossians occur at the end of the letter as references to the local assembly in Col 4:15 ("to Nympha and the church in her house") and in Col 4:16 ("in the church of the Laodiceans"). Neither reference is included in Ephesians, where *ekklesia* is used only to designate the cosmic mystical entity and not the local church.

Colossians emphasizes the change in the status of believers as a result of Christ's death and resurrection.[27] This change of status is described in terms of believers in general. The author addresses the audience using the second person plural and employs a variety of dramatic language to describe the transformation of Christians. Much of this language refers explicitly to baptism. For example, in Col 2:12–15 the author states:

> When you were buried with him in baptism, you were also raised with him through faith in the power of God, who raised him from the dead. And when you were dead in trespasses and the uncircumcision of your flesh, God made you alive together with him, when he forgave us all our trespasses, erasing the record that stood against us with its legal demands. He set this aside, nailing it to the cross. He disarmed the rulers and authorities and made a public example of them, triumphing over them in it.

---

[27]D' Angelo ("Colossians," 314) points out the similarity between the eschatological perspective of the letter to the Colossians and that of the women prophets in Corinth. See also Wire, *Corinthian Women*, 168–69.

This transformation is described elsewhere in terms of deliverance from evil powers: "He has rescued us from the power of darkness and transferred us into the kingdom of his beloved Son" (Col 1:13–14). The author refers to the resurrection of believers as a present reality: "So if you have been raised with Christ, seek the things which are above where Christ is" (3:1).

The similarity of the eschatological perspective of those whose language is reflected in the letter to the Colossians with those with whom Paul argues in 1 Corinthians has been frequently pointed out.[28] Both share a cosmology expressed in the language of powers: ἀρχή, ἐξουσία, βασιλεία, θρόνοι. The emphasis of the language in Colossians is on the present triumph effected by Christ's resurrection. Col 2:12–15 is strong evidence that such a "realized eschatology," in which baptism meant a present resurrection, was not permanently eclipsed after 1 Corinthians.

The author of Colossians uses language of resurrection, victory over the powers, and baptism to argue against "false teachers" (Col 2:16–23). The language that the author uses to characterize the "false teachers" begins in Col 2:8 and continues in verses 16 to 23. The historical identity of the Colossian "opponents" has been the major question of Colossian scholarship. Generally, scholars have tried to read the verses that characterize the "false teachers" and match the description with some form of philosophy or teaching known from contemporary sources. Lohse characterizes the opponents as adhering to "Hellenistic syncretism."[29] Recently, Troy Martin has argued that Cynic philosophy is the best candidate for the Colossian opponents.[30] This reconstruction of the historical situation of Ephesians does not require a precise label for the "opponents" in Colossae. However, it is clear that according to the rhetoric of Colossians, the polemic against false teachers is closely linked with the extraordinary claims about the supremacy of Christ and

---

[28]Schüssler Fiorenza (*In Memory of Her*, 252) notes: "The so-called enthusiastic theology ascribed to Paul's opponents in Corinth is fully expressed here." See also D'Angelo, "Colossians," 314. Wire (*Corinthian Women*, 168–69) states: "Only in what is probably the post-Pauline letter to the Colossians does the New Testament express a present resurrection triumph as bold as that attributed to the Corinthians."

[29]Lohse, *Colossians*, 97.

[30]Troy Martin, *By Philosophy and Empty Deceit: Colossians as a Response to Cynic Critique* (JSNTSup 118; Sheffield: Academic Press, 1996).

the effectiveness of baptism over the "rulers and authorities" (2:15) and the "elemental spirits of the universe" (2:8). Against the assertion that various ritual and ascetic practices were the means to achieve victory over the powers, the author presents Christ.[31] Ascetic practice and visionary experience are not the means of exaltation.[32] False teachers cannot pass judgment on the audience because they have been raised. Scholars have often noted that Colossians's argument against false teachers does not play a role in Ephesians. This fact relates to the overall vagueness of the audience and situation of Ephesians. However, the shift in the language of opposition in Ephesians, from preoccupation with false teachers to ongoing combat with cosmic opponents, also may be related to the historical situation of Ephesians.

The author of Colossians also argues that the believers' status necessitates their putting on various virtues in their relationships with one another (Col 3:5–17). In the exhortation to a change in moral behavior, a variation of the baptismal formula occurs in Col 3:11. This version does not include the pair "not male and female," nor does it use the image of "one in Christ Jesus." Rather, it uses phraseology typical of Colossians: "Christ is all and in all."

The author of Ephesians changes the purpose of the emphasis on the contrast—through baptism—in the believer's state from "then" to "now." In Colossians, the Christian who was dead and is now alive (2:13) demonstrates that no one can pass judgment with regard to any regulations or specific kind of worship (2:16–18). In Ephesians, however, the contrast between the former state of sin and the present state of being alive is used to show, not that the regulations of outsiders are now irrelevant but that the community should remain separate from the outsiders and prepare for the final battle (2:1–3, 4:17–19, 5:6–8).

The different perspectives of Colossians and Ephesians are illustrated in the different connotations of key words in the two letters. In Col 2:19, σῶμα refers to the cosmos, while in Eph 4:15–16 it refers to the church. While in Colossians πλήρωμα refers to the fullness of God, resident in

---

[31]D'Angelo, "Colossians," 319. Harold A. Attridge, "On Becoming an Angel," in Lukas Bormann, Kelly Del Tredici, and Angela Standhartinger, eds., *Religious Propaganda and Missionary Competition in the New Testament World: Essays Honoring Dieter Georgi* (Leiden: Brill, 1994) 481–98.

[32]D'Angelo, "Colossians," 320.

Christ, in Eph 1:23 it refers to the church. The word μυστήριον is used with different connotations in Colossians than in Ephesians. In Col 1:26 and 27, the content of the mystery is Christ, and this mystery occurs among the Gentiles. In Eph 3:3–6, the mystery involves the Gentiles becoming one with Jews. In Colossians, the recipients of the mystery are "the saints," but in Ephesians the mystery is revealed to a narrower group, the "holy apostles and prophets." The identification of the mystery with the union of Christ and church, which concludes the argument of Ephesians, is absent from Colossians. The difference in connotations between key words in the epistles may correlate with the different perspectives of their authors. Commentators have summarized this difference as a greater christological emphasis in Colossians and a greater ecclesiological emphasis in Ephesians. Because christological and ecclesiological emphases should be complementary, and because the author of Ephesians builds upon imagery already present in Colossians, scholars emphasize the harmony between Ephesians and Colossians without noticing the critical differences between them.

Broad observations about how Ephesians shifts the major images in Colossians are further supported by analysis of Ephesians's redaction of specific phrases from Colossians. In her examination of the use of Col 1:14 in Eph 1:7, Jennifer Maclean notes that in Col 1:12–14 and Col 2:12–15, the cross is understood as a place of eschatological rescue.[33] This rescue is not attributed to Christ's blood but to triumph over divine power.[34] By putting together the two phrases "through his blood" and "redemption," which were separated in Colossians, the author of Ephesians reasserts the traditional meaning of redemption in contrast to Colossians's understanding of redemption as eschatological rescue. Baptism is redefined from "rescue from cosmic powers which enslaved them to Jewish practices" to "the believer's experience of the efficacy of Christ's blood to forgive sins."[35]

In another case, Maclean illustrates how in the adaptation of a phrase from the Colossians Christ hymn, the author of Ephesians challenges the central claim of the Christ hymn—that Christ is God's agent in creation (Col 1:16; Eph 1:10). She argues that in Ephesians, Christ is God's

---

[33]Maclean, "Ephesians," 40.
[34]Ibid., 40–41.
[35]Ibid., 43.

agent in the process of salvation and sets the pattern for believers' continuation of that process after his resurrection. The author of Ephesians ignores or transforms all aspects of the hymn that betray its origin in Wisdom speculation. Although in her thesis Maclean attributes Ephesians's transformation of Colossians primarily to the desire of the Ephesians author to portray a continuous divine plan between Israel's past and redemption, her observations about the redaction of Colossians could also be explained in another way. The view of the cross primarily as a place of triumph would be a dangerous view for those with whom the author to the Ephesians is arguing. The high christology of the Wisdom hymn, in which Christ is claimed to be the reconciler of "all things," could also be called on for support by those who assert that they are not to be enslaved by anything or that in Christ there is no male and female. I propose a variation upon Maclean's argument by linking the shifts she observes in the first two chapters of Ephesians with other shifts in the later chapters.

Col 3:18–4:1—Exhortation to Submission and the Ephesians Adaptation

The pattern of submission in the letter to the Colossians is more loosely connected with its context than the exhortation to submission in Ephesians. Although most scholars note that it is difficult to link the exhortations to submission with the polemic against false teachers, which seems to dominate the first part of the letter, most argue that the instructions to the members of the household have an "anti-ascetic function."[36] If the false teachers were urging ascetic practices, as seems to be the case in 2:21–23, then conventional moral teaching about the household would counter an emphasis on celibacy. In the second part of the letter, the author of Colossians specifies that freedom from the principalities and powers does not mean freedom from traditional social structures.

In Colossians, the exhortations to different members of the family are made in the section of general ethical exhortations about new life in Christ. The conventional teachings of Hellenistic popular philosophy,

---

[36]For example, Troy Martin (*By Philosophy and Empty Deceit: Colossians as a Response to Cynic Critique* [JSNTSup 118; Sheffield: Academic Press, 1996] 201–4) argues that the Cynics rejected marriage, childbearing, and slavery.

indicated by the phrases "as is fitting" (3:18), "acceptable" (3:20), "justly and fairly" (4:1), are brought into the letter at this point and given a Christian motivation with the phrase "in the Lord."[37] Obedience to one's social superiors is interpreted as obedience to the *kyrios*. The purpose of the theological elaboration is to relate the address to obedience to the ambiguous word *kyrios*.[38] Wives are to obey their husbands "as its fitting in the Lord." Children are to obey parents because "this is your acceptable duty in the Lord." The lord and the master are identified with one another in the address to slaves in verses 3:23 and 4:1. The more extensive address to slaves and masters has led some commentators to conclude that there was a particular problem with slaves in the audience of Colossians.[39] Lohse argues that these verses address the relationship between the freedom granted in Christ and the *douleia* that slaves had to continue in order to serve their earthly masters.[40] Therefore, this problem receives "specifically Christian instruction." Lohse accepts this articulation of the problem as it is constructed by the author of Colossians.

In his adaptation of the pattern of submission in Colossians, the stance of the author of Ephesians is not one of critique. The position of the exhortation near the end of the letter is retained. All the same classes of individuals are addressed in the same order. Most of the language of Colossians is repeated and expanded. The exhortation to wives and to husbands is integrated into the argument of the whole letter.

The language of *kyrios* in Colossians is loosely connected with the language of the rest of the letter, which, except for Col 1:10, is Christ language. The author of Ephesians retains the *kyrios* language in Eph 5:21–6:9 in the initial address to wives (5:22), but he supplements it with Christ language. He also integrates Christ language into the exhortations to slaves (6:5–6). This is another example of how he integrates the exhortation to submission into the letter as a whole.

The author of Ephesians expands the exhortation to wives, husbands, children, parents, slaves, and masters that he found in

[37]Lohse, *Colossians*, 156.
[38]D'Angelo, "Colossians," 321.
[39]Crouch, *Origin*, 129.
[40]Lohse, *Colossians*, 159–60.

Colossians. He devotes the most energy to emphasizing and elaborating the wife and husband pair.[41] He introduces the identification of husband and lord in Eph 5:22: "be subject to your husband as to the lord," and extends the analogy with the Christ-church analogy. The author of Ephesians expands the exhortation for husbands to love their wives that is present in Col 3:19. This emphasis corresponds to an increase in the references to God's love and Christ's love within Ephesians (2:4, 3:18, 5:2). He extends the christological justification in the address to wives and husbands and to slaves and masters, and he integrates it into his argument about church, mystery, and unity.

The author of Ephesians's treatment of the address to wives and husbands, children and parents, slaves and masters, which he knew from Colossians, may now be put into the context of his overall adaptation of the material in Colossians. Although he uses some similar language, the context in which he puts that language and his interpretation of it is different. For example, Christ as the place of reconciliation of "all things" in Col 1:22 is described in Ephesians as reconciliation of Jew and Gentile (2:16). The author of Ephesians does not reproduce the Christ hymn of Col 1:15–20, with its description of Christ as Wisdom. Although he employs the language and traditions of baptism frequently throughout Ephesians, he does not repeat the baptismal formula of Col 3:11. Where Colossians explicitly refers to baptism, traditions about baptism are incorporated into the rhetoric of Ephesians without the vocabulary of baptism (see Eph 2:11–20). He shifts attention from Christ being supreme, in the sense of reconciling all things and creating all things, to Christ being supreme as the head of the church. The shift from a cosmological meaning of "body" to an ecclesiological meaning, which can be seen in the interpretation of the Christ hymn within Colossians, is extended by the author of Ephesians. This same author uses Colossians's strong emphasis on the present resurrection of believers and their victory over the powers in order to argue that they should demonstrate unity as the church in opposition to the powers and principalities. All the features operating within the letter to the Ephesians—the identification of the meaning of baptism to the oneness of Jew and Gentile in the church,

---

[41]Sampley (*One Flesh*, 20–21) notes the christological expansion of the Colossian household code in Ephesians. Sampley does not depend on any particular theory of the literary relationship between Colossians and Ephesians.

the subordination of baptismal language to marriage imagery in Eph 5:26, and the identification of the mystery with Christ and the church— appear to be consistent with the way the author of Ephesians treats Colossians.

These observations show that in reworking the material of Colossians the author of Ephesians omits material that emphasized the present res- urrected state of believers (as a result of their baptism), their freedom from rulers and authorities, and the suffusion of Christ in all things. All of the language expressing this perspective could lend support to those who argued that baptismal oneness applied to the relationship of male and female and slave and free. At the same time, the author of Ephesians expands that part of Colossians that is most useful in order to counter the baptismal understanding in which the distinction between male and female and slave and free did not belong in the new creation. Therefore, the writing of Ephesians may be read as evidence that the rhetoric of Colossians was unsuccessful in suppressing the ascetic views and the views in which baptism made male and female one in Christ that were current in the community. In fact in its repetition of the baptismal rheto- ric and its emphasis on the new resurrected life in Christ, Colossians may have had the opposite of its intended effect.

The transformation in the language of opposition from the concrete in Colossians to the cosmic in Ephesians may have operated within this rhetorical strategy. In Colossians, the author argues powerfully for the reality of Christ's conquest of the rulers and authorities in order to con- front the "opponents" inscribed in the letter, who are recommending ascetic practices and angel worship. The author's logic is that the audience's being raised with Christ means that neither the opponents nor their practices can have power over them. Therefore, the audience is exhorted to be subordinate in marriage, family, and slavery rather than to be celibate or to observe dietary laws *because* they have been raised with Christ. In contrast, the author of Ephesians shifts the language of opposition from "false teachers" to the less specific and more cosmic "sons of disobedience." According to the logic of Ephesians, unity that equals subordination is necessary to oppose the powers of darkness. While the author of Colossians argues that the battle is already won, and therefore one can be free from regulations and laws, the author of Ephesians intensifies the language of cosmic opposition in order to jus- tify further his injunctions to obedience and subordination. Subordination is necessary to win the battle. By shifting the language of opposition, the author of Ephesians curtails the power of the language of victory and provides a further justification for the exhortation to obedience.

The greater ecclesiological emphasis of Ephesians has been read as a harmonious development from the christological emphasis of Colossians. However, when Ephesians is read as a rhetorical reworking and correction of Colossians, then one can recognize that the author's construction of church, reinforced in Eph 5:21–32, is a response to the consequences of Colossian christology, with its stress on baptism as victory and the cross as a place of triumph. The presence of Col 3:18–4:1 was ineffective in countering the rhetorical power of the language of resurrection and victory in the Christ hymn in Col 1:15–18 and in Col 2:12–18. The author of Ephesians responded by omitting the Christ hymn and by subordinating baptismal language to marriage imagery.

Using the material of Colossians to write a new letter was a strategy of the author of Ephesians to correct the wrong interpretations of those in the Colossian community.[42] Andrew Lincoln characterizes Ephesians's use of Colossians as "free and creative dependence." His assumption is that Ephesians adapts Colossians in a positive appropriation and not a criticism or correction of Colossians. However, the evidence of the shifts in emphasis between the two letters suggests that the "free and creative dependence" of Ephesians on Colossians was not done out of admiration but in order to control the damage created by the proliferation of wrong interpretations of Colossians. The canonization of both letters preserved both the dangerous letter and its reinterpretation but guaranteed that Colossians would always be read in light of Ephesians.

Conclusions—The Historical Situation

This reconstruction has arrived at an alternative explanation for the lack of precise description of the audience and the situation of the letter to the Ephesians. The author does not describe the situation

---

[42]Jennifer Maclean's dissertation argues persuasively that reinterpretation of Colossians was the primary factor in the composition of Ephesians. She illustrates how the relationship between the two documents in the instances she investigates is not congenial but disputed. My proposal, based on broad observations of the two texts as a whole, is a variation on hers. Unlike her reconstruction, which emphasizes the relationship between Jewish and Gentile Christians in the first century as a primary issue motivating the author of Ephesians, mine

explicitly, not because he does not view the rhetorical problem as severe, but because it *was* urgent. The lack of precise description is part of the author's rhetorical strategy. By building his argument the way he does, culminating with the exhortation to submission in 5:21–6:9, the author can critique alternative understandings of *ekklesia* without repeating and amplifying them in the way that the author of Colossians does.

The language of opposition shifts in Ephesians from warnings against false teachers to warnings against current cosmic powers. In the reconstruction presented here, the shift can be understood as a rhetorical strategy. By viewing the powers as cosmic and still at work, the author links opposition to them with maintaining a particular structure in the *ekklesia*. The author does not directly oppose any teaching in Ephesians but rather builds a symbolic universe of hierarchy to reinterpret the unity of baptism.[43]

The author writes to a predominately Gentile audience that includes women and men. By using the vocabulary of mystery and revelation and using the style of prayer, he claims to be the authoritative interpreter of the mystery. His claim to apostolic authority is intensified beyond that of Colossians. Ephesians is written to address issues that remained unresolved since the writing of Colossians. The situation requires "Paul" to write again in order to readdress the issue, using similar language, and creating a text that repeats much of the material of its predecessor. The major issue that remains unresolved is not the relationship between Jew and Gentile in the church but the relationship between male and female. The expansion of Col 3:18–19 by the author of Eph 5:21–32 is evidence that it was the male and female relationship that was most at issue. Ephesians stresses the continuity with Judaism over those parts of Colossians that imply a break with Judaism. This is

---

sees the relationship of men and women in the church, especially the ministry of women, as primary. My focus on the second half of the letter may account for this difference. Also, I read the earlier part of Ephesians as an effort to establish common ground with the audience. With her focus on source and redaction criticism, Maclean does not use a rhetorical method.

[43]My interpretation of the language of opposition differs from that of Clinton Arnold (*Ephesians: Power and Magic: The Concept of Power in Ephesians in Light of Its Historical Setting* [SNTSMS 63; Cambridge: Cambridge University Press,

related with but secondary to the unresolved gender issue. By stressing the oneness of Jew and Gentile in Eph 2:11–20 and then defining oneness as structured according to the pattern of subordination of the kyriarchal family, the author reasserts that the break with the law does not mean transformation of gender roles.

This reconstruction finds that the best historical explanation of the author's presentation of the argument in Ephesians is not a crisis between Jewish and Gentile Christianity or a crisis of persecution but a dispute over interpretation of the oneness of Christian baptism and how that oneness plays itself out in the church.[44] The motivating factor in this re-presentation by the pseudonymous author of Ephesians is not the death of Paul, and therefore the "loss of Paul as the unifying source of authority,"[45] but the ongoing vitality of diverse viewpoints about how the *ekklesia* is envisioned. When one reconstructs the alternate language and symbolic universe of these Christians, which remain visible within Colossians and Ephesians, one sees these perspectives to have been well represented in early Christianity in the traditions used in Galatians, Corinthians, and Philippians. The language of obedience, in this case ὑποτάσσω, was typical in the literature of Hellenistic moralists. However, its conventional existence in that setting does not completely explain its presence in Eph 5:21–6:9. The author of Ephesians builds a symbolic universe beginning with the subjection of all things to Christ (Eph 1:20–22) taken from the interpretation of Ps 8:7. For some early Christians, particularly those whose self-understanding was akin to the theology of Col 1:15–20 and Col 2:15, the subjection of all things meant freedom from rulers and authorities. For women and slaves such free-

---

1989]). He reads the purpose of Ephesians as counteracting the audience's fear of hostile powers and links this fear to evidence of Artemis cult in Asia Minor. His reconstruction does not explain the shift between Colossians and Ephesians nor why the author of Ephesians would portray the powers as still at work, when Colossians portrayed them as defeated.

[44]The theory that Ephesians was written to maintain the unity of Jewish and Gentile Christians was proposed in Ernst Käsemann, "Ephesians and Acts," in Leander E. Keck and James L. Martyn, eds., *Studies in Luke-Acts* (London: SPCK, 1968) 288–97. Andreas Lindemann ("Bemerkungen zu den Adressaten und zum Anlass des Epheserbriefes," *ZNW* 67 [1976] 235–51) proposes that persecution under Domitian was the historical impetus of the letter.

[45]D. G. Meade, *Pseudonymity and Canon* (Tübingen: Mohr, 1986) 142–48.

dom could be interpreted as freedom from the hierarchical social relationships of slave and free and female and male. The language of obedience is used by the author of Ephesians to limit those who express their experience of victory over the principalities and powers. By interpreting the subjection of all things to Christ as the subjection of certain subordinated members of the household to others, the author of Ephesians counters and erases other interpretations.

The historical reconstruction presented here differs significantly from earlier historical reconstructions that read the author's rhetoric as a mirror of the historical situation. Many commentators are convinced by the rhetoric of Ephesians, which portrays the maintenance of the unity-as-hierarchy structure elaborated in Eph 5:21–6:9 as necessary to define the *ekklesia* over and against the Gentiles and the cosmic opponents. The exploration of the language of obedience in Philo and Josephus and scholarship on ethics of the period, however, shows that the sharp separation that the author draws between the symbolic structure of the *ekklesia* and that of the world outside is not so rigid as the rhetoric presents. Rather, the language of opposition, which frames the exhortations to wives, children, and slaves to obey, can be read not as accurately reflecting a historical situation but in terms of its rhetorical effects—it intensifies the sense of urgency about conforming to this structure.

Among those commentators who have recognized the conventional nature of these injunctions, some have emphasized that the christological grounding of the injunctions to submission and love makes them distinctively Christian. However, when the author's directions to wives, children, and slaves are evaluated within the wider context of early Christian interpretive language of baptism, resurrection, and christological reflection, then what the author of Ephesians does in his letter may be reframed not as the christological grounding of conventional morality but as the limitation and circumscription of christological reflection by analogy with the symbolic universe of kyriarchy.[46]

As many scholars have suggested, the author of Ephesians did use the language of obedience to respond to a problem as he understood it. He tailored his rhetoric to fit a problem that he did not name. He used it

---

[46]This may be similar to the insight expressed in Käsemann's phrase "the domestication of the gospel." Critical as he was of this development, Käsemann continued to work with the model of Paul and the "enthusiasts" and thus did not recognize the diversity of Christian christological articulations.

to reassert and to justify the reestablishment of the gender hierarchy of patriarchal marriage in the face of other positions within the community that envisioned baptismal unity as transforming the conventional hierarchical dualism of Jew/Greek, slave/free, male/female. But unlike other reconstructions that evaluate the author's uses of obedience language in the historical situation as necessary, because they judge the alternate positions as misunderstandings of Christian language, this reconstruction illustrates *both* how the author's development of the images of unity, body, and mystery was one choice among different possibilities *and* how the various features of the author's rhetoric work to make the author's logic appear inevitable.

The Diversity of Early Christian Theological Language

This study analyzes the function of the language of obedience in two letters of the Pauline tradition. It critically explores how that language operates in the logic of the author's argument and reconstructs the historical situation of each letter using evidence from other parts of the New Testament and from sources outside it that give evidence of the activity of women in the ancient world and in early Christianity. In this way, I describe and clarify two specific instances in early Christian history in which the language of obedience was employed: first by Paul in the letter to the Philippians and second by one who writes in Paul's name to the Ephesians. The method of investigation focuses on the particularities of each rhetorical context rather than on generalizations drawn on the basis of other statements in Paul's letters.[1] Rather than using a preconceived understanding of the development between letters,[2] I explore each letter individually in order to let points of comparison emerge.

This approach has yielded specific observations of the similarities and differences between Philippians and Ephesians. First, in both letters, the language of obedience operates in concert with the dynamics of opposition and identification with the author, and with the rhetoric of oneness. In the argument of Philippians, Paul links ongoing "oneness" of the community with his former presence and current absence and

---

[1]This marks a crucial distinction between this study of obedience language and Norman Petersen's reconstruction of Paul's symbolic universe (*Rediscovering Paul*).

[2]For example, I do not judge Ephesians to be either a degeneration into early catholicism or a complete flowering of the Pauline legacy.

juxtaposes exhortation to unity with the language about "opponents" and "enemies" (Phil 1:27–30, 3:18–21). By presenting positive and negative examples of behavior, Paul constructs "being of the same mind" as identification with and unity with himself. The rhetoric of obedience participates in the rhetoric of oneness, because when Paul describes being unified with each other as "obeying" (Phil 2:12), modeled on the example of Christ in 2:6–11, he calls on the symbolic universe of the father-son and master-slave relationship. The conventional connotations of obedience language in the social contexts of the patriarchal family and in the political context of ruling and being ruled are not transformed within Paul's argument, despite the reversal of that system proclaimed in Phil 2:6–11. By using the language of obedience within his argument, Paul defines partnership and friendship in a particular way. The harsh harangue against "dogs" in Phil 3:2–21 heightens the language of enmity while leaving ambiguous the status of Euodia and Syntyche as friends or enemies.

In another distinct rhetorical and historical situation, the author of Ephesians explicitly links the language of obedience with the rhetoric of unity. In fact, the author's argument can be read as a presentation of how unity and obedience are related in the symbolic universe of the Christian community. The rhetorical efforts of the author attempt to resolve the conflict among different views of oneness present in the community, specifically centering on the position of women within the symbolic universe and their role in the community. He attempts to resolve that conflict by presenting a picture of oneness described hierarchically, with obedience of subordinate to superordinate as the organizing principle. The author intensifies the sense of urgency about establishing the structure by projecting cosmic opposition that poses an ongoing threat to the community. While the author of Colossians speaks of opposition to the audience in terms of "false teachers," the author of Ephesians envisions that opposition as heavenly and as not yet conquered by Christ's victory on the cross.

The tension between unity-as-equality and unity-as-hierarchy in Ephesians and the tension between partnership and obedience in Philippians are parallel. In the case of Philippians, Paul subtly calls upon the language of obedience, adapted from the Christ hymn and put in context of commendation of Timothy and Epaphroditus and the criticism of Euodia and Syntyche, in order to critique and limit the vision of partnership represented by the latter. In the case of Ephesians, the author overtly uses obedience language and the kyriarchal system in which it conventionally operates in the culmination of the argument as a way to circumscribe the interpretation of oneness.

Second, the individual analyses of Philippians and Ephesians have shown that both authors make a similar interpretive move when adapting earlier traditional material that employs the language of obedience and subjection.[3] When Paul deploys the Christ hymn in Philippians, he states that congregational obedience is the conclusion to be drawn from it. In so doing, he points to the first half of the hymn, which narrates Christ's renunciation of status, as the relevant moment in the drama. What in its earlier setting proclaimed Christ's rulership of the cosmos, Paul uses to emphasize human obedience to God. He interprets an assertion that Christ's victory is a present reality as necessitating obedience to God. The shift from present victory to future expectation is exemplified in Phil 3:20–21, where Paul reinterprets subjection of all things to the Lord Jesus Christ to mean a future transformation from heaven, rather than a present transformation of relationships of power.

The author of Ephesians executes a similar shift. Eph 1:20–23 interprets Christ's subjection of the powers to mean that God has put all things under Christ's feet "on behalf of the church." By the end of the letter, the author has interpreted Christ's subjection of all things for the church to mean that the church must be subject to Christ, and specifically, wives must be subject to husbands. Subjection in the present is a necessary defense against still unsubjected powers: the powers of darkness in the heavenly places. Here, as in Phil 2:2–12, the stress shifts from the benefits of freedom of Christ's victory to the necessity of obedience and submission. Ephesians's "correction" of Colossians provides additional evidence of this move. The author of Ephesians does not reproduce the Christ hymn in Col 1:15–20, which proclaims Christ's preeminence, nor does he repeat the expression of belief in the present efficacy and victory of baptism in Col 2:12–15. Instead, the author of Ephesians emphasizes the present subjection required to fight for the still unrealized victory.

---

[3]In his study of the use of hymnic material in the Pauline corpus, Stephen Fowl (*Story of Christ*, 210–11) notes the consistency in the way in which the hymnic material functions in the epistles of Colossians and 1 Timothy. My study finds this consistency to be true in Philippians and in Ephesians and reads it as a similar way of interpreting traditional material still valued by the Christian communities.

Finally, in both instances presented in this study, the language of obedience is involved with the construction of the authority of the author. In Philippians, the rhetoric of obedience supports Paul's construction of a symbolic universe where son obeys father and congregation obeys God. In Ephesians, the author does not use obedience language to construct his relationship with the community. Rather, he claims authority for his construction of the hierarchically structured symbolic universe of 5:21–6:9 by presenting the story of the election of the community in the language of prayer and doxology and by phrasing his projection of the symbolic universe of obedience in the language of mystery. Rather than reiterating his own history with the community, as Paul does in Philippians, the author of Ephesians retells the primordial history of the community with God. The author uses the name of Paul but constructs the persona of Paul in a way that will appeal to the values of some members of his audience.

In both Philippians and Ephesians, the authors use the language of obedience to respond to alternative languages and symbolic universes within early Christian communities. Evidence of these visions survives in the early Christian traditions that Paul and the Pauline author employ in their arguments. When exegetes and theologians label a christological position that stresses the presentness of the resurrection, Christ's victory over oppressive powers, or the abolition of male privilege within patriarchal marriage, as "utopian," "enthusiastic," or as representing "over-realized eschatology," they follow the directions indicated by the author's rhetoric and further marginalize those voices. Strengthening the rhetoric of the author at the expense of the voices of other traditions results in the broad assertions that Paul views human life as slavery, that the most important question for an early Christian was whose slave you were, or that the early Christian vision of baptism, which removed divisions between slave and free and male and female, operated only on the symbolic level. This position reinforces both the slavery metaphor and the kyriarchal social system implied with that metaphor as a given in early Christian discourse. It curtails the diversity of Christian language in both early Christian history and current theological discussion.

Index of Biblical References